CW00517572

The PCW LOGO Manual

Robert Grant

SIGMA PRESS
Wilmslow, England

Typesetting and graphics: LocoScript2, Protext, Dr LOGO and MicroDesign 3.

Camera Ready Copy: Starjet SJ48.

Cover Design: Design House, Marple Bridge.

First published in 1992 by
Sigma Press, 1 South Oak Lane, Wilmslow, Cheshire SK9 6AR, UK

First printed 1992

ISBN: 1-85058-334-X

British Library Cataloguing in Publication Data
A CIP catalogue record for this book is available from the British Library

Printed and bound in Great Britain by: The Cromwell Press, Melksham, Wiltshire

CONTENTS

PART ONE: TUTORIAL

PART TWO:

PART THREE:

PART FOUR:

APPENDICES:

USER DISK

A PCW disk containing all of the programs in PARTS TWO and THREE is available by sending £9.95 (inclusive of VAT, postage and packing in UK and Europe) to:

SIGMA PRESS, 1 South Oak Lane, Wilmslow, Cheshire SK9 6AR
Telephone 0625 - 531035

ACCESS and VISA welcome. Cheques payable to Sigma Press. Price correct at September 1992. Please check with Sigma Press after December 31st 1992.

IMPORTANT: Please state machine type (PCW 8256/8512/9512, PcW 9256/9512+) and disk size (3"/3.5") when ordering.

INSTRUCTIONS FOR USE: Load LOGO (see page 5 of this book), put the USER DISK in drive A: (all machines) and, at the ? prompt, type `'load "readme readme'`. From there on, follow the on-screen instructions.

PART ONE: TUTORIAL

INTRODUCTION

Some time back a good friend of mine told me that he was going to 'treat himself' to an electronic typewriter. Naturally I soon put him straight about that! Within no time he had a bright new PCW 8256 up and running, and was as delighted with it as we all are.

A couple of weeks later he said to me:
"So what's this Doctor Logo business then?"
"The Dr stands for Digital Research actually. It's a programming language. Have a look at the back of the manual," I suggested.
"Oh I've drawn a square, if that's what you mean. Pretty boring. Is there a book?"
"Well, no, not really..."

Which is how this book came to be written. I hope it will take you, as well as my friend, far beyond that boring square, into the exciting world of LOGO.

Dr LOGO was amongst the software that Amstrad bundled with the PCW when it was launched in 1985, and it's been with us ever since - much despised by some who should know better. Unfortunately the manual writers seem to have run out of steam when they got to Part III and what little information about LOGO that they allowed to escape is not very helpful and occasionally not strictly accurate. Digital Research, having created an excellent implementation of LOGO, also seem to have lost interest. What little written information we have is either elementary, or written for other machines and versions. The book recommended by Amstrad - 'Soft 160, Guide To LOGO' - was written for the CPC machines, comes in a nice box, and deals extensively with matrices and genealogy.

Dr LOGO has been bundled with all the Amstrad PCW's since their inception and still comes packaged with the new PcW's, and there is still no definitive text-book. Yet LOGO is probably the best introduction to computer programming ever devised. It is simple to understand, contains virtually all the elements found in other high-level languages (and a good many that are not) and is capable of producing surprisingly powerful and useful programs. And it has one major attraction for us cost-conscious Amstraders - it's free!

I hope that this book may fill the void. By the time you have worked your way through PART ONE, the TUTORIAL section, you should have a sound knowledge of how to program in LOGO. PART TWO contains a number of LIBRARY procedures, functions and utilities which may be incorporated in your own programs. PART THREE contains some working programs as examples of what LOGO can achieve. PART FOUR is provided for reference, and for the first time gives descriptions of all the 167 primitives, system properties and operators in the Digital Research implementation, together with syntax and examples. Finally there are a number of APPENDICES containing useful reference material, printing programs, machine-code programming, and so on.

Whilst this manual has been written specifically for the Amstrad PCW's and PcW's, owners of other machines will find that LOGO is a very portable language, and the various implementations are very similar. Most of the examples and programs in this volume will work with very little alteration on most other machines. There is a list of the most common version equivalents in APPENDIX VII.

LOGO is much more than just a means of teaching children computing – although it does this very well – it is a powerful and exciting (if somewhat slow) computer language. On the PCW it also provides a straightforward graphics facility, which can produce excellent results both on screen and on paper; and we're not just talking about screen-dumps.

LOGO is an interpreted language, which means that it cannot produce stand-alone .COM files as can languages such as PASCAL and C, but must have the interpreter present whilst its programs are being run, in just the the same way as Mallard BASIC.

The name LOGO comes from the ancient Greek *logos*, meaning 'word', and by computing standards LOGO is itself a pretty ancient language. It was devised in the late sixties by a team led by Seymour Papert at the Massachusetts Institute of Technology (MIT). Papert had previously left MIT for five years to study developmental psychology with Jean Piaget in Geneva, and it was during this period that he came up with the concept of turtle graphics, which was to form the starting point for LOGO and which still distinguishes it from most other computer languages.

At that time LISP (LISt Processing) was the flavour of the month for workers in the field of Artificial Intelligence and doubtless Papert was influenced by it. One can see many similarities between LISP and LOGO. From 1967, in a room in MIT which Papert called 'Mathland', LOGO was developed. Subsequently much work on the language was done at Edinburgh University, and there is a version, little used today, called 'Edinburgh LOGO'. There are two main forms of LOGO in use at present: MIT and LCSI (Logo Computer Systems Inc). Dr LOGO is a development of the more commonly found LCSI type.

CONVENTIONS USED IN THE TEXT

Throughout the text the term 'PCW' may be taken as a blanket reference to any of the Amstrad PCW or PcW models, except where otherwise stated. In spite of the preference in the Amstrad User Manual for 'disc' over 'disk', I have used the latter spelling in line with Dr LOGO's error messages and the rest of the computer industry.

I have assumed that the reader has at least a reasonable working knowledge of the PCW, if not there are many excellent books on the subject and it is not the intention of this work to teach general computing.

Therefore, and to avoid the need for endless repetition, I have taken it for granted that he or she will know that, in command mode, <RETURN> must be pressed at the end of each line to cause the instructions in that line to be executed. However, where its use may be in doubt, it is represented as <RETURN>. The angle brackets <> have been used to enclose <RETURN>, <EXTRA>, etc, instead of the more usual square brackets [] to avoid confusion with LOGO's square bracket list-markers. The keypresses <ENTER> and <RETURN> are synonymous in LOGO on the PCW, and either may be used. However <ENTER>, unlike <RETURN>, auto-repeats if held down.

Primitives, in the text but not in the listings, are printed in bold type, thus: **make list memberp**.

Programs that may be found in PARTS TWO and THREE are printed in upper case thus: POLYGONS. Procedure names are put in single quotes in the text (but not in the listings). Thus the entry 'loop' refers to the procedure 'to loop'.

Where optional parameters (inputs) to a command are to be entered, they are shown in italics, thus:

save "*filename*
(list *item1 item2..itemN*)

You should enter the appropriate name or item in place of the italicised words.

Where a range of numbers, letters, or items is used, the range is represented thus:

a..z	All the letters between and including a and z.
5..10	All the numbers between and including 5 and 10.
item2..itemN	All the items between and including item 2 and item N, the N'th item.

Indenting lines in programs is generally not necessary, although there is no harm in using indentation occasionally to make a listing clearer. However wherever in this book line-indents are used you must observe them.

Program fragments are shown thus:

```
...
make "x first :list
...
```

Items enclosed in braces {} are optional. Neither the braces nor the italicised word should be entered, only the required instruction. Thus the entry:

{*drive*}

might be interpreted as:

b:

If the option were omitted here, the default drive would be assumed.

The entry <STOP> should not be confused with the LOGO primitive **stop**. The first refers to the <STOP> key, the second to the LOGO operator **stop**. Pressing the <STOP> key always stops the execution of a program and returns you to the ? prompt. The primitive **stop** is quite a different fish, and one we'll deal with in due course.

Although lines of programs are not numbered as in BASIC, some programs in this book have been numbered purely for ease of reference. Line numbers must *not* be typed in when writing or copying programs.

Remarks, or comments, in programs are delineated by a semi-colon preceding them, thus:

```
to loop :st :en :step          ;looping procedure
```

Neither the semi-colon nor the remark following it need be typed in, although if you wish to retain the remark, you may do so. LOGO will not read anything that is beyond the semi-colon and *on the same line*. This facility is entirely equal to BASIC's REM statement. Remarks can be very useful when you're developing a program.

You cannot 'type ahead' in LOGO as you can in some programs, for example Protext and LocoScript, where a number of commands, including <RETURNS>'s, may be typed in without waiting for each command to be executed. In LOGO you must wait until the ? prompt returns after each press of <RETURN> in command mode. The interpreter will however usually accept one keypress in advance.

<RETURN> may be pressed when the cursor is anywhere in a command line. The whole line will still be executed as if the cursor were at the end of the line. A virtually unlimited number of commands may be included in one command line: however there are exceptions, which are duly noted in the text.

To avoid confusing the numeral 1 (one) with lower-case letter L (l), especially since a sans-serif typeface has been used for the listings, lower-case L is not used anywhere as a variable name. So when you see something like:

```
make "x 1
```

in the listings, you may be sure it is the numeral one that is intended.

1

LOGGING ON TO LOGO

1.1 Setting Up The System

Before we switch on the PCW, there are a few terms specific to LOGO that we need to understand. The commands, or keywords, are called 'primitives'. There are 167 of them including system properties, arithmetic operators, etc, and a full list is given in APPENDIX I. In addition they will all be found fully described in PART FOUR, the REFERENCE section.

A chunk of a program that performs a particular operation or sequence of operations is called a 'procedure'. A procedure always starts with the primitive **to** and ends, cleverly enough, with the primitive **end**.

Now we can switch on and prepare a LOGO self-starting disk. For 8000 series machines, you will need to do a couple of disk-swaps. The programs are the same on the other machines, but no disk-swapping.

1. Switch on, or re-set your PCW with <SHIFT><EXTRA><EXIT>.
2. Put your copy of the CP/M system disk in drive A (side 2 for 8000's).
3. When CP/M has loaded, format a fresh A drive disk using DISCKIT.
4. <EXIT> from DISCKIT. Put the system disk back in drive A (side 2 for 8000's) and enter:

```
A>pip
```

At the asterisk prompt, enter:

```
*m:=a:j*.em?
*m:=a:setkeys.com
*m:=a:submit.com
```

5. 8000's only, put side 4 of the system disks in drive A (the disk containing LOGO.COM, LOGO.SUB, and KEYS.DRL). Everybody enter:

```
*m:=a:logo.*
*m:=a:keys.drl
```

6. Put the LOGO start-of-day disk in drive A and enter:

```
*a:=m:*.*
*<RETURN>
```

7. Enter:

```
A>rename profile.sub=logo.sub
```

Label this disk 'Dr LOGO START-OF-DAY'. Re-set the computer by holding down <SHIFT><EXTRA> and pressing <EXIT>, and try out your new disk. Provided you've done everything correctly, CP/M will load automatically, followed by LOGO. Here's a little short-cut: when you have to enter many similar commands in succession (as in PIP above), type in the line, press <RETURN> and then <COPY> or <PASTE> to repeat the previous command, and then edit it. This works in LOGO command mode as well as in CP/M.

When you load LOGO, you will see the copyright message come and go and finally you will be left with a question-mark in the top left corner of the screen. This is LOGO's command prompt and is equivalent to CP/M's A> prompt and BASIC's Ok. For details of LOGO.SUB see APPENDIX IV.

1.2 Drive Selection

As you have loaded LOGO from the A drive, this is now the default drive, but we're not stuck with it. All PCW's have at least one other drive, drive M:. To set the default drive to M:, simply type:

```
?setd "m:
```

Notice that almost all primitives in Dr LOGO must be typed in lower case. There are a few exceptions, but we'll deal with those later. Try typing:

```
?SETD "M:
```

You get a reasonably friendly "I don't know how to ..." message. If you have a B: drive fitted you can equally well make B: the default:

```
?setd "b:
```

You will have noticed that LOGO simply repeats its ? prompt each time. So far you have no means of knowing whether the command has been obeyed or not. Now type:

```
?defaultd
```

This primitive is short-hand for "what is the default drive?" Up will come the appropriate answer, A:, B:, or M: (or even C:, D:, etc, if you have a hard disk). If you have conscientiously typed in all the commands up till now, your screen should look like this:

```
?setd "m:
?SETD "M:
I don't know how to SETD
?defaultd
M:
?
```

You may find that you are typing a '2' instead of a double-quote mark (") quite a lot, because of having to keep using the shift key. In 'CHAPTER 15: HINTS AND TIPS' you will find a handy tip for resetting the 1/2 key to a double-quote mark, which will save you a lot of grief! In APPENDIX VI there are suggestions for a number of other keys to re-assign.

1.3 Working Space

Before we go any further we'll clear the screen and start afresh. There are several ways of doing this, but for the moment we'll use the clear text command:

```
?ct
```

and all the writing will vanish. With this command we've only cleared the screen, not the memory. To demonstrate this, type:

```
?nodes
```

and a figure of about 3574 will appear. Now type:

```
?recycle
```

Wait for the ? to re-appear and then type **nodes** again. This time the figure will be about 3633. In fact an empty workspace is more like 3636 nodes: the comand **nodes** itself uses up three **nodes** (temporarily). Later on we shall see how we can enlarge this workspace.

The primitive **recycle** is more or less equivalent to Mallard BASIC's FRE ("") command: it clears the 'garbage' out of the memory. Garbage is just another word for deleted variables, procedures, commands, etc, which hang about in memory until the space is needed for new data. It is much the same idea as LocoScript's limbo files and these areas of memory can be overwritten by new commands. **recycle** clears these areas and makes them instantly available to new material. Like almost all of Dr LOGO's primitives, **recycle**'s name pretty well describes its function.

LOGO doesn't measure its program space in kilobytes like CP/M and BASIC, but in **nodes**. Just as a very rough guide we can think of two bytes as being equal to one node, which means that we have something like 7k of LOGO workspace in which to create and run our programs. This may seem miniscule compared with BASIC's 31k, but there are ways round this problem and programs of much greater size can be run quite happily.

LOGO's greatest drawback is not lack of workspace, but lack of speed. There are no two ways about it: LOGO is slow. But even this may not prove to be as great an obstacle to useful programming as you might think.

The trick with programming is always to use the language best suited to the application, and to yourself, and you will find that LOGO can do a lot of things on the PCW that BASIC, for one, cannot. However if you want a racehorse go for BASIC or Pascal. LOGO is a friendly hack, but one built for comfort rather than speed. That said, it is also a lot easier ride!

1.4 The Three Screens

So, now we have a clear screen and an empty workspace, we'll take a look at the screen in more detail. The ? prompt has returned to the top left corner, which, when we are talking about text, is position [0 0] that is, [zero space zero], not capital letter O's. Spaces are very important in LOGO. They are used as separators between instructions, in the same way that BASIC uses commas, colons and semicolons. In LOGO commas are not used at all, and colons and semi-colons have quite different meanings.

The PCW screen is 90 columns wide and (as far as LOGO is concerned) 31 rows deep, so top left is [0 0], top right [90 0], bottom left [0 31] and bottom right [90 31]. The X axis (horizontal) always comes before the Y axis (vertical) just as in maths, or other languages.

When we refer to LOGO screen positions we put them in square brackets [], with one space between the numbers, whether they are text or turtle positions. Anything in LOGO that is put in square brackets becomes a 'list'.

We have three different types of screen to consider: the text screen the graphics screen and the split screen. The entire physical screen can at one time either be wholly text, wholly graphics, or split between the two. Now type:

```
?fs ts pr [text screen]
```

When you press <RETURN> the message (which is a 'list' of words) will be printed out. **pr** not only prints out a list, but also executes a line-feed and carriage return. You may care to think of it as 'print return' instead of just print. Now type:

```
?ss pr [split screen]
```

You will see that the cursor jumps to a position about two thirds down the screen. The top two thirds have now been given over to graphics, the bottom third to text. **ss** means split screen, but it doesn't have to be split in this ratio. Type:

```
?setsplit 3 type [split screen]
```

Note we have used an alternative primitive to **pr**, **type**. It prints a list to the screen, but without a line-feed and carriage return. To return to the default split, we simply type 'setsplit 10'. With split screens, the top part is always graphics, the bottom part text.

Now enter:

```
?fs <RETURN>
?pr [This is a graphics screen]
```

Chances are you stopped typing almost at once, because after you typed **fs** and pressed <RETURN>, nothing more happened. **fs**, short for full screen, gives us a full *graphics* screen, so we can't enter text in this state. In fact, when we actually get down to programming proper, we shall constantly be switching between these two states, text and graphics. To get to a text screen we need another primitive: **ts** (text screen).

When you enter **ts**, it gives over the whole screen to text, and if you now enter text it will start at the top left of the screen. There are two ways of changing from a graphics screen to a text screen and moving the cursor to [0 0]:

```
?fs ts
?ts ts
```

1.5 Stringing Commands Together

Note that we have been putting two or more commands together on one line in these examples. In LOGO any number of commands may be put on one line, without any punctuation between them, just spaces. LOGO sorts out where one command ends and the next begins.

In BASIC we might write:

```
INPUT "Enter a number ";n%:GOSUB 150
```

We can do exactly the same thing in LOGO:

```
type [Enter a number] make "n rq subprocedure
```

Don't worry if the actual commands in either language are Double-Dutch to you, what both lines say is: "Type the message 'Enter a number' on the screen and wait for the input. When the user types in a number, assign it to the variable called 'n' and then jump to another part of the program." The point is that LOGO will accept a whole string of commands and deal with them one at a time from left to right. This makes program writing easier, but reading rather more difficult. We look for punctuation to tell us where commands begin and end, but there is none. However we are allowed comments in LOGO programs, the equivalent of BASIC's 'REMS'. Anything on a line typed after a semicolon (;) will be ignored when the program is run, so we could write:

```
...
type [Enter a number]
make "n rq subprocedure              ;assigns input number to var n
```

and the program will ignore the comment when we run it. However the comment will show up when we list the program, making it easier to read. Unfortunately remarks use up memory, so use them sparingly. Later on we shall find a way of getting rid of all remarks in one fell swoop.

Up till now we have been typing in some simple commands, pressing <RETURN> each time and watching the commands being obeyed. We have been using 'command mode' waiting for the ? prompt each time. In proper LOGO programs we shall never see the ? prompt, any more than we see BASIC's Ok prompt when we run a BASIC program.

1.6 Programming Proper

So how do we write a real program? Type:

```
?ed "demo
```

ed is short for edit. The double quote-mark " signals to LOGO that the word that follows it is a *name*, the name of a variable or a procedure. In this case 'demo' is the name of a procedure. We'll deal with the rules governing procedure names in CHAPTER 5. We are now in the edit screen, where we shall be doing most of our program writing. We shall be spending many happy (hopefully) hours in edit mode, so let's get to know it.

You'll be pleased to hear that LOGO's editor is a full screen editor and that it understands most of the PCW's special keys LINE, EOL, DOC, etc. The full set of editing commands can be found in APPENDIX II, but the most useful are these:

move cursor	cursor keys
move to end of line	EOL
move to start of line	LINE
delete character	DEL->
delete previous character	<-DEL
finish editing & define procs	EXIT
abandon edit	STOP

When you start to access LOGO's flexible friendly editor, you will quickly appreciate just how friendly and flexible it really is, especially when compared to BASIC's restrictive line editor, to say nothing of CP/M's ghastly ED. But we are not ready to write a program yet, so press <EXIT> to return to command mode. You will notice that the message 'program defined' has come up on screen, followed by the ? prompt. For the moment we'll ignore this message and end the chapter with a few notes on 'syntax'.

1.7 Program Punctuation

In case you're new to programming, syntax simply means grammar: the exact shape and form in which commands must be entered. Just as in writing English we use commas, full-stops, etc, to make our meaning clear, so in programming (whatever the language) we must use various 'punctuation marks' to make our meaning clear to the computer.

In LOGO, as in all computer languages, the syntax must be correct, or the program simply will not run. We've already seen a couple of examples of precise syntax. Instead of 'fs ts' try typing:

```
?fsts
```

and you'll see what I mean. Without the separator (space) between the commands, LOGO doesn't recognise them.

As a general rule each command must be entered in lower case and separated from the following command by a space. There may be as many commands on a line as you like, but if the line is longer than the screen width, an exclamation mark (!) will appear at the end of the line to indicate that the line is carried over onto the next line. Even if a command is split in the middle in this way, it will still be obeyed as if it were all on one line. For example, in the following, where we might assume that the row of dots represents various instructions and the half-word 'setc' occupies columns 86..89:

```
.......................................................setc!
ursor [24 6] pr [This is a very long line]
```

the command **setcursor** will still be obeyed in the normal way. However, for clarity's sake, avoid lines that are longer than the screen width if you can. Long lines are almost never necessary. The program line:

```
...
if wordp :alist [op :alist] if emptyp :alist [op []] if (and (wordp first!
:alist) (emptyp bf :alist)) [op :alist]
...
```

is entirely equal to:

```
...
if wordp :alist [op :alist]
if emptyp :alist [op []]
if (and (wordp first :alist) (emptyp bf :alist)) [op :alist]
...
```

Short lines are easier to write, easier to read, and easier to debug. It really doesn't matter what all the above means at the moment. It probably looks like complete gobbledegook at this stage: in no time at all you'll be tearing off much more complex stuff without a second thought.

1.8 Reservations

Finally a few notes about LOGO's special characters. The following symbols are LOGO operators or delimiters, and are reserved 'words':

+ - / \ * [ ] ( ) " : ; > < =

If you wish to use any of them as simple text characters, you must precede them with a backslash (\), obtained by pressing <EXTRA><1/2>, or f3.

Round () and square [] brackets have special meanings in LOGO, which we'll come to later. The double-quote-mark " has two meanings: to indicate that the word following it is a name, or to indicate a null entry, thus these:

```
pr "
type "
```

will execute a line feed and carriage return, but type nothing. Actually in certain circumstances they will type a space. The entries:

```
pr []
type []
```

will always type a space.

None of the primitives and system properties in the LOGO vocabulary may be used as filenames or procedure names. A chunk of a program (Papert called them 'mind-sized chunks') is called a procedure. Virtually all LOGO programming is done from within procedures. 'Mind-sized' is a very good description: we should not write longer procedures than we can comfortably encompass in our minds at one time.

Data may be expressed in LOGO by using objects, properties and values. These words (object, property, value) are not reserved words, nor are they primitives. They are merely convenient labels for different levels of information.

2

SPEAKING GRAPHICALLY

2.1 Writing A Simple Graphics Program

This is where LOGO tutorials usually begin: with turtle graphics. If you type, at the ? prompt:

```
?fs st
```

a small triangular beast will appear in the middle of the screen. This is the famous turtle, even though it does look more like an arrow-head.

Again, most LOGO tutorials start with a routine like:

```
pd fd 50
rt 90 fd 50
rt 90 fd 50
rt 90 fd 50
```

This sequence produces a square - that boring square. The Amstrad User Manual manages to get as far as 'squareanysize', which, apart from being a horrible word, is also pretty boring. If we'd started off by drawing a square, you could have been forgiven for giving up LOGO there and then. So let's plunge in a little deeper and give ourselves a tiny foretaste of what LOGO can do. Type in the following and don't worry about what it means:

```
?ts
?ed "demo
```

When the editing screen comes up, you will see that LOGO has obligingly entered 'to demo' and 'end' for us. Press <EOL> then <RETURN> to make a space between the two lines and enter the rest of the procedure:

```
to demo                          ;this has been entered for you
cs ts ts
type [Enter a number between 20 and 100, press RETURN]
make "radius rq
cs fs ht pd fd 50
circle :radius
end
```

```
to circle :radius
ct seth 270 pd
repeat 36 [fd :radius / 5.75 rt 10] pu
end                                  ;this has been entered for you.
```

Quite a mouthful! Don't bother to type in the remarks following the semi-colons. Now check your typing. The important syntax bits are: no space between (") and (radius) in 'make "radius rq', no space between (:) and (radius) each time. So ':radius', not ': radius'. Now press <EXIT>. The edit screen will vanish and

```
demo defined
circle defined
```

will appear on screen. Now at the ? prompt enter 'demo' and obey the program prompt. A line will be drawn with a circle on it. Try entering various radii in the range 20..50. Finally try a radius of 150 and watch what happens.

Let's break down the program and see how it does what it does. Look at the first line 'to demo'. **to** tells LOGO we are going to write a procedure, which we shall call 'demo'. The first instruction **cs** clears the screen, **ss** sets a split screen. **ht** hides the turtle, **pd** puts the imaginary pen down and 'fd 50' moves the (hidden) turtle forward 50 units. When LOGO is first loaded, the turtle starts in its 'home' position, in the middle of the screen pointing upwards, or North. When we talk about 'units' we are more or less talking about pixels for all practical purposes.

The text 'Enter a number...' will appear in the lower third of the screen. 'make "radius rq' says "read the quote (ie: whatever is typed in by the user) and assign it to the variable 'radius'". Suppose you entered '75' ':radius' will now contain the value '75'. The name of the variable is "radius, the variable itself is :radius and its value is 75. More about variables later, so don't worry if it's as clear as mud at the moment.

The line 'circle :radius' needs a little explanation. In LOGO, unless a word is not a primitive, nor a number, nor has it a quote mark, nor a colon either side of it, then it can only be the name of a procedure. Look at these and you should get the idea:

```
type          is a primitive
"radius       is the name of a variable
:radius       is a variable containing a value
b:            is a drive letter
demo          is the name of a procedure
```

That's all there is left for 'demo' to be. You must of course define (write) a procedure before you can use it. In this short program there are only two procedures defined 'demo' and 'circle'. However, when we've finished with procedure 'demo', we want to jump to procedure 'circle', which we do simply by naming it. This is referred to as 'calling' the procedure, and is more or less equivalent to BASIC's 'GOSUB' command. A procedure can even call itself – but more of that later.

The call to procedure 'circle' takes some hand-luggage with it: the variable ':radius'. So the line 'circle :radius' means "jump to the procedure 'circle' and execute that procedure, using whatever value the variable ':radius' holds as the radius of the circle to be drawn". 'seth 270' means **set** the **h**eading of the turtle to 270 degrees. Look at Figure 2.1 which shows how absolute turtle headings are worked. Up, or North, is 0°, or 360° if you like. All angles in LOGO are in degrees.

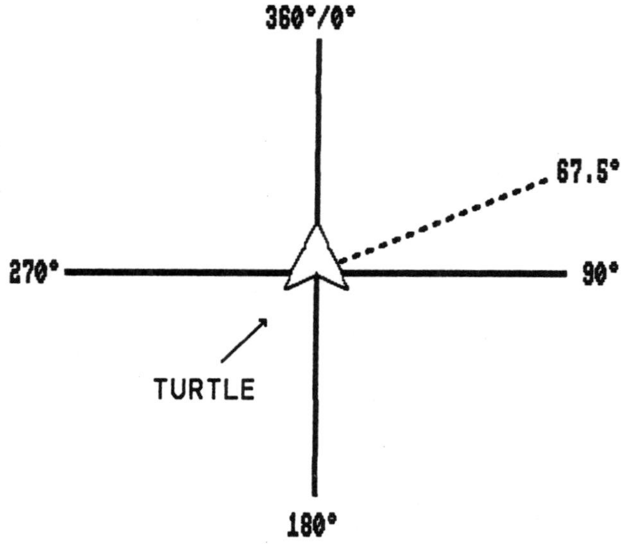

Figure 2.1 Absolute turtle headings. If the turtle was pointing right to 90°, then the command 'lt 40' would make it turn to an absolute heading of 50°

The turtle can be made to point in any direction you want. 'seth 67.5' would make it point in the direction of the dotted line in Figure 3. **seth** doesn't move the turtle forward, merely turns it towards an absolute heading.

Now we come to the line 'repeat 36 [fd :radius / 5.75 rt 10]'. 'repeat 36' simply means what it says: repeat the following (list of instructions) 36 times. The actions to be repeated may be as complex as you like, but they must be in the form of a list. Ergo, they must be enclosed in square brackets.

In this case we want the turtle to move forward by an amount to be calculated. The computer will do the calculation for us. The slash / is LOGO's division sign, as in most computer languages. The final part of the action is 'rt 10', meaning "turn the relative heading of the turtle 10 degrees to the right".

The procedure finishes with the command **pu** – take the pen up off the paper – and is just there for neatness in this example. If we now wanted to move the turtle to another part of the screen, we could do so without drawing a line.

If you haven't got the first idea of writing procedures and assigning variables yet, we shall be going over it all in much greater detail later, so don't despair. At least we've managed to draw something slightly more interesting than a square. We've written a program that draws a lollipop, or a balloon on a string, or whatever you like to call it. We could of course have done the whole thing from the command line, instruction by instruction, but it would actually have been more difficult.

2.2 The Circle Formula

For the mathematically-minded amongst you, this is how we get to the formula 'repeat 36 [fd :radius / 5.75 rt 10]', where 'radius=50' and 'factor' is one thirty-sixth of the circumference:

```
circumference of a circle      = 2 * pi * radius
                               = 2 * 3.1415927 * 50
                               = 314.15927
factor for circle formula      = 36 * 50 / 314.15927
                               = 5.7295779
```

which, to save LOGO having to do a lot of intricate sums and waste time and space, we round up to 5.75. In practice this gives us as true a circle as our screen will allow.

2.3 The Turtle Commands

Just so that we get the idea of how the turtle commands work, try these five examples one at a time from the ? prompt:

```
?cs ss ht pd repeat 10 [fd 10 pu fd 10 pd]
?lt 90 pd fd 100 pu bk 100
?repeat 5 [fd 10 pe fd 10 pu]
?lt 60 pd repeat 3 [bk 50 lt 120] pu
?seth 270 wrap pd fd 500 pu window home st
```

Quite a few new primitives here. The first line is straightforward, we've already met all those primitives. In the second line we have **bk**, meaning "move **back**". In line three **pe** is **pen erase** - erases anything the pen moves over. In line four, **lt** is **left** and sets the turtle heading however-so-many degrees to the left, relative to its present heading.

Suppose the turtle is pointing vertically upwards (seth 0). The command 'seth 90' will turn it so that it points horizontally to the right. Now the command 'lt 40' will turn it *relatively* 40° to the left, to the *absolute* heading of 50°.

The last line is rather more complicated. We must first understand that the graphics screen can be in one of three states: **window**, **wrap**, or **fence**. **window** is the default state and the one we mostly use. It means that the physical screen is a window onto a theoretically infinite turtle world, into or out of which window the turtle can freely roam. **fence** does what it says: it fences the turtle in to the physical screen. If he tries to move out of it, an error message ('turtle out of bounds') is generated.

Finally **wrap**: an interesting one. If you send the turtle off the screen on one side, he'll immediately re-appear on the equal and opposite side. Try typing the last line again, substituting **fence** for **wrap**, just to see exactly what happens. You might like to try this simple 'program'. Enter:

```
?fs seth 45 wrap fd 3000
```

It quite frequently occurs, when you're playing about like this, that you forget what screen state you're in, or whether the pen is up or down, or where the turtle is heading. And that happens when you're programming too. Fortunately there's an extremely useful primitive we can use: **tf**, which gives us a list of the turtle facts. Type:

```
?cs home tf
```

You should get the answer:

```
[0 0 0 PD 1 TRUE]
```

The first number is the X co-ordinate, the second the Y co-ordinate, the third the heading, item four is the pen-state (**pd pu pe px** - down, up, erase, xor). Item five is the current pen-colour (always 1 with the PCW), and the final item shows whether the turtle is visible or not. TRUE means it's visible, FALSE means it's hidden. Now enter:

```
?ht pd fd 100 rt 90 fd 100 pu
?tf
```

and see the result:

```
[100 100 90 PU 1 FALSE]
```

Although it may not be too obvious at this stage, **tf** can be very useful in a complex program, when, for example, we may wish to pass the turtle's co-ordinates or absolute heading from one procedure to another. This, for example, would extract the turtle's heading:

```
?type item 3 tf
90
?
```

2.4 More Graphics Operators

Before concluding this chapter, we'll look very briefly at the other graphics primitives. Don't try and remember everything at this stage - just play about with them to see what they do. Fitting them into programs will come later. First the ones to ignore completely!

```
pal setbg setpal setpc setpen wait
```

(palette, set background-colour, set palette, set pen-colour, set pen-condition & colour, wait). They all refer to the CPC (colour) machines and are of absolutely no use on the PCW whatsoever. Some aren't even implemented, even though they're listed.

Now for the ones you *can* use:

dot [*X Y*]	Puts a dot (turns on the pixel) at the position [*X Y*].
dotc [*X Y*]	Returns 1 if the pixel at position [*X Y*] is switched on, returns 0 if it isn't.
setpos [*X Y*].	Sets the turtle at position [*X Y*].
setx *X*	Sets the turtle X co-ordinate, keeps the old Y co-ordinate.
sety *Y*	Sets the turtle Y co-ordinate, keeps the old X co-ordinate.
px	Sets the pen to Exclusive Or state (XOR). That is, green/white pixels are changed to black and vice versa.
st	Shows the turtle if it has previously been hidden. The opposite of **ht**.

setscrunch — Sets the aspect ratio of the vertical and horizontal distances. The default is 0.46875. Interesting results can be achieved by altering the aspect ratio, but if you want *round* circles, stick to the default. On print-out 0.5 may be preferred using the bundled dot-matrix printer.

towards [*X Y*] — Returns the turtle heading necessary to point the turtle towards the point [*X Y*]. If the turtle is at the position [0 0], 'towards [100 0]' will return '90'. It does not actually turn the turtle however. The point may be well outside the visible screen if required.

fill — Fills an area with green/white pixels if the pen is down, unfills it if the pen is erase. USE WITH CARE! If the area is not totally enclosed, **fill** will fill the screen! You can't stop it. Wait till you've progressed a little further before you experiment with this one. It comes with a health warning!

Figure 2.2 DESIGNER drawing exported and printed from Microdesign3 unretouched. LOGO's 'fill' operator has been used to paint the sails.

3

PUTTING IN THE TEXT

3.1 Positioning The Cursor

For a moment let's forget all about the turtle and examine LOGO's textual talents. After all, virtually every program we write will have to display words as well as graphics. Unlike Mallard BASIC, LOGO has a very simple way of presenting text precisely where you want it on the screen. First of all type:

```
?cs erall recycle ts ts
```

This will clear the screen, clear the memory and place the cursor at the top left of the screen. It is now actually in the position [1 0]. Position [0 0] is occupied at present by the ? prompt. Figure 3.1 shows how the X and Y axes are numbered for cursor positions.

If you have a single drive computer, you should disable the status line - the line where the "Drive is..." message appears - in order to clear row 32. If you look at APPENDIX IV you will see that the code for this is ESC 0. In LOGO this becomes:

```
(type word char 27 "0)
```

and the "Drive is..." message will disappear. 'char 27' is the same as CP/M's 'ESC' (escape), or BASIC's 'CHR$(27)'.

```
(type word char 27 "1)
```

restores the status line to normal use. Note, that's the figure '1', not the letter 'l'. As in all graph work, columns (X axis) always come before rows (Y axis), so to put the cursor at column 5 row 10, we simply enter:

```
setcursor [5 10]
```

and that's where it will go. If you've just tried this out from the ? prompt, you're going to call me a liar! It did go there, I promise you. What happened was this: the cursor jumped from [1 0] to [5 10] and then control passed back almost instantaneously to the ? prompt and the cursor jumped back to [1 10]. But it looked as if the cursor had jumped straight from [1 0] to [1 10]. It went via [5 10], but too quickly for you to see.

So how do we get the cursor to stick at [5 10], or anywhere else for that matter? The answer is, it won't, not in command mode. However in program mode it will go wherever we like, and stay there for as long as we like.

For a change we'll write this procedure in definition mode. That means, a mode in which procedures can be defined without using the editor.

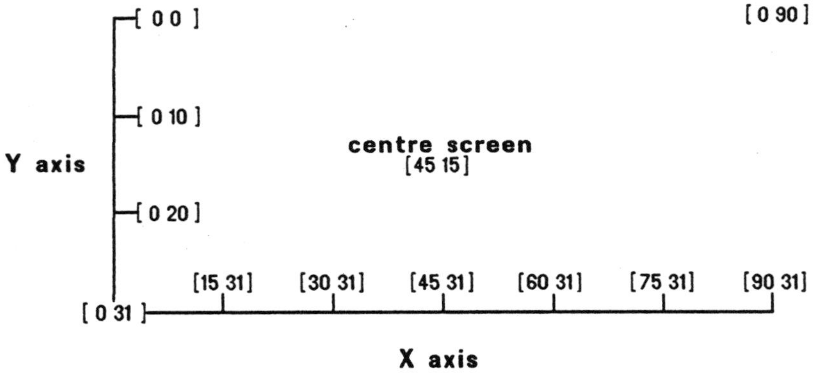

Figure 3.1 X and Y cursor co-ordinates. LOGO cannot use row 32. If anything is entered in column 90, a ! will be inserted and a line feed and carriage return executed.

3.2 Definition Mode

At the ? prompt, type:

to test

When you press <RETURN> you will see the cursor jump down a line and a '>' (greater than) sign will appear. This is because using the primitive to in command mode takes us into definition mode. The procedure we type in will be defined as soon as we type **end** and press <RETURN>. The snag is, definition mode reduces us to line editing. I wouldn't advise you to use it overmuch if your typing is as erratic as mine. If you do make mistakes and don't notice them at the time, you will have to go into the editor to correct them anyway, so you might as well have gone there in the first place! However you should know how definition mode works, even if you only use it once in a blue moon, so try it now. This is what the screen will look like when you've finished. LOGO puts the '>' signs in for you automatically:

```
?to test                        ;procedure name
make "inp rl                    ;read list, assign to variable "a
make "x item 1 :inp             ;assign elements of input list
make "y item 2 :inp             ;  to "x and "y
setcursor se :x :y              ;position the cursor
test                            ;loop back and wait for next input
end
test defined
?
```

Once again, don't bother to type in the remarks. This is what it all means: 'make "inp rl' takes the input from the keyboard and, when <RETURN> is pressed, assigns it to a variable named "inp. The primitive **rl** (**read list**) reads the input as a list, whatever it is, but doesn't do anything with it until <RETURN> is pressed. The instructions 'make "x item 1 :inp' and 'make "y item 2 :inp' assign the first number of the input to "x and the second to "y. Next the instruction 'setcursor se :x :y' is obeyed. The primitive **se** (**se**ntence)makes the variables :x and :y into a sentence and puts square brackets round it, turning it into a list, which is just what **setcursor** is looking for.

The eagle-eyed amongst you may have spotted an 'error' here. **rl** gave us the input as a list: we then stripped out the elements of the list using **item**, and reconstituted the list with **se**. Rather a long-winded way of going about things admittedly, but it serves to illustrate the use of **se** and **item** for the first time.

If we enter 'test', press <RETURN> and enter, say, 18 20 and press <RETURN> again, 'setcursor se :x :y' is translated by LOGO into 'setcursor [18 20]', which is where it will now send the cursor. The only way out of the program is by pressing the <STOP> key, since the program calls itself in the last line with 'test'. We shall explain what this 'calling itself' business is all about later. For the moment think of it as being an endless loop: the program simply goes round and round in circles.

3.3 Naming Names

It is good programming practice to use variable and procedure names that mean something to you six months later. You may understand your program perfectly just after you've written it, but with the passage of time it can become almost incomprehensible. I have to confess that some of my programs become totally incomprehensible to me almost as soon as I've finished writing them! So I'm afraid this is a bit of 'do as I say' rather than 'do as I do'.

Whenever possible use 'x' and 'y' as the variable names for the cursor co-ordinates. They make sense because the represent the X and Y axes, and, as they will often be used in the form 'se :x :y', they're also very sexy! Easy to remember. You could use 'col' and 'row' for column and row if you prefer. Whatever you do, be consistent, and your programs will be easier to read and, more importantly, to debug. A procedure for sorting a list of names into ascending alphabetical order could be called 'salph' LOGO will accept it as a name but something like 'sort_az' would make a lot more sense and again is perfectly acceptable. A procedure to add numbers together called 'adnum' would be pretty self-explanatory, as would a variable ':num'. A procedure called 'an' and a variable ':n' could be almost anything. That said, bear in mind that long names take up more memory space than short ones, and if you invent many variables called 'anynumberyoucanthinkof' you'll very soon run out of memory and get typist's cramp into the bargain! But back to the cursor. Type:

```
?ed "test
```

and insert the words 'show cursor' just after the line 'setcursor se :x :y'.

Run 'test' (by simply entering 'test' at the ? prompt) and see what happens. Wherever you send the cursor, it now prints out its own co-ordinates. In fact the exact position is where the first '[' sits. The primitive **cursor** outputs two elements, the present X and Y co-ordinates of the cursor.

3.4 Printing Text To The Screen

The actual printing of characters to the screen is done by using one of three primitives: **pr**, **type**, and **show.** Just to remind ourselves, **pr** prints and then executes a line-feed and carriage return, whilst **type** prints the text and leaves the cursor on the same line. The new one, **show,** is in a class of its own, because, unlike **pr** and **type**, it doesn't strip the outer brackets away from a list, and secondly it only takes one input. Compare these:

```
?pr [A] pr [B]
A
B
?type [A] type [B]
AB
?show [A] show [B]
[A]
[B]
?
```

Note that **show** executes a line-feed and carriage return. Here are some more examples, together with their results:

```
?pr "hello
hello
?pr [hello]
hello
?pr hello
I don't know how to hello          ; " missing before 'hello'
?type [yellow] type [hammer]
yellowhammer
?type "fruit type cake
fruit
I don't know how to cake           ; " missing again
?type [fruit cake]
fruit cake
?show [fruit cake]
[fruit cake]
?make "a "willow make "b "herb
?pr se :a :b
willow herb
```

```
?show :a show :b
willow
herb
?show [:a :b]
[:a :b]
?show [This is a sentence]
[This is a sentence]
?show [a [b] [[c]]]
[a [b] [[c]]]
?type [a [b] [[c]]]
a [b] [[c]]
?
```

The error messages are obvious enough. 'I don't know how to...' is saying "the input word, having no colon or quote mark, must be a procedure, but there is no such procedure in my workspace, so, 'I don't know how to...'". Look at the line 'type "yellow type "hammer'. It prints out one word: 'yellowhammer'. If we want a space between the words, we must tell LOGO this. We can either put the sentence in square brackets, in which case **type** will put in the space, or we can use 'char 32', the ASCII code for a space.

```
?type "yellow type char 32 type "hammer
```

will print: 'yellow hammer'. However we cannot write:

```
type [column 1          column 2]
```

and expect it to come out like that. It will close up to:

```
column 1 column 2
```

The trick is either to use char 32 and **repeat**, like this:

```
type [column 1] repeat 12 [type char 32] type [column 2]
```

or use **setcursor** if there is a lot of tabulating to be done.

There is a way that we can avoid having to keep entering **type** or **pr** in a line and that is to enclose the whole thing in parentheses or round brackets (). Suppose :runs holds the value 257 and :wickets a value of 8, then:

```
(type [Total score:] :runs [runs for] :wickets [wickets])
```

would print out as:

```
Total score: 257 runs for 8 wickets
```

Now we'll introduce a new primitive, **word**.

Try these:

```
?pr [post card]
?pr word "post "card
?pr (word "picture "post "card)
?pr (word 1 2 3 4)
?pr (se 1 2 3 4)
```

And, so long as you haven't lost the variables :a and :b from the previous example (if you have, 'make' them again) try this one:

```
?pr word :a :b
```

The primitive **word** joins up the inputs to it, whilst **se** makes them into a sentence, with spaces in between. Note that numbers don't need to have a quote mark in front of them. Note also that both **word** and **se** don't require round brackets if there are precisely two inputs, but for one, three, or more, the whole bang shoot must go into round brackets, including the primitives **word** and **se**. Compare these two:

```
?pr [word :a :b]
word :a :b
?pr word :a :b
willowherb
```

Quite a different result. Anything inside the square brackets is printed out, literally, just as it is. So if you want any calculations done or variables deciphered within a print line, either leave out the square brackets, or get your program to do the calculating or deciphering first, and then put the result in brackets.

Before we leave the text screen – temporarily – there are two primitives we need to look at in a little more depth: **ts** and **ct.**

ts we've already come across: it makes over the whole screen to text input. Meaning that no new graphics input will be shown. The corollary is that no text typed in when a full (graphics) screen is in operation will be shown. The point needs to be made that, although nothing will be *shown* in a full screen, it does not mean that nothing is *happening*. Even in a **fs** state, text typed in will be obeyed, if it contains relevant instructions. Try these out:

```
?ts type "hello fs type "hello
?pd fd 100 ct
?cs
?ss type "hello fd 100
?ct
```

Experiment with a few more like this and you'll soon see how the three different screens treat text and graphics. **ct** will only clear text in a full text screen, or the text part of a split screen. **cs** clears everything from a full screen, whether text or graphics, but only from the graphics part of a split screen. Look at the REFERENCE section for more details. Never guess at the result of anything, test it first. Put this up on the wall in big letters: "WHEN IN DOUBT, CHECK IT OUT!"

3.5 Bracketing the Target

Finally in this chapter, a few words on brackets. LOGO uses two types of brackets: round () and square []. Round brackets (parentheses) are used in arithmetical expressions in the normal way to indicate precedence (see CHAPTER 9). They are used with the primitives **se**, **word** and **list** (CHAPTER 10), and with the the logic operators **and**, **or**, and **not** (CHAPTER 9 again). In addition they are needed to enclose multiple **type** and **pr** statements as we've just seen. They may also be used almost anywhere else, either to clarify an expression to the interpreter, or, more likely, to the programmer!

Square brackets are only used in one way: to delineate a list. Lists are central to LOGO, so here, a bit ahead of its time, are a few examples. The contents of each of them may mean absolutely nothing to you at the moment, but that doesn't matter, they soon will. First a conditional test:

```
if :a > :b [type :a] [type :b]
```

If the condition is TRUE, that is if the value held in variable :a is greater than the value held in variable :b, then the first list of instructions '[type :a]' is executed. If FALSE, then the second list is carried out.

The primitive **repeat** needs a list of instructions on which to operate:

```
repeat 8 [fd 50 rt 45]
```

will draw an octagon, but that's beside the point. What we need to note is that once again the list is contained in square brackets, or to put it the other way, what's contained in the square brackets is a list!

The primitives **pr** and **type** will print out a list of words:

```
pr [Type these words, then execute a RETURN]
type [Type this without a RETURN]
pr []
```

The last one prints an empty list, ie: nothing! Well actually it prints a space, and it does still execute a line-feed and carriage return, so it's a lot more useful than it looks at first sight.

If you want to use brackets in text just as brackets, not as delimiters, like this for instance:

```
pr [(1)...DATABASE]
pr [(2)...[EXIT] to CP/M]
```

you must preface them with a backslash '\'. The backslash can be obtained with with f3. So you would type the above like this:

```
pr [\(1\)...DATABASE]
pr [\(2\)...\[EXIT\] to CP\/M]
```

The backslash tells LOGO that whatever follows is to be treated as a simple text character, not as a delimiter. It looks complicated at first sight, but you will soon get into the habit of doing it. If you miss out a backslash or two, you can be sure of one thing: LOGO will let you know soon enough, one way or another! Try entering the above without backslashes and you'll see what happens.

4

TEXT, GRAPHICS, AND THE SPLIT SCREEN

4.1 Splitting The Screen

Unlike any other computer language I know, LOGO has a unique concept: the split screen. We've already looked at it briefly: the top part a graphics screen, the bottom part a text screen. We've also noted the way in which we can change the proportions of each using **setsplit**. The default division is 10 lines of text, 21 lines of graphics. But:

```
?setsplit 21
```

would reverse this proportion. **setsplit** takes as its input the number of text lines we require. Even:

```
setsplit 31
```

is possible, but pretty pointless.

The command **ct** clears only the text part of the screen, **cs** and **clean** affect only the graphics part of the screen. Any turtle moving commands will move the turtle within the limits of the graphics part of the screen. If it tries to stray into the text screen, it will either disappear, wrap around, or generate the error message 'turtle out of bounds', depending on whether **window**, **wrap**, or **fence** is in force at the time.

But why, we may well ask, do we need a split screen, when we have already seen how easy it is to swap from text to graphics and back again, using **fs** and **ts**? The simple answer is that there are occasions when it is more convenient not to have to keep swapping. A game, for instance, which may require constant text input from the keyboard whilst the graphics are going about their business, can be much easier to program using **ss**. For one thing, text input need not have constant **setcursor** assignments to keep it away from the graphical content. Then again in a program like DESIGNER (*vide* PART THREE) the split-screen allows us to view some fairly complex commands as we enter them, to make sure they're correct.

But there are snags. For a start, if we jump from a full text screen to a split screen, all the text is wiped in the process! Not a very desirable result. But, as always, there's a way round it.

4.2 Jumping Around

Whenever we jump from a text screen to a split screen, we must go via a full graphics screen. Odd, but true. This is how it looks:

```
...
fs fd 100
ts type [Going to a split screen]
fs ss type [Split screen]
...
```

and the graphics will be preserved. And in reverse:

```
...
ss type [Split screen]
fs ts type [Text screen]
fs fd 100
...
```

The same rule applies whenever you jump from one screen type to another within a procedure, or from one procedure to another: always go via **fs** and all will be well. But when you go from, say, a graphics screen to a split screen, you will lose any graphics in what is now given over to text. The same thing happens when jumping from a text screen to a split screen.

One thing you cannot do, and that is to leave a split screen with text in it and later come back to it whilst preserving that text. Every time you enter a split screen, the text part is wiped. Once again there is a rather devious way of getting round this. Suppose you had two lines in a split screen (setsplit 10) which you wanted to preserve when you returned from a full screen, this is how we might manage it:

```
...
ss pr [This is an example of a dodecagon:]
pr [a plane figure of twelve sides.]
fs ts setcursor [20 12] type [ANGLE (360/12) = 30]
setsplit 8
fs ss
...
```

This will have kept the two lines of text from the previous **ss** by making the new **ss** two lines less deep. Here's a program to demonstrate the use of **ss**. Type 'ed "polygons' to get into edit mode and enter:

```
to polygons
setsplit 12
cs ss seth 270 pu setpos [50 -50] pd
make "planes 3 make "len 80
figures :planes
end

to figures :planes
(pr [Number of planes:] [] :planes)
make "ang 360 / :planes
ht pd repeat :planes [fd :len rt :ang]
if :planes = 12 [type [Program completed] stop]
figures :planes + 1
end
```

Leave the editor with <EXIT> and run the program by entering 'polygons'.

Watch how the program moves from the text part of the screen to graphics and back again without any effort. We won't concern ourselves with the details of this program at the moment: it's here for a bit of fun and to demonstrate the viability of a split screen.

4.3 Screen Facts

Time to meet one more graphics command: **sf** (screen facts). If you type it in at any time, you will get a reply that looks something like this:

```
[0 TS 10 WINDOW .46875]
```

The first figure refers to the background colour of the screen and will always be 0, so from now on forget about it. The second item shows the screen state, which will either be TS, FS, or SS. Item three shows the number of text lines reserved for the text part of a split screen. Item four is the graphics border state (**window wrap fence**). Finally the last figure is the aspect ratio of the screen, which we can alter with **setscrunch**.

Now we've got the general idea of how to enter graphical commands, and what most of them mean, we'll move on to some more interesting and involved graphics.

4.4 The Graphics Screen

First of all we need to know the dimensions of the screen in turtle, as opposed to cursor, terms. In the graphics screen top left is [-360 263], top right is [359 263], bottom left is [-360 -265], and bottom right is [359 -265]. The easy one is centre screen (the **home** position) which is [0 0]. The graphics co-ordinates are rather more complicated than the cursor co-ords.To demonstrate the actual boundaries of the graphics screen, type in this little program, which consists of only one procedure, and run it by typing 'graphscr':

```
to graphscr
cs ct fs pu ht setpos [-360 263] pd
repeat 2 [rt 90 fd 719 rt 90 fd 528]
end
```

This will draw a line round the perimeter of the screen. If your screen is different to mine (unlikely), alter the figures to suit. If your screen hasn't shrunk in the wash or grown overnight, you should find that you cannot go any further out without losing the line.

4.5 Matching Cursor To Turtle

The interesting problem here is to relate cursor positions to turtle positions. We need a program to do the job for us.

Exactly what do we want the program to do? It is helpful to write a program statement before diving in and writing the actual program. That way hopefully we shan't miss out a vital ingredient.

1. Take any turtle position on the full graphics screen and place the cursor at that exact position.
2. Make it possible to write text starting at the position of the cursor.
3. Enable cursor movement anywhere on the visible screen and make it possible to write more text.
4. Enable us to return to the graphics screen at any point.

This last raises a point worthy of your consideration: do you want the turtle to be positioned where the cursor has got to, or should it be left where it last was? I have chosen the latter, but it would be simple enough to write a line or two to reset the turtle to the cursor. In the LIBRARY section you will find a program 'TURPOS' that converts cursor positions to turtle positions – the reverse of this program. You could easily take out a part of 'TURPOS' and meld it with 'CURPOS' to answer this problem if you so desired.

Look at para 1 in the program statement. We know that **tf** will tell us what the turtle co-ords are, so that bit's easy. Using variables "cx and "cy as the cursor co-ords and 'curpos' as the procedure name, we begin with:

```
to curpos
make "cx item 1 tf
make "cy item 2 tf
```

But these are still turtle position numbers, so we need the conversion factors. Each character position occupies eight pixel positions across the screen, so to convert turtle positions on the X axis, we need to make every eight turtle positions into one cursor position. If the left of the screen is –360 and the right is 359, we need the absolute sum of the two figures (ignore the minus sign for a moment) to know how many pixels the screen is wide. This gives us 719 – call it 720 – divide by 8 and we get the answer we want: 90, which is the number of columns.

Do the same thing with the Y axis. Each row occupies, not 16 as you might expect, but 17 pixels. Top of the screen is 263, bottom is –265, sum of the numbers: 528 – call it 527 – divide by 17 and up comes the answer 31, which is of course the number of rows available. So in go the formulae:

```
make "cx item 1 tf make "cx round (:cx + 357) / 8
make "cy item 2 tf make "cy round (:cy - 255) / 17
```

The primitive **round** simply rounds the number up or down to the nearest whole number: **setcursor** can't handle fractions. The brackets around '(:cx + 357)' and '(:cy – 255)' are there so that, just as in ordinary arithmetic, the sum within the brackets will be executed first; only afterwards will the division be made. Also watch the spaces between the operators – and + and the numbers. ':cx + 357 / 8' without the brackets is a very different sum, since in this case LOGO would first divide 357 by 8 and then add the value of :cx to the result. Also watch the spaces between the operators – and + and the numbers.

The curious figures '357' and '255' haven't been plucked out of thin air: they are there to make the turtle co-ords of top left of the screen more or less [0 0] to start with. I say more or less, because some small adjustment had to be made to both figures to make sure that they gave cursor co-ordinates of exactly [0 0], when the numbers were rounded. All we need to do now is actually to place the cursor in the position we've worked out for it. Remember, we're in a **fs** state, so we add the line:

```
ts setcursor se :cx :cy
```

and we've taken care of para 1 of our program statement.

Para 2 asks for the ability to write text at the position of the cursor. This would best be done in a separate procedure - a subroutine if you like:

```
to curwrite
local "a make "a rq
if :a = " [stop]
end
```

Anything typed in will be printed to screen and we can amend it with the <DEL> keys if we like. Pressing <RETURN> will assign the input to the variable :a. But how do we get to 'curwrite'? We need an input code to take us there. Call the input from the keyboard "inp and we have:

```
make "inp rq
```

The Primitive **rq** is **r**ead **q**uote. Now anything typed in at the keyboard will be stored in :inp. Which neatly brings us to para 3 of the program statement: "Enable cursor movement anywhere on the visible screen and make it possible to write more text".

Take my word for it at the moment that the cursor keys return the following ASCII numbers:

right arrow	char 250
left arrow	char 254
up arrow	char 242
down arrow	char 240

You will find in the LIBRARY section a program called ASC which prints out the ASCII values of all the characters available from the keyboard.

We also need keypresses to get us into 'curwrite' and to exit from 'curpos', which last will fulfil para 4's requirement. I have chosen <EXTRA><!> (which gives the upside-down exclamation mark) to exit to the graphics screen, and <EXTRA><+> (which gives the 'not equals' sign) to jump to 'curwrite'. The reason these were selected is simply because they are the first and last characters on the top row, so they are easy to remember; also they are unlikely to be needed for writing to the screen.

However, you can use any characters you like. Just be sure that they aren't used in writing text, or everything will go wrong. Don't use the <STOP>, or <EXIT>, or <RETURN> keys: they'll be no use to you in a program; anyway the first two would stop it in its tracks, the last would crash it completely.

We're nearly there now, but we must be able to keep moving the cursor around the screen, that was one of the requirements of para 3. The simplest solution here is to make a loop within the procedure, using **label** and **go**. It is supposed to be a sign of sloppy programming using **label** and **go** and the practice is much railed against by the pundits. I fully expect that there's a really nasty corner of hell specially reserved for programmers who do it: I'll see you there!

The finished program will look like this:

```
to curpos
(local "cx "cy "inp)
make "cx item 1 tf make "cx round (:cx + 357) / 8
make "cy item 2 tf make "cy round (:cy - 255) / 17
fs ts label "X                    ;this is where we jump back to
setcursor se :cx :cy
```

```
make "inp rc                          ;reads input character
if :inp = char 175 [fs ss stop]       ;EXTRA !
if :inp = char 222 [curwrite]         ;EXTRA +
if :inp = char 240 [make "cy :cy + 1]
if :inp = char 250 [make "cx :cx + 1]
if :inp = char 242 [make "cy :cy - 1]
if :inp = char 254 [make "cx :cx - 1]
go "X                                 ;loops back to label "X
end
to curwrite
local "a make "a rq
if :a = " [stop]                      ;returns control to 'curpos'
end
```

Ignore the references to local for now: we'll deal with them in CHAPTER 6. Type the whole program in, leaving out the remarks if you like, and try it out. With the program in the workspace, at the ? prompt type:

```
?ss pu cs ht home pd fd 126 rt 64 fd 73 curpos
```

You will see a couple of lines drawn, then the cursor will appear and jump to the head of the second line, to where the turtle is sitting. You can move it around with the cursor keys, and write to the screen by pressing <EXTRA><+> and typing in your message. When you've finished, press <RETURN>, and you'll be able to move the cursor around again. Use the <DEL> keys to erase, or, after you've 'fixed' the message with <RETURN>, use the spacebar to erase. You will be dumped back to the text part of the split-screen when you type <EXTRA><!>, which will allow you to enter more turtle-moving commands.

Now that we've written a program, it's time to examine the process in a bit more detail, which is what the next chapter is all about.

5

MIND-SIZED CHUNKS

5.1 Procedure Names

As LOGO programs consist of one or more procedures, everything that a LOGO program *does* must be contained within procedures, although variables and properties can *exist* outside procedures.

Wherever possible keep procedures short. The less work a particular procedure has to do, the less prone to programming errors, and hence to run-time errors, it will be. If you try to cram too much into a procedure it is very easy to lose track of all the possible paths through it that the program can take. Try, if at all possible, to make each procedure perform one main function. A counsel of perfection: it isn't always possible.

Procedures must have names. Any name will do, it needn't even be a 'real' word, but there are a few things it must not be. It must not be the name of a LOGO primitive or reserved word, or begin with a number, or have the same name as another procedure within the same program, or be in upper case letters. Otherwise the world's your oyster.

It makes sense to give a procedure a name that reflects what it does, if you can. For example, we could call a looping procedure 'xyz', but 'loop' would be a lot more sensible.

A procedure name must consist of only one word. If you want to call a procedure 'draw graph', you must link the two words in some way, other than with a space. Remember, to LOGO a space is a separator or delimiter, not just a gap between words. The most usual ways of linking words in procedure names are using either '_' (the underline character) or '.' the full-stop or period. So 'draw_graph', or 'draw.graph' are both perfectly acceptable.

Remember, you can't use hyphens, colons, or brackets, or any of the maths operators: * / + - < >. But you can use exclamation marks, numbers (but not at the beginning of the name), commas, dollar signs, or whatever, but not colons or semi-colons. Decide which linking symbol you're going for and stick to it. Personally I find the full-stop the easiest, since it saves shifting to get the underline character. If I use the underline character I usually forget to press <SHIFT> and type in a hyphen (minus sign) instead! So procedure names in this book are linked with full-stops. What you use is up to you, but you must not use full-stops in file-names. LOGO will accept them, but CP/M will not, and you might want to use PIP to do some file-shifting. You can however use the underline character in filenames quite safely.

It makes sense to keep procedure names reasonably short, to save on typing and memory-space. Also it is quite common to use the name of the main procedure as the filename, and filenames must obey the CP/M rules, that is they must be no longer than eight letters. LOGO adds the .LOG or .PIC extension to filenames automatically, but we'll come to that in good time.

5.2 Loops

Now let's look at a ready-made procedure. Type this one in, in whichever mode you prefer (edit or definition):

```
to loop :st :en :step
   perform.action
   if :st = :en [stop]
   make "st :st + :step
   loop :st :en :step
end
```

You don't have to indent the lines as I have done here, but it sometimes does help, especially with longer programs, to show where procedures begin and end. Use the <TAB> key: it is set to give four spaces, but it's not a true tab.

All this procedure does is perform a loop (just the same as a BASIC FOR...NEXT loop). The parameters (inputs) :st and :en are the starting and ending figures and :step is the value by which the count is incremented or decremented. 'perform.action' is a procedure (which we haven't written yet) which will perform a certain action the appropriate number of times.

We then increment :st by adding the :step value, which will be a minus value if we want to start high and work down. Finally the procedure calls itself in the last line. The line 'end' is never reached it's only there to tell LOGO that that is where the end of the procedure is, even though we never actually get there!

When at last :st equals :en, the procedure stops. Note, the *procedure* stops, not necessarily the *program*. In fact the primitive **stop** passes control back to the instruction that follows the original call instruction. It works in precisely the same way as BASIC's RETURN command from a GOSUB.

Now for a simple 'perform.action' procedure:

```
to perform.action
pr :st
end
```

Couldn't be much simpler than that, could it? Notice how this time we do reach the word 'end', which causes the procedure to stop, returning us to 'loop', to the instruction following the call to 'perform.action', ie: to the instruction 'if :st = :en [stop]'.

Now set the ball rolling with:

```
?loop 1 5 1
```

and watch what happens. Try any other figures you fancy, and try a decrementing loop:

```
?loop 8 0 -2
```

This isn't terribly exciting as it stands, but it serves to illustrate an important point. These two procedures perform one function each. As a result they are short and easy to read.

It is interesting to note this variation of 'loop':

```
to loop :st :en :step
perform.action
if :st = :en [stop]
loop (:st + :step) :en :step
end
```

We improve our programming by avoiding 'make "st', reducing our procedure by one line, and saving on memory. A small improvement, but every little helps. And it illustrates a very useful function that we shall use a great deal: altering the values of parameters each time a procedure loops round. Take a look at Figure 5.1, which shows the program path through these two procedures.

The final version of 'LOOP' is in PART TWO, the LIBRARY section.

When writing a program you should always start with pen and paper, never with the computer. Write down in simple terms what you want your program to do. Forget the language for the moment. It doesn't matter whether it's going to be written in LOGO, PASCAL, FORTH, ALGOL, or whatever. The program statement will be the same whatever the language you finish up using.

Taking our 'LOOP' program, the program statement might look like this:

1. Repeat a given action a given number of times in increasing or decreasing steps of a given size.
2. Test to see if the condition has been met: if it has, return control back to the main program.

From this statement we see that there are two distinct operations: the action itself and the procedure that controls the number of repeats.

Now start to develop the statement:

1. State the number of repeats and the size of the steps.
2. Start the loop.
3. Perform the action.
4. Test for the end of the loop, if reached then stop, if not reached...
5. Increment or decrement the number of loops and loop again (jump back to 2).

From this we can write a looping function in any language: all the requirements have been stated.

Progressing from a general statement of intention in steps to a finished program is called 'stepwise refinement', and is heartily to be recommended.

Never try to write a complete program on the computer from scratch... unless your name happens to be Papert or Wirth. You may get away with it if the program is very simple, but it is a bad habit to fall into.

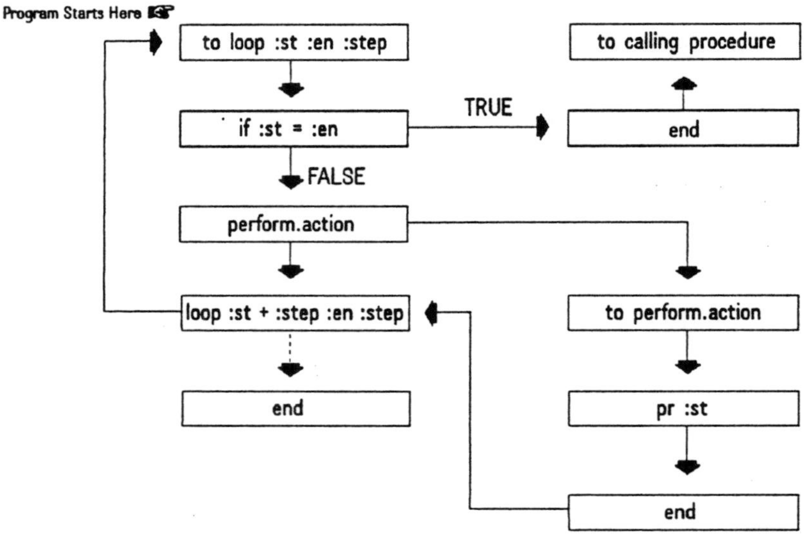

Figure 5.1 Program path of the procedures 'loop' and 'perform.action'

Write down your program statement on paper, develop it step-by-step, and put in the bells and whistles right at the end when you're sure the basic idea works. As you write each procedure you can test it before going on to the next. LOGO lends itself to this kind of discipline, since it forces you to use procedures, which in turn forces you to break up your program into chunks - Papert's 'mind-sized chunks'.

5.3 Error Traps

It would now be easy to add some 'bells and whistles' to our 'loop' program. For example, an entry such as:

```
?loop 10 1 1
```

is obviously incorrect. It should be:

```
?loop 10 1 -1
```

since steps down from 10 to 1 must be minus steps. We could add an error-trap to detect this:

```
...
if and :st > :en not equalp piece 1 1 :step "\-
   [pr [step must be minus] stop]
...
```

This would do, but it would throw control back to the calling procedure, which may not be what we want. Another approach would be to correct the mistake automatically. Note that in both versions the indents are vital.

```
...
if and :st > :en not equalp piece 1 1 :step "\-
   [make "step word "\- :step]
...
```

You may or may not have followed what's going on here: we are jumping ahead a little, but for the inquisitive among you, this is what all that means, very briefly.

If the starting number is greater than the end number (if ... :st > :en) and the first bit of :step (piece 1 1 :en) isn't equal to (equalp) the minus sign ("\-), then make the end number a minus one ([make "en word "\- :en]). Remember that backslash is there to stop LOGO thinking we mean the operator, rather than just the sign for it. Don't worry if it's still confusing you: we shall deal with all these commands properly later.

The message behind all this is clear: build the scaffolding of your program first and then gradually add the refinements. If you try and do it all in one go, you'll finish up with a load of garbage, which will be hell to sort out, and you'll probably have to start all over again anyway.

One of the greatest strengths of languages like LOGO and PASCAL is this ability to create a procedure to perform a particular function which is not already part of the language. For example, neither language has an inbuilt tangent function, but we can easily write one. Again in LOGO there is no function to raise a number to a power. Both these and many others will be found in the LIBRARY section.

5.4 Recursion

Now, take a deep breath, we're about to grapple with recursion. Strong men have been known to quake at the very mention of the word, but I really don't know what all the fuss is about. Put simply it means going round in a circle. The procedure is executed once, then when we reach the end, or some other given point in the procedure, we make it loop back to the beginning again. We can easily control how many times this happens. We've already used recursion in 'loop'. The last line is a 'recursive call': in other words, the program calls itself:

```
loop (:st + :step) :en :step
```

What we're saying is 'go to the beginning of the procedure called 'loop', which happens to be the procedure we are already in, taking along the parameters :st (which please increase by the amount of :step), :en and :step itself'. And round we go again. And that is more or less all there is to recursion. It can get a little more complicated, but not much.

Look at this procedure:

```
to infinite.loop
type "X
infinite.loop
end
```

Don't bother to type it in: all you'll get if you run it is a screenful of X's. In fact if there were an infinite amount of memory available it would go on looping round for ever and ever. Once again we have used recursion, but this time there is no way out of it; no condition which, when fulfilled, will stop the procedure looping. Let's try something else.

```
to infinite.loop
type "X
infinite.loop
type "Y
end
```

Now we've got two problems. First the loop is still infinite, and second we never reach the line 'type "Y'. However this in itself creates a third problem. Each time the program loops round it looks to see if there are any further instructions in the procedure. If it finds any, it makes a note of the fact. Each time it goes round it makes another note. These notes, or 'flags', are stored in part of the memory called the 'stack buffer': quite literally it stacks the reminders one on top of the other. Now the stack buffer, like the rest of the computer's memory, is anything but infinitely large. It very soon fills up, the program crashes and an error message is generated.

We'll tackle these problems one by one. Firstly, to get out of a loop, we already know we must put in a condition. Suppose we make it a numerical condition:

```
to condition.loop :maxtimes :check
type "X
if :check = :maxtimes [stop]
condition.loop :maxtimes (:check + 1)
end
```

Run the procedure by entering something like:

```
?condition.loop 10 1
```

Ten X's will be printed out and the program will stop, because :check has reached 10, and is therefore equal to :maxtimes. For the moment don't concern yourself with the construction of the 'if' line, just follow the logic. We have created a procedure called 'condition.loop'. It could be called 'raspberry' for all the difference it would make, but it wouldn't help our understanding of its purpose overly. The procedure asks for two parameters (inputs) to be entered, :maxtimes, which is the maximum number of times we want X to be typed, and :check, which obviously starts at 1 and is incremented by 1 each time an X is typed.

Because the last instruction in the procedure is a recursive call and it is at the very tail-end of the procedure, we have what is called, sensibly enough, 'tail-end recursion'. And because of this LOGO doesn't have to make a note about any unfinished business in the procedure, so no flag is set and the stack buffer doesn't get filled up. Remember, the word 'end' is not an instruction, simply an end marker, so LOGO doesn't need to make a note of it in the stack buffer.

So that's solved two of our three problems. But what about 'type Y', which we've quietly ignored in this version?

Look at these two side by side:

```
to loop1 :maxtimes :check           to loop2 :maxtimes
type "X                             repeat :maxtimes [type "X]
if :check = :maxtimes [go "A]       next
loop1 :maxtimes (:check + 1)        end
label "A                            to next
type "Y                             type "Y
end                                 end
```

In the first program, 'loop1', we've used the equivalent of BASIC's GOTO statement. As we don't have line numbers in LOGO, we use 'labels' to jump to, but only within a procedure, you can't jump out of a procedure using a 'go "label' instruction; we use another technique to do that. **label** can have any name you like, even a single letter, but being a name it must have the quote mark in front of it every time it's mentioned, thus:

```
...
go "places
...
label "places
...
```

Or the other way round:

```
...
label "jump.back
...
go "jump.back
...
```

'loop1' works perfectly well, so now look at 'loop2'. This one works perfectly well too. So what's the difference? Have a look at the two programs again and consider an input of, say, 500 for :maxtimes. That means, in 'loop1', that the stack buffer has to hold 500 memos to the effect that there is more to be done after the recursion is completed. I'm here to tell you it won't! It won't even hold 300. However, in 'loop2' we have used *repetition* instead of recursion. There is no question which is the better program. If you don't believe me, try them out for yourself with an input of 2000 for maxtimes and (in 'loop1') an input of '1' for 'check'. 'loop1' chugs along and soon collapses, exhausted. 'loop2' is a Nigel Mansell of a program and will happily zip through as many thousands of repeats as you like. It uses about 20 nodes per three thousand repeats. 'loop1' uses about 3000 nodes to get through a mere 260! Often recursion is not the best way of doing things and we must use repetition instead, as in this case. Which leads us to another technique, accumulation. We'll come to that one in good time, and don't worry: that too is very simple.

6

A VARIETY OF VARIABLES

6.1 Different Data Types

Unlike BASIC, which recognises different data types, and PASCAL, which insists on them with a zeal that can be infuriating at times, LOGO treats all variables the same way. Thus in LOGO the value held in a variable could be any of the following types:

A	character
6	integer
3.142	real
example	character string, or word
days.in.week	constant

LOGO doesn't distinguish between these. It is only when we try to compare variables that we run into trouble if they are not of the same type. Obviously if variable :a contains a number and variable :b contains a word, we cannot write:

```
make "c :a * :b
```

Even if :a contained the value '6' and :b contained the value 'six', the two are still not consistent, because '6' is a number and 'six' is a character string. Therefore we will do well to use variable names that describe the type of variable we are using. Variable names like "n and "s are all very well, but they give us no clue as to what sort of data they might contain. Names like "number and "sentence would be much more descriptive. At the same time we have to consider that long variable names take up more memory space than short ones. It's a delicate balancing act.

There is one slightly confusing aspect to this lack of data 'typing'. LOGO treats numbers as words as well as numbers. So it treats '1234' as both the number 'one thousand two hundred and thirty-four' and as a word '1234'. In practice this doesn't matter too much, but it's as well to bear in mind; it can be very useful at times and confusing at others.

We shall see later on how we can test variables to find out what type they are, which will often be the source of useful error-traps.

6.2 Variable Names

It is interesting to note that you can use names of primitives as variable names (but not procedure names), but it's not a terribly good idea. If I tell you that **list** and **count** are both primitives, I think you'll agree that the following is more than a little difficult to follow:

```
...
make "list list count :a count :b
make "count count :list pr :count
...
```

This all makes perfect sense to LOGO, but would drive us silly trying to fathom it out. The answer is, don't use primitive names as variable names, even though it's legal.

We've already suggested "x and "y as variable names for X and Y co-ordinates; how about "inp for keyboard input and "ctr as a counter variable? Work out your own system, but once you've settled on one, stick to it and you'll find life is a lot easier.

6.3 Locals

Using short variable and procedure names may save a little memory space, and may even make the program run a little faster (in theory at any rate), but there's a much better way of conserving memory: using local variables. 'Local' because they are only available to ('local to') the procedure in which they are declared, *and to any procedure called by that procedure.*

We've already seen local variables in action in 'condition.loop' as :maxtimes and :check. By putting them as parameters (inputs if you like) to the first procedure and declaring them at the command prompt, we made them local to 'condition.loop'.

Look at this example:

```
?make "a 10
?:a
10
?
```

We create (with **make**) a variable called "a, give it the value '10', and then ask LOGO for its value by simply typing in ':a'. Now type in this test procedure:

```
to test
local "a
make "a 5
type :a
end
```

Run this by entering 'test' and you will see '5' printed to the screen. Now type ':a' and you will get the answer '10'. How come it isn't '5'? Because when we created the variable "a in command mode, we created a *global* variable, but within the procedure in which the *local* variable was created, :a has the value '5'. The global variable :a has been suspended whilst 'test' is running. But once 'test' has finished, the local variable :a disappears and global :a comes into its own again.

The difference is that a global variable, once it has been declared and assigned a value, can be used by any part of the program, except within a procedure where a local variable of the same name has been declared, even if the local hasn't yet been assigned a value. The safest bet is not to use the same names for local and global variables, that way you won't get them mixed up.

Local variables can have their values passed on to other procedures called from within the procedure in which they were declared, and in turn they can be passed on to other procedures. This is a very useful facility and one which we make great use of. It is economical of memory and an efficient means of passing on information from one procedure to another. However for this trick to work, the variables must be used as parameters - hand-luggage as it were - to the call.

6.4 Locals As Parameters

This program demonstrates this better than pages of chat. Read it first - there's a deliberate mistake in there somewhere; see if you can spot it:

```
to proc.one
(local "num "guess "goes)
make "num random 100
type [Guess the hidden number, 0 to 99 , in 6 goes:]
make "guess rq
make "goes 1
proc.two :num :guess :goes
end

to proc.two :num :attempt :goes
if :attempt > :num [pr [Too big] proc.four :num :goes]
if :attempt < :num [pr [Too small] proc.four :num :goes]
if :attempt = :num [proc.three :num :attempt :goes]
end

to proc.three :num :try :goes
(pr [You guessed:] [] :try "in :goes "goes)
(pr [You win!!!])
proc.one
end

to proc.four :num :goes
local "newguess
if :goes = 6
   [(pr [You've had your 6 goes...you lose!] :num) stop]
(type [Try again:] [])
make "newguess rq
proc.two :newguess :goes + 1
end
```

Yes, I admit it, it's a sloppy bit of programming, it jumps about like kangaroo with St Vitus' dance, but that isn't the point of the exercise. We're just looking at the way local variables behave. We run the program by entering 'proc.one', but before we do that, let's just examine it .

The first line in 'proc.one' declares three local variables, "num and "guess and "goes. Because there is more than one, the whole expression must be put in parentheses. The line 'make "num random 100' outputs to the variable :num a random number between 0 and one less than the input to **random**. In other words :num will now have a value between 0 and 99. If we wanted values 1..100 we would write 'make "num (random 100) + 1'.

The last line of the procedure calls 'proc.two' and takes with it the values of the variables :num and :guess. However when we look at 'proc.two' there is no mention of :guess. Instead there is a new variable :attempt.

This little trick is quite permissable and indeed sometimes it can help our understanding of how the program works. I've only done it here to show you that it is allowed. LOGO requires two inputs to 'proc.two' and it doesn't care what they are *called*, it only looks at the *values*. To all intents and purposes :guess and :attempt are one and the same variable. The identical trick has been used in calling 'proc.three'

Everything is straightforward from then on, until we get to 'proc.four'. Did you spot the deliberate mistake? Look at the last line of 'proc.four':

```
proc.two :newguess :goes + 1
```

and then look at 'proc.two': it requires three inputs and the call only had two. The correct line would be:

```
proc.two :num :newguess :goes + 1
```

6.5 Local Declarations

We can create as many local variables as we like from within a procedure, they need not be carried in as parameters. For example:

```
...
(local "n "m "group "sum)
make "n 12
make "m 3
make "group :a
make "sum :n + :m
...
```

The odd man out here is :a, which we can assume is a global variable previously declared and assigned a value. What we should not write would be something like:

```
...
make "n 12
(local "n "m "group "sum)
make "n 7
...
```

What value do you think :n would now hold, '7' or '12'? The answer is the local variable :n is '7', but the global variable :n, which was assigned before the local declaration, still holds the value '12'. LOGO doesn't look backwards within a procedure: the local variable must be declared before it is assigned a value. In fact no variable, whether local or global, can be used before it has been declared and assigned. You might think this is too obvious to mention, but it is surprising how often we forget this simple fact. In the above example :n still has a global value of '12' and as soon as the local :n has been dispensed with, global :n will swing back into action. Forgive me if I seem to labour the point, but it is a cause of much confusion: local variables always take precedence over global variables of the same name, for just so long as the local variable is available to the program. We could perfectly well write:

```
...
local "n
make "n 12
local "m
make "m 3
...
```

but that would be messy and confusing. The place for local declarations is immediately after the procedure declaration (the 'to "*procedurename*' line).

6.6 Examining The Workspace

Now let's whizz through some primitives we use in command mode:

pots Prints out titles of all procedures in the workspace.
pops Prints out definitions of all procedures in the workspace.
pons Prints out names of all global variables in the workspace. (Local variables are lost as soon as the procedure ends.)
po "*procedure* Prints out the definition of the procedure *procedure*.
poall Prints out the definitions of **all** procedures and names and values of all global variables in the workspace.

Type any of the above at the ? prompt and you will be given the appropriate information. Don't use **pots**, **pops** and **pons** inside programs – there are better ways of getting the information should we require it during the execution of a program, which we'll come to later. There's even a couple of better ways of getting the information that **po** would give us.

Before we leave variables, let me introduce our first System Property: **.APV**, which stands for Associated Property Value. It's the first operator we've come across that takes upper case – and don't miss out the leading full-stop. All the System Properties (there are seven of them) have a leading full-stop and are in upper case.

We use **.APV** like this:

```
?glist :a ".APV
```

glist is a new one too. It means **g**et the **list** of properties. We'll deal with **glist** properly in CHAPTER 11. For the moment ignore it, **.APV** is the animal we're interested in. Suppose we enter:

```
?make "a 25
```

at the ? prompt, and then:

```
?glist ".APV
```

we shall get the answer '[a]' and maybe a few others. What we get from 'glist ".APV' is a list of the variables in the workspace. Now for another new primitive, **gprop** (**g**et **prop**erty), which gets the property of anything we specify, always pre-supposing it's got one of course! Enter:

```
?gprop "a ".APV
25
?
```

And 25 is indeed the value that we put into "a.

7

WORKING IN THE EDITOR

7.1 Moving Round the Editor

We've already looked briefly at editing, but before we start to write more complex programs , we need to study the editor a little more closely. To re-cap: we can get into the editor with 'ed *procedurename*', or even with just 'ed', which gives us a completely blank editing screen. We can also use 'edall' if there is room for all the procedures that are in the work-space. Once in edit mode, the following commands allow us to work more quickly:

COMMAND	EFFECT
CURSORS	Move up, down, left and right.
LINE	Move to beginning of line.
EOL	Move to end of line.
DOC	Move to end of edit buffer.
RELAY	Move to top of edit buffer.
PAGE	Move to end of page.
ALT + PAGE	Move to top of page.
DEL->	Delete character under cursor.
<-DEL	Delete previous character.
ALT + DEL->	Erase to EOL.
COPY or PASTE	Recall the last line deleted.
EXIT	Finish editing and define all procedures in the edit buffer.
STOP	Abandon edit without defining procedures.

There are some others: you'll find the full list in APPENDIX II.

It is interesting to note that in command mode and definition mode <PASTE> and <COPY> actually *repeat* the last line typed, whilst in edit mode they *recall* the last line deleted with <ALT><DEL->>. Very useful. If you have to repeat more or less the same line several times in the editor, type it in once, go back to the beginning of the line and delete it with <ALT><DEL->> and then copy it back in with <COPY> as many times as you like. Subsequent lines then need only be edited as appropriate. Unfortunately the LOGO editor doesn't boast block-copying or Find-and-Exchange functions, but as we shall see there's a way round that one too.

Whilst writing programs in the editor there is no need to space out the instructions on separate lines, nor need they be indented, but it is good practice to make your lay-out pretty and easily readable. Programs are hard enough to read at the best of times.

7.2 The Editing Commands

ed	Puts up an empty editing screen.
ed "*procedure*	Puts the procedure called procedure into the editor.
ed [*list of procedures*]	Puts the procedures named in the list into the editor, if there is room.
edall	Puts all the procedures and global variables into the editor, if there is room.
edf "*filename*	Loads the file filename from a disk in the default drive, and puts it directly into the editor, if there is room. When editing of the file is finished, pressing <EXIT> automatically re-saves the file to disk, overwriting the previous version. Disks may be changed between loading and saving. If there is no file of that name found, a file will be opened on the default or named drive and written to from the editor in the normal way.

We've met **ed** before. **edall** is obvious enough, but **edf** is a tricky one. Very useful in that it doesn't interfere with the workspace, but awkward in that it overwrites the previous version of the file when you press <EXIT> and re-save to disk. If you want to keep both versions, swap disks before you exit from edit mode and **edf** will save the new version to the new disk. The old version will remain intact on the other disk.

Both **edall** and **edf** share a common problem. The edit buffer is not large and you will often see the error message 'My edit buffer is full' when you try these two commands. This doesn't really mean what it says. What it actually means is 'I haven't got enough room in my buffer for what you are trying to put there'. You will just have to put smaller chunks of the program into the editor at any one time. The only other way out of it is to use a word-processor or text-editor that will edit larger files. Which of course will give you the missing block-copy and Find-and-Exchange functions!

Now for the erasers:

er "*procedure*	erases the named procedure.
er [*list of procedures*]	erases all procedures named in the list.
ern "*variable*	erases the named variable.
ern [*list of variables*]	erases all the named variables.

Use all these commands with caution, It's all to easy to erase the wrong thing, even to wipe out an entire program by mistake. Note that **ern** (always makes me think of Ernie Wise - 'Little Ern') actually erases only the *name* of a variable, but of course in doing so it automatically erases its value as well. Because you're erasing the name, that is why you must preface it with the quote mark. Remember, all names must be properly addressed with their due title.

An interesting point about **er** and **erall** is that, if they are used in a program, the remainder of the procedure in which they are used will still be executed, even though that procedure itself may have been erased before it's finished working.

What is happening of course is that LOGO does the same in principle as your printer does: it stores up a certain amount of the program in its buffer - to the extent of one procedure at a time, or less - so it can continue up to the end of the current procedure even after it has been erased. This is an idiosyncracy of Dr LOGO - some other versions of LOGO don't do this.

Try this one out to see how this strange phenomenon works. Start with a clear workspace by typing 'erall' first, then enter:

```
?to test.erase
make "a 20
(pr [Before erasing :a \=] [] :a)
er "test.erase ern "a
(pr [After erasing :a \=] [] :a)
end
?
```

Run it and then type 'pots' and 'pons'. Amazing isn't it? Even after the procedure was erased, the procedure still carried out its instructions, even after death. What a noble procedure!

This magic trick can be very useful, but always thoroughly test it before relying on it: sometimes it won't work because there's too much information left over for LOGO to carry. With care however it will come up trumps every time. One thing you must not do: do not put in a **recycle** command between the erasing and the remainder of the procedure - it wipes the buffer deep-down clean!

If you're clearing the workspace prior to loading another chunk of your program, leave the last procedure intact until the last minute and then let it erase itself just before it gives the load command. Now this really is jumping ahead, so I won't say any more just now, except to mention that you'll find examples of this technique in PART THREE.

7.3 Preserving Programs

It is worth mentioning that the Digital Research implementation of LOGO is not entirely bug-free. For example the program will sometimes lock-up when exiting from an **edall** situation. There is only one way out of this: re-set the computer with <SHIFT><EXTRA><EXIT> - and lose everything in the workspace in the process! What seems to help is to use the command 'recycle edall', rather than just 'edall'.

So, remember the golden rule of programming: SAVE TO DISK AT FREQUENT INTERVALS. The same rule applies to writing manuals: I have just had the embarrassment of losing an hour's work because I got so carried away with telling you all about LOGO, I forgot to save what I was writing and we had a power-cut! Red faces all round. No good saving to the M: drive in a case like that. Always have a disk with plenty of free space in the default drive and keep saving your workspace to it. Boring? Yes. A chore? Certainly. Necessary? AN ABSOLUTE MUST - as I've just proved to my cost.

Here's a little program consisting of just one procedure that will make the process simpler and quicker. First type 'erall', then:

```
to upd :file
erasefile :file
save :file
end
```

When you've typed this in, make sure you've got a disk with some space on it in the default drive and enter:

```
?save "upd
```

Wait for the ? prompt to return and the job is complete. Put this program onto every LOGO disk you use and load it in with every program. It takes up hardly any space (about 20 nodes) and saves a lot of typing. Just leave it tacked onto your programs when you save them: you're bound to fiddle about with them later and 'upd' will still be there to help you keep up to date.

To use it you simply type 'upd "*filename*'. However don't use it the first time you save to disk. That time you must use **save** in the normal way - saving is dealt with in detail in CHAPTER 8. You will need to load 'upd' into your workspace if you're writing a new program from scratch, but thereafter it will always be at your command whenever you load that program. The alternative is typing:

erasefile "*filename* save "*filename*

every time, which is probably at least three times as much typing and you are therefore three times as likely to mistype something. LOGO, like every other computer language, is very unforgiving of typing mistakes.

I promise you, this little habit will save you hours of re-working, tooth-gnashing and hair-tearing. It is an immutable law of computing that when you have no back-up, you will lose the only copy you have, due to electrical interference, or coffee-spillage, or dog-chewing. It is equally true that, when you have not saved your workspace to disk, that is when the computer will lock-up for no good reason at all.

I am quite convinced that all computers have a magic chip inside them that knows when we haven't backed up disks: it then springs into action and wipes the only version we had.

By the way, with LOGO it doesn't matter a jot what order you write your procedures in, or what order they are in when they are saved. It does however make sense to put the procedures that are called the most at the top of the program, since it does speed things up a little. It also makes good sense to write the program in logical order for the sake of clarity. The snag is that the order of procedures often gets muddled up whilst you are writing the program. In CHAPTER 15 you'll find a handy tip which will take the hard work out of re-ordering procedures. When you enter **pots** it will show you the order of the procedures in memory.

Incidentally LOGO is rather sluggish at loading and saving. Saving in particular is done in two very noticeable parts with quite a pause in between: wait for the ? prompt to come back before you try entering fresh commands.

7.4 Errors

One of the friendliest things about the LOGO editor is how it brings your attention to the exact spot where an error has occurred. Suppose you have mis-typed something in your program and when you come to run it, you get an error message. If you now enter 'ed' you will be taken into the editor with the appropriate procedure entered and with the cursor either on or just past the error. Which makes it very easy to see where you have gone wrong. The hard part usually is putting things right - but that's the subject of CHAPTER 13. Occasionally LOGO will put the wrong procedure into the editor when you use this method: you will have to go back to command mode and use **ed** with the correct name.

LOGO error messages are all in APPENDIX III, but you will find most of them self-explanatory

You may sometimes decide that you don't like the name you have chosen for a procedure. So you pop it into the editor, delete the old name, type a new one and exit from the editor. And that's that. Well, it isn't actually, because LOGO thinks you have written a new procedure and it's kept the old name, together with it's definition, in the workspace, as you'll discover if you type 'pots'. Just erase the old procedure with 'er "*procedurename*', and all will be well. Incidentally the same sort of thing applies to variables: deleting them in the editor doesn't mean you've erased them from the workspace. You must use **ern** in command mode.

8

DISK HANDLING

8.1 Filenames and Saving To Disk

We've already touched on saving programs to disk, now it's time to examine the process in more detail. When you save a LOGO program, you save everything in the workspace, so make sure you know exactly what's there before you do it. At the ? prompt type **pots** to list the procedures in the workspace and **pons** to list the global variables. You should also get into the habit of using another primitive: **pps** (**p**rint **p**roperties). We haven't entered any properties yet, so you won't find any in the workspace, but remember to use it every time, along with **pots** and **pons** - not pots and pans, please note!. You'd be amazed at how much garbage can collect unnoticed in the workspace and get saved with programs, making them unnecessarily long and often causing them to malfunction.

Now choose a filename for the program: the filename and the program name are one and the same in fact. The filename may be the name of one of the procedures in the program if you like, or conversely it need not be. What it must not be is more than eight letters long and it must not have a file extension. LOGO adds '.LOG' to the end of all text files and '.PIC' to the end of all picture files. Nor must a filename start with a figure (0..9), although it may *contain* figures. Nor must it have any gaps in it: we've already mentioned this one. Use whatever linking character you decide on, but avoid any of the following:

< > = ! ¦ * ? / & $ [ ] ( ) . : ; \ + -

because CP/M won't like them, and you never know when you may want to juggle files around in CP/M.

When you type **dir** or **dirpic** (**dir**ectory of **pic**ture files), you will not see the '.LOG' and '.PIC' extensions, but if you do a directory listing in CP/M, Protext, LocoScript, Mini Office, MicroDesign, etc, there they will be. It really is a lot safer to keep separate data-files for your LOGO programs, and not mix them up with data-files from other disciplines.

We should just note here the difference between a picture file and a text file in LOGO. A text file can contain all the instructions for drawing a picture (as well as other things of course), whilst a picture file simply contains a snapshot of the screen. So when you save a picture file, you are not saving any instructions for re-drawing that picture, you are merely saving the picture itself.

For the technically minded, LOGO makes a bit-image record of the screen, which bears no relation whatsoever to the instructions that needed to be carried out to produce that picture. Later we shall see that we can turn this very much to our advantage, since it allows us to transport a LOGO picfile into other programs, such as desk-top publishing programs.

Text files are saved by typing in, at the ? prompt:

?save "*filename*

and pressing <RETURN> of course. Picfiles are saved by typing:

?savepic "*picfilename*

In both cases the quote-mark preceded by a space is obligatory and the filename must be entered in lower case. Should you wish to save a picture that you have laboured long over and don't want 'savepic...' etc splattered all over it, make sure you type **fs** first:

?fs savepic "*picfilename*

The command will be obeyed, but because we have made it a graphics screen with **fs** no text will appear on screen. You can't afford to make any typing errors though. A good trick is to use 'setsplit 1' and then issue the **save** command. That way any error messages will be confined to row 31. They then scroll off screen anyway, so they won't wreck your picture.

However these commands need not necessarily be entered from the ? prompt, they can also be executed from within a program. The filename or picfilename may also be assigned to a variable and 'save "*variablename*', or 'savepic "*variablename*', are perfectly in order.

The program 'DESIGNER' in PART FOUR contains an example of this technique. In fact it offers all the facilities you need for drawing, saving and re-loading pictures, and you'll find it easier to use a program like this, rather than trying to save pictures from the command line.

Here's a brief extract:

```
...
make "plist (dirpic "design??)
if emptyp :piclist
[make "fn "01 savepic word "design :fn stop]
if count :piclist = 1 [make "fn piece 7 8 first :piclist]
[high :piclist :temp]
make "fn :fn + 1
savepic word "design :fn fs
...
```

What this snippet does is first to use **dirpic** to get a list of the picfiles on the disk that are called 'design-something-something', which it then puts into the variable :piclist. If there are no picfiles on the disk that match, it automatically calls the picfile it is about to save 'design01'. However even if there is only one file called 'design*number*' on the disk, it looks to see what the *number* is and puts that value into :fn, which it duly increments by 1. This prevents the program trying to save two picfiles with the same number, which would throw up an error message all over the screen and completely ruin the picture beyond recall.

If it finds that there is more than one file on the disk, called 'design..', it passes the problem to a procedure called 'high' which sorts through the list stored in variable :piclist and duly outputs the highest number of all the 'design' picfiles on the disk. The variable :fn is then given that number, which it increments by one and the new picfile is saved with a number 1 higher than the highest on the disk.

savepic saves the whole of the current screen to disk, but beware. Each LOGO picfile takes up 23k of disk space on the 173k disks (24k on double-density disks, because they save in 2k blocks). If there is insufficient space on the disk you will get an error message all over your lovely picture. An 8000 A: drive disk can only hold 173k of information on each side, which means you can only put seven picfiles on one side of an A: disk, assuming it has no other files on it.

Double-density disks are rather more generous, with 706k available. This allows twenty-nine picfiles to be stored (just). But a word of caution. LOGO's **dir** only shows LOGO textfiles, **dirpic** only shows LOGO picfiles, neither show any other sort of files you may have stored on the disk. Check in CP/M or whatever before you start a session just what you have on what disk and how much space there is left. There is no way that you can access this information from inside LOGO, you must do it outside.

Saving in LOGO is done in two parts. The red drive light will go off in the middle of the operation and the drive may stop whirring, but you must wait until the second part of the operation is complete. In command mode this means wait until the ? prompt comes back. In program mode, you just need to sit it out. A well-written program should have some sort of message to tell you when it's safe to remove the disk, or whatever.

Picfiles in particular take quite a time to save and there is an appreciable gap between the two parts of the operation.

8.2 Loading Files From Disk

Loading is done in more or less the same way as saving. The primitives are **load** and **loadpic** which load textfiles and picfiles respectively:

?load "*filename*
?loadpic "*picfilename*

Each will load the named file from the default drive. It is important to remember that picfiles, when they load, wipe the screen, so you can't expect anything to be left over from before. However you can now work on the loaded picfile, altering the graphics, adding new ones, altering and adding text, to your heart's content. Very useful if you're trying to create something that requires constant updating, like a crossword-puzzle for instance.

With either saving or loading, you can use the drive letter as a prefix if the file you want is not in the default drive. Suppose the default drive is A:, the following would be perfectly acceptable and would retain A: as the default:

?load "m:filename

As a text file loads you will see the list of procedures it contains come up on the screen one by one. If you want to prevent this happening in a program, as well you might, use this format for loading:

```
?fs load "filename
```

and then stay in **fs**, or revert to **ts** or **ss** as appropriate. The file will be loaded as normal, but the list of procedures will not be printed to the screen.

It is possible to assign a file to be loaded to a variable as with saving, either in command mode, which would be pretty pointless, or program mode. The import of this is enormous. It makes it possible to run a program of great size by loading it in smallish chunks and erasing unwanted bits, all from within the program itself. This means that we can run programs vastly larger than the 7k or so of the workspace. Without this facility LOGO would be a very small fish indeed. If you use this technique you should first load the program into the M: drive and run it from there: it is immeasurably quicker.

Of course the default drive can be changed at will as we already know, and this can be done from within programs, permitting the saving and loading of files to and from whichever drives we want. Although it is much quicker to work in the M: drive, you may well want to save and load to and from other drives and then revert to M: to carry on working. All this can be done using **setd**.

8.3 Checking the Directory

You will have observed that **dir** and **dirpic** give us directory listings in upper case, in spite of the fact that we saved the files in lower case. This can be a problem at times, because when we search the directories from within a program we have to remember that our search string (the name of the file we are looking for) must be in upper case.

We have two primitives to help us here: **uc** and **lc**, which respectively turn lower case to upper and *vice versa*. They work like this:

```
?type uc [capital letters]
CAPITAL LETTERS
?type lc [LOWER CASE LETTERS]
lower case letters
```

Suppose we had a disk with one file on it called 'dummy', and we wished to check whether the file was present or not. Of course in command mode it's simple, we just type **dir** and the list is displayed for us, but in a program we probably don't actually want to see the list, we just want to test for the presence or absence of a particular file. I'll demonstrate how this works in command mode, because it's easier to understand, but normally it would be built into a procedure:

```
?save "dummy
?dir
[DUMMY]
?memberp "dummy (dir)
FALSE
?
```

memberp is a primitive which asks the question: "is the first input a member of the second?" We must put **dir** in round brackets when we use it in this way. For example:

```
memberp "dummy dir
```

would print out the directory, as well as testing the truth of the **memberp** test, which is probably not what we want in the middle of our program.

But why did 'memberp "dummy (dir)' return 'FALSE', which is LOGO's way of saying "no"? Simply because LOGO is very precise. It distinguishes between 'DUMMY' and 'dummy', because it doesn't look at letters in the same way as we do, by recognising the shapes. To a computer the letter 'D' is the ASCII number 68 and 'd' the ASCII number 100, so as far as the interpreter is concerned we might just as well be talking about apples on the one hand and aeroplanes on the other. To the computer 'd' and 'D' are as alike as chalk and cheese - or indeed, apples and aeroplanes!

So we must be equally precise and watch our cases. The simple solution is to reduce the **dir** entry to lower case, or the search string to upper case, using **lc** or **uc**. So either of these would work:

```
?memberp "dummy lc (dir)
TRUE
?memberp uc "dummy (dir)
TRUE
?
```

When we use **dir** and **dirpic** in a program, we should always assign the value (the directory list) to a variable, otherwise each time we mention either of these primitives in the program, the directory commands will be executed, which is an awful waste of time. Something like:

```
...
make "d (dir)
if not memberp "file :d [.....]
...
```

will do the trick. This is especially important if you are using recursion or repetition in the procedure containing the directory command, since the command would otherwise be repeated a number of times, quite unnecessarily. A good way of wearing out your disk drives and your patience.

And last, but not least, **dir** and **dirpic** can be used in the forms 'dir "a:' and 'dirpic "b:' thus allowing access to drives other than the default. If there are no files present (of the type specified), an empty list will be displayed: '[]'. Remember, don't be fooled into thinking that this means the disk is empty. It may be full to the brim with files of a different type, or non-LOGO files. There is even more to **dir** and **dirpic** than we've mentioned here: it's all in the REFERENCE section.

8.4 Erasing Files and Name-Changing

Erasing files and picfiles is done with **erasefile** and **erasepic** in the usual ways, either in command mode, or within a program:

?erasefile "*filename*
?erasepic "*picfilename*

Both erasefile and erasepic will accept the ? wild-card, so this would erase all files beginning with the letter 'w':

```
?erasefile "w???????
```

Be warned, with LOGO there is no 'Are you sure, y/n?' business. Once you've issued the command, away goes your file forever.

Finally a primitive for renaming files on disk: changef. The syntax is:

?changef "*newfilename* "*oldfilename*

Well that's the theory at any rate. My copy of Dr LOGO stubbornly refuses to implement **changef**, and so far I haven't managed to debug it. I hope you're luckier. If you aren't and it won't work for you either, here's the alternative:

```
to ren :new :old
erall fs load :old
erasefile :old
save :new erall ts ts
end
```

To change the name of a file called 'ancient' to a new name 'modern', enter:

?load "ren ren "modern "ancient

The program REN automatically erases itself from the workspace, so be sure to save it to disk before you use it for the first time! Obviously to use it you have to load it into the workspace first, but it does at least automate the process for you. Not as good as **changef** I'll grant you, but if **changef** doesn't work...

9

MATHS AND LOGIC

9.1 The Arithmetic Operators

LOGO could never be accused of being a great mathematician. It has some useful operators, but is woefully lacking in other departments. We can of course write procedures to fill the gaps, but number-crunching is is not really what LOGO is about. That said, it can handle graphs, and geometric and trigonometric problems with comparative ease, even if not with the lightning speed of C or PASCAL. As a balance however, it is a good deal easier to write! First we'll look at the simple operators:

```
* (asterisk)    multiply
/ (slash)       divide
- (hyphen)      subtract
+ (plus)        add
```

All these operators can be used in 'infix' or 'prefix' form. Infix is what we normally use:

```
2 + 3
```

This is the infix form of two plus three, and probably the way you are used to writing sums. The prefix form is:

```
+ 2 3
```

It produces exactly the same result. Sometimes you may find that a particular sum will not run properly: try using the opposite form (infix if you are using prefix, and *vice versa*). Usually it will make no difference which form you use, but occasionally LOGO seems to prefer one to the other. The other operators may be used similarly and in combination. For example, both the following give the same answer 10 (not 14 as you might have supposed):

```
+ * 4 3 2
4 + 3 * 2
```

If your maths is a bit rusty, you should note that * and / take precedence over + and -, and so are acted upon first.

Bracketed expressions are recognised and will change the precedence. Thus we could write:

```
(4 + 3) * 2
```

which would indeed give us the answer 14. Anything inside the brackets takes the precedence over anything outside. Bracketed expressions may be nested:

```
(3 * (5 + (6 / 2))) - 4
```

The answer will be 20, made up like this:

6 divided by 2	= 3 (the innermost pair of brackets)
5 plus 3	= 8 (the next pair)
3 times 8	= 24 (the outermost pair)
24 minus 4	= 20

We are not likely to want to use a powerful computer to perform a simple calculation like this – we could probably do it quicker in our heads, if we're over forty that is! If we're younger we shall use a cheap pocket calculator. I'm not telling you which I am, even if you offer me ten shillings.

However the power of a computer language is its ability to use variables rather than constants. So if we rewrite the above sum using variables, it can become a formula which can be used with variable inputs of any value. If we were to set up some variables like this:

```
make "a 9 make "b 14 make "c 3
```

and then enter:

```
(3 * (:a + (:b / 2))) - :c
```

we get the answer 45 for the inputs we have used, and this can of course be part of a program, so that we don't have to enter the appropriate numbers, the program does it for us. No pocket calculator can handle this, because it can't handle variables. Even an expert mathematician might have difficulty working out a string of such problems in his head, and he certainly couldn't do it at the speed a computer does it.

9.2 Accumulation Versus Recursion

We'll digress for a moment at this point and take a look at accumulation, which was mentioned briefly in CHAPTER 5. The general idea is to use less memory (stack space) and speed things up. Recursion tends to be a touch memory-hungry and not especially Speedy Gonzales, especially if the program has a lot of arithmetic to do.

Take as an example a program to work out the raising of a number to a power. Here's a perfectly good recursive program that does the job very well:

```
to raise :num :exp            ;inputs are number and exponent
if :exp = 1 [op :num]
make "num :num * raise :num :exp - 1
op :num
end
```

Suppose we enter as inputs '6' to the power of '6', and if we were then to examine the workings of this program we should see that it goes to a depth of [6] and then all the way back to [1] again. In other words it's using up a great deal of memory. We'll deal with how we do this later.

Here's a second way of achieving the same result, but at more than twice the speed and with far less memory being used:

```
to power :num :exp
local "ans
make "ans :num
repeat :exp - 1 [make "ans :ans * :num]
op :num
end
```

This time if we were to examine its workings we should see that the depth of call is never any more than [1], and with far less steps. It is a much more efficient program. What 'power' does is to accumulate the result of each multiplication in the variable :ans, so that it never has to go back and pick up the pieces as 'raise' has to do. If you try these two programs with large numbers, say 49 to the power of 16, you'll soon see which is the better of the two. Motto: use accumulation with arithmetical programs whenever you can.

As an example of the efficiency of accumulation over recursion in this instance, here are some comparisons:

Program	Calculate	Time	Memory Used
RAISE	49 to power 16	3 secs	113 nodes
POWER	49 to power 16	1 sec	81 nodes
RAISE	105 to power 48	8 secs	337 nodes
POWER	105 to power 48	3 secs	243 nodes
RAISE	89 to power 195	......	....
POWER	89 to power 195	12 secs	983 nodes

'RAISE' couldn't manage the last sum. After about 14 secs it ran out of stack space, having used over 3000 nodes. 'POWER' produced the astonishing answer 5.23742497263383e+151. And that's an awful lot of noughts. Not bad going for a non-mathematical language. I have to accept that the answer is correct: my calculator couldn't cope with the sum either, and I'm not about to do it in my head.

9.3 More Arithmetic Operators

Now back to arithmetic proper. We have various primitives which can be used with arithmetical problems:

numberp quotient remainder int round random rerandom arctan cos sin

numberp (**number p**roperty) tests whether the input is a number, and so is particularly useful in error-trapping ('mug-trapping' in the vernacular), where the program asks the user to input a number. Here's a typical **numberp** error-trap:

```
to input
pr [Enter a number]
make "num rq
if not numberp :num [input]
...
```

numberp returns TRUE if the input is a number, and FALSE if is not. In this example we have used 'not numberp', so if the number is not a number the output will be TRUE. so if the user enters anything that is not a number, **numberp** returns TRUE and control is thrown back to the beginning of the procedure, and no error message is generated. If we didn't have this error-trap and a non-numerical character were input, the program would almost certainly crash.

Of course another way of testing for numbers would be to test the ASCII number of the input, but **numberp** is much easier.

quotient is a useful variation of the division operator '/'. Whereas '/' outputs a real number (one with decimal fractions), **quotient** performs integer division and therefore gives an integer (whole number) result, discarding any remainder there may be. For example:

```
?quotient 102 5
```

would give the answer 20, ignoring the remainder 2. On the other hand:

```
?102 / 5
```

returns 20.4, a real number. If we try:

```
?quotient 6.9 2.4
```

we get the answer 3. The reason for this is that quotient reduces both its inputs to integers before it performs the division. Note that it doesn't round up, only down. On the other hand:

```
?6.9 / 2.4
```

yields 2.875. The partner to **quotient** is **remainder**, which outputs the remainder, if any, of integer division of the first input by the second. **remainder** is used like this:

```
?remainder 102 5
```

which outputs 2. There is a snag with both these primitives: they will not accept input numbers greater than 32767. For numbers greater than this we must use:

int (*dividend / divisor*)

to give the equivalent of **quotient**, and:

dividend - (int (*dividend / divisor*))

to give the equivalent of **remainder**. **int** converts real numbers to integers (strips away any fractional part). Its partner is **round**, which rounds up or down to the nearest whole number. Look at these:

?int 7.8	?round 7.8
7	8
?int 44.2	?round 44.2
44	44
?int 3.5	?round 3.5
3	4
?int 9.99	?round 9.99
9	10
?int 12.0	?round 12.0
12	12

As you can see, **int** always rounds down, whilst **round** rounds up or down. Numbers having a fractional part of .0 to .4 are rounded down, those with the fractions .5 to .9 are rounded up. Any further decimal places are ignored. For instance 5.449, which in arithmetical terms would normally be rounded up from right to left to 6, will still produce 5 in LOGO. It is important to realize that there is a difference between, say, 12.0 and 12; they may seem to be expressing the same number, but the first is a real number, the second an integer. We can look at 12.0 and know that it is a precise figure, whereas 12 could be 12.4 in disguise. If **int** is used like this:

```
int 9.9 / 3.3
```

the answer will be 3, but:

```
(int 9.9) / 3.3
```

outputs 2.72727272727273, which is quite a different basket of numbers.

We should mention that LOGO will accept and output real numbers with up to fifteen decimal places. Any decimal places after that are ignored. If you require greater accuracy, scale the input up by a factor of 10, 100, 1000, or more. Whole numbers of greater than 15 figures are given in scientific notation, as are fractions of less than 0.1, but only if there is no whole number part, or the number is very large. For example, 0.08 will be represented as 8.e–2 and 0.004 as 4.e–3. However 6.0007 will still be shown as 6.0007. Since LOGO supports floating point arithmetic we may enter all numbers in scientific notation. For example we may use any of the following forms, and note that it may be 'e' or 'E' as you wish:

```
5.8e6
34e+0.7
9.25E-6
```

random we have already seen working. It takes one input, an integer, and outputs a non-negative random integer between 0 and one less than the input number. Very often we don't want an output of 0, we would prefer the output to be between 1 and the maximum. So all we need to do is to write it like this:

```
make "num (random 100) + 1
```

and we shall not get a zero result. Note that we must put the brackets in to make sure that **random** is run first and then 1 is added to the result.

Actually **random** outputs a pseudo random number. If you use **random** a few times immediately after you have booted up LOGO, then reset with <SHIFT><EXTRA><EXIT>, reboot and use **random** again, you will see the same sequence of numbers coming up. If you try:

```
random 100
```

ten times, you will most likely see the sequence:

```
66 23 95 8 38 10 60 22 37 73
```

every time you reset the machine (it may be a different sequence on your model, but it will still repeat). Now enter **rerandom** (**re**set **random**) at any time and try ten 'random 100' entries and you will get exactly the same sequence of numbers. Well, that's what **rerandom** does, it resets the seed for the random number generator. The only conceivable use is when testing a program that uses random numbers and you wish to do repeat testing on the same set of inputs. If you can find any other use for it, perhaps you'll let me know!

The real problem is not getting back to the pseudo random series, but getting away from it. In PART TWO there is a very short program called 'RANSEED'. This sets a random seed for **random**, which is then virtually guaranteed to give truly random output, or as near to it as you'll ever get with a computer. Which is why ERNIE picks out your Premium Bond numbers with a gas plasma device and not a PCW. Yes, I know, it doesn't matter what he picks them out with, he never seems to pick yours, does he? Anyway, execute 'RANSEED' just before any of your programs that use random numbers and all will be well, even if your ERNIE number still doesn't come up! Before we leave **random**, it might be worth mentioning that it will accept a variable as its input.

9.4 Trigonometry Functions

LOGO has three inbuilt trigonometrical functions: **sin (sine), cos (cosine)** and **arctan (arc tangent). sin** and **cos** each take one input, an angle in degrees, and output the sine and cosine of that angle respectively. **arctan** outputs the arc tangent in degrees of the input number. Note that in this respect LOGO is different from BASIC, which uses radians. Minutes and seconds must be represented as decimal fractions of degrees. Thus:

30° 45'

would be represented in LOGO as:

30.75

Easy enough to write a conversion procedure if you need to output in minutes and seconds. Once again, inputs to all the above may be variables.

There are several useful mathematical functions missing from Dr LOGO: some of these will be found in PART TWO, but we should remember that maths is not one of LOGO's strongest points. What LOGO is very good at is drawing graphs from input data, and is especially good at creating geometrical and trigonometrical drawings.

9.5 Boolean Logic and Comparisons

Now we came to something at which LOGO is very adept: Boolean logic. Don't be put off by the name, if you've never come up against it before: it's really very simple. Just as a matter of record, it commemorates it's progenitor, George Boole (1815–1864), the great English mathematician. His book, *The Laws Of Thought*, laid the foundations for the science of what is now called Boolean algebra.

LOGO has the Boolean operators **and, or,** and **not,** the values TRUE and FALSE, and the comparators '<' (less than), '>' (greater than), and '=' (equal to). There are no signs for 'equal to or less than' or 'equal to or greater than', but we shall have no difficulty in writing expressions for these. The primitive **equalp (equal p**roperty) may be used instead of '='. It is always used in prefix form (see PART FOUR). All the Boolean expressions may be used in conjunction with the arithmetic operators.

The broad principal of Boolean logic is that when we test a comparison, we get an answer of either TRUE or FALSE. For example:

```
?4 > 3
TRUE
?19 < 17
FALSE
?42 = 2 * 21
```

```
TRUE
?
```

TRUE and **FALSE** are also LOGO properties, but they don't actually do anything, they simply represent the values 'true' and 'false'. They can also represent the truth of certain primitives, such as **ERRACT** (see CHAPTER 13) and **keyp** (*vide* CHAPTER 12), but that's another story.

Although we only have the three comparators available in Dr LOGO, '>', '<' and '=', we can write 'equal to or greater than' and 'equal to or less than', using the Boolean LOGO primitives **or**, **>** and **<**. 'Greater than or equal to' becomes;

```
...
if or :a > 6 :a = 6 [action]
...
```

The main thing to note is that **and**, **or**, and **not** must be used in the prefix form. You cannot write:

```
if :a > 6  or :a = 6 [...]
```

LOGO will not accept this. Where there is more than one 'and' or 'or', they must be enclosed in brackets. See the REFERENCE section for details.

There's sometimes a problem with the comparators '<' and '>'. If the numbers compared are more than single digit numbers, the interpreter will occasionally only compare the first digit of the first number with the first digit of the second number. If you do run up against this little bug, the answer is put the numbers into variables and compare the variables, and, *hey presto!* no problems.

9.6 Conditional Statements

We need to mention the primitive **if** again here. We've already met it a number of times, but it's worth making a formal statement of its use and syntax here. **if** is a conditional operator, takes one or more inputs and outputs the logic value of each comparison or statement as TRUE or FALSE. It must then be followed by a list containing an instruction or instructions to be carried out if the output is TRUE. If the output is FALSE, control is passed to the next line following the 'if' comparison. if may optionally take a second instruction list to be executed if the output is FALSE.

`if [`*`instructionlist`*`] {[`*`instructionlist`*`]}`

is entirely equivalent to BASIC's 'IF...THEN' and 'IF...THEN...ELSE' statements. Here's an example of the use of Boolean logic operators and comparators:

```
to compare :a :b :c :d
if (and and :a > :b :a < :c not :a = :d) [pr "TRUE] [pr "FALSE]
end
```

This translates as "*if* :a is greater than :b *and* :a is less than :c *and* :a is *not* equal to :d, then the conditions have been met, so 'TRUE' will be printed, if not 'FALSE' will be printed. This is of course an unnecessarily complicated way of writing this expression, but it does show how various elements can be combined. Try out with these two entries with the procedure 'compare':

```
?compare 16 10 20 15
?compare 15 10 20 15
```

It is standard practice in computer language text-books to print 'truth tables' for 'AND, 'OR' and 'NOT', and who am I to depart from standard practice? I will say, however, that the best way to understand Boolean logic is by trying it out on the computer. Attempting to learn truth tables by heart is a thankless task, but here they are anyway, just for reference:

AND	condition1	condition2	result
	TRUE	TRUE	TRUE
	TRUE	FALSE	FALSE
	FALSE	TRUE	FALSE
	FALSE	FALSE	FALSE

OR	condition1	condition2	result
	TRUE	TRUE	TRUE
	TRUE	FALSE	TRUE
	FALSE	TRUE	TRUE
	FALSE	FALSE	FALSE

NOT	condition		result
	TRUE		FALSE
	FALSE		TRUE

9.7 TRUE and FALSE As Output Values

TRUE and **FALSE** are primitives, but they are more often used as values, particularly when associated with **if** statements. Look at this line:

```
if :a > 100 [make "a 0] [make "a :a + 1]
```

LOGO first tests to see if :a is indeed greater than 100. If it is it outputs TRUE, but it doesn't print it to the screen. Instead it notes the *value* TRUE and executes the first list of instructions, in this case '[make "a 0]'. If :a is less than 100, the test will return FALSE, which tells LOGO to ignore the first list of instructions and execute the second list ('[make "a :a + 1]'), or to go to the next line of the procedure if there is no second list. This is an example of the use of TRUE and FALSE as values. Later we shall see how the *primitives* **TRUE** and **FALSE** are used.

9.8 'Running' Variables

Finally there is another way in which we can use the outputs TRUE and FALSE. We need to know about yet another primitive: **run**. Normally we use run to execute a list of instructions contained in a variable. But there is another way in which **run** can be used, namely to test the truth value of a variable. Suppose we have put a list into a variable:

```
make "compare [:a = :b]
```

We could now 'run' the variable, like this:

```
...
if run :compare [action1] [action2]
...
```

In other words, **run** is running the instructions contained in ':compare' and outputting the values TRUE or FALSE. We can see this working in a utility program 'WHILE' which you will find listed in PART TWO. The variable :action must be presumed to contain an instruction to perform some action or other. It might, for instance, contain the name of a procedure, or a print instruction.

```
to while :condition :action
if not run :condition [throw "TOPLEVEL]
run :action
end
```

And here's a simple example of 'WHILE' working, in this case to print a list in a vertical column. All we need, apart from the procedure 'WHILE', is a declared list and a procedure to do the printing. Try entering:

```
?make "alist [A B C D E F G]
```

and then:

```
to printv :alist
while [not emptyp :alist]
   [pr first :alist printv bf :alist]
end
```

Run the program with 'printv :alist'. Rather a large sledge-hammer to crack a very small nut, you might say, but it demonstrates an important point. The line '[pr first :alist...' must be indented by *at least* one space from the line containing the 'if' test (see **if** in the REFERENCE section). Now as to how the 'run' bit works. In line two of 'while':

```
...
if not run :condition [throw "TOPLEVEL]
...
```

the variable :condition contains a test 'not emptyp :alist'. So long as that condition is met (ie the list is not empty), the loop will continue and 'printv' will print the next item on the list: that is what 'run :action' is saying in 'pr first :alist'. So, **run** can be used to run a list of instructions or a procedure, or as a logical test operator when used in conjuction with the comparator **if**.

And that brings this chapter to a logical conclusion.

10

WORDS AND LISTS

10.1 Word For Word

'Word' in LOGO doesn't mean quite the same thing as it does in English. A 'word' in LOGO can consist of one or more alphanumeric characters (and a few more besides), which contain no delimiters – spaces in effect. All the following are LOGO 'words':

hello
xyz16
good.bye
good_bye
R
32

The last one may seem surprising. As we discovered earlier a number can be used arithmetically, but can also be treated as word for the purposes of word-processing. In practice this does not present any real problems. There is a test we can use to see whether a word is a word or not: **wordp** (**word** property). Try 'wordp 32' and you'll get the answer 'TRUE', which could be confusing. We could always double check using **numberp** (**number** property), which will return 'TRUE' for '32', but 'FALSE' for a word made up of alphabetic characters, like 'hello'. That would sort out the sheep from the goats. Try this:

```
?make "alist (list "a "b "c "d)
?wordp :alist
FALSE
?wordp first :alist
TRUE
?
```

Why is this? Because :alist is a *list*, but the list is made up of *words*, so the first (or any other) element of that list is a word and **wordp** will return TRUE.

If we wish to join together two or more inputs to make them into a word, we use the primitive **word**. **word** takes one or more inputs, but if there are more or less than two, **word** and its inputs must be enclosed in round brackets. It works like this:

```
?word "break "fast
breakfast
?(word "user "\- "defined " "graphics)
user-defined graphics
?
```

Bear in mind that, since **word** joins words together, we must specifically enter a space if we want one included. **word**, funnily enough, accepts a space as a word if we tell it that that's what it is! But why don't we simply type in 'user-defined graphics' in the first place? Because we can use **word** with variables, and this is where it becomes really useful. Suppose variable :la holds the number of the last file saved to disk and the variable :file contains the name 'design'. When we write:

```
...
make "la :la + 1
make "file word :file :la
savepic :file
...
```

we are saying: "take the name of the file ('design') and suffix it with the number of the last picfile saved plus 1, then save it to disk". So if the last picfile saved was 'design10', the next one saved will be named 'design11' automatically. If we didn't use **word** we would get a file called 'design 11', and we know filenames must consist of one word, not two, so 'design 11' would be illegal.

10.2 Making Sentences

From words to sentences - again not the same meaning as in English. The primitive is **se**, which makes a list of its inputs. Like **word**, **se** takes any number of inputs, and if there are more or less than two, **se** and its inputs must be enclosed in round brackets. For example:

```
?se "full "stop
[full stop]
?(se "common "place "things)
[common place things]
?
```

Notice how **se** puts spaces between words. You can even combine **word** and **se**:

```
?se "average word "rain "fall
[average rainfall]
```

Note that 'word "rain "fall' counts as one word as far as **se** is concerned, so no outside brackets are needed. Since **se** creates a list, it produces the right sort of input for such primitives as **setpos**, **cursor** and **pr** - we've already seen the first two at work with **se**. **pr** works in exactly the same way. Suppose :a holds the value 'print' and :b the value 'text':

```
pr se :a :b
```

would output 'print text'. This is what happens: first the variables are translated to give 'print' and 'text', and then **se** puts them into a list '[print text]'. Finally **pr** prints the contents of the list to give 'print text'.

10.3 Making Lists

List processing is the very essence of LOGO. Amongst other things, it shows its parentage: namely LISP. LISP (LISt Processing) is the father and mother of all list-processing languages, and it's well-worth looking at and comparing it with LOGO. But why all the fuss, you may well ask? After all, a list is a list, and that's all there is to it. Look at the following:

[1 [2] 3 4 [5 6 7] [[8] 9] 10]

How many lists are there? One...three...? Actually there are five. The easy way to count them is to count the total number of brackets and divide by two. That's also a good way of checking whether you've missed out an opening or closing bracket somewhere: if the count is an odd number, you have. Just to make sure this is absolutely clear, this is how the list of lists breaks down:

```
              [1 [2] 3 4 [5 6 7] [[8] 9] 10]
level 1       [1.........................10]          1 list
level 2          [2].....[5 6 7].[[.] 9]              3 lists
level 3                           [8]                 1 list
                                        TOTAL:        5 lists
```

Yes, a list can consist of only one item. You can even have an empty list like this [] which still counts as a list. There is no limit to the depth of lists, theoretically anyway. PART TWO contains a program 'DEPTH' which measures the depth of nesting of a list of lists. The primitive used to create a list is, sensibly enough, **list**. It behaves just like **word** and **se**: it can take any number of inputs from one up, but if there are more or less than two, the whole lot must be enclosed in round brackets:

```
?make "numlist list 5 9
?:numlist
[5 9]
?make "addrlist (list "name "addr1 "addr2 "addr3 "addr4)
?:addrlist
[name addr1 addr2 addr3 addr4]
?
```

Although numbers need not be prefaced with quote-marks, they may be if you wish. But such symbols as '£', '$', '#' and '%' must be prefaced with quote marks, as must all words and letters.

10.4 List Manipulation

For the purposes of demonstrating what we can do with a list, we will create a simple first-level list which we'll call 'rainbow':

```
?make "rainbow (list "red "yellow "green "blue "indigo "violet)
?:rainbow
[red yellow green blue indigo violet]
?pr first :rainbow
```

```
red
?pr last :rainbow
violet
?
```

The primitives **first** and **last** are obvious enough: **first** outputs the first element of a list and **last** outputs the last one.

```
?bf :rainbow
[yellow green blue indigo violet]
?bl :rainbow
[red yellow green blue indigo]
?
```

Again pretty self-evident. **bf** outputs a list of all but the first element of the list, and **bl** all but the last. The distinction needs to be made that **first** and **last** extract the *items* from the list, whereas **bf** and **bl** output *lists*. We can repeat any of these four commands as many times as we like:

```
?bf bf bf :rainbow
[blue indigo violet]
?first last :rainbow
v                                ;the 'v' of 'violet'
?last bl bl :rainbow
blue
?bf bf bl bl bl :rainbow
green
?last first :rainbow
d                                ;the 'd' of 'red'
?
```

Two more primitives allow us to add to a list, **fput** and **lput** (first **put** and (last **put**):

```
?make "rainbow fput "infra_red :rainbow
?:rainbow
[infra_red red yellow green blue indigo violet]
?make "rainbow lput "ultra_violet :rainbow
?:rainbow
[infra-red red yellow green blue indigo violet ultra_violet]
?
```

Just to give you a taste of what, for instance, **bf** can do for us in a program, here is a simple little utility that will print out a list in a column rather than in a row, that is, it prints vertically. It's a simplified version of 'printv' that we met earlier:

```
to pv :alist
if emptyp :alist [stop]
pr first :alist
pv bf :alist
end
```

Call this with something like:

```
pv [a b c d e f g]
```

or any other list you like. The procedure uses tail-end recursion and calls itself, using :alist as a parameter. Each time it goes it round it reduces the list by taking away the first element. When the list is empty (**emptyp** is **empty** property) it stops. Remember, **stop** only stops the procedure, not the program. Try 'pv (dir)': it gives a clearer list of the directory, but

DIRCOL, which is part of STARTUP in PART THREE, does it even better. If you want to print the list in reverse order, use **last** and **bl**.

Here's a way to reverse the contents of a list, rather than just print it backwards. The first procedure simply initialises the variable :temp, whilst 'rev.work' does the actual work:

```
to reverse :alist
local "temp
make "temp []
op rev.work :alist :temp
end

to rev.work :alist :temp
if emptyp :alist [op :temp]
make "temp fput first :alist :temp
op rev.work bf :alist :temp
end
```

Call this program with 'reverse [1 2 3 4 5 6 7 8 9]' (any list you like). Procedure 'reverse' creates a local variable called 'temp', which is given a null value '[]', which is an empty list, and then calls 'rev.work' with the parameters :alist and :temp. This is a slightly different call to the sort we're used to. **op** (**output**) calls the procedure 'rev.work' and at the same time asks it to output its result. In 'rev.work' the list :alist is checked to see if it's empty: if it isn't, the first element of :alist is put into :temp, using **fput**. Then rev.work calls itself, but chopping the first element off :alist in the process, and again using **op** rather than a straight call. This goes on until the list is empty, when the conditional instruction '[op :temp]' is obeyed. The result is output to the calling procedure ('reverse'); in the example above, the output will be '9 8 7 6 5 4 3 2 1'. **op** throws control back to 'reverse', which in turn outputs the result, and the program stops.

10.5 Outputting From Procedures

The primitive **op** is a very useful command: it allows us to output the result of a procedure to another procedure without assigning it to a variable. It further has the action of stopping the procedure in which it appears when it is executed. Even if we were to add another instruction after 'op' in 'op :temp' it would not be obeyed. It is also important to note that **op** can only hold one value, which can of course be a list as it is in our example – so that's how you get round that one! If we wrote:

```
...
make "a :a * :b
make "b :a / :b
op :a op :b
...
```

we would never reach 'op :b', because 'op :a' stops the procedure there and then. But we *can* write:

```
...
op list :a :b
...
```

which neatly outputs two values. Very handy. If you study the LIBRARY and WORKING PROGRAMS you will see the many ways in which **op** can be used. In particular notice how it can automatically output the result of a procedure by using the form 'op *procedure-name*'.

10.6 Extracting Items From Lists

But how do we extract the contents of a list? No problem with a first-level list: we can use **type** and **pr**, or we can use **item**, or **first** and **last**. All very fine as far as it goes, but what about our list of lists?

```
[1 [2] 3 4 [5 6 7] [[8] 9] 10]
```

If we try type on this, all we shall lose are the outermost brackets: not very helpful. And this is no use at all:

```
?item 6 [1 [2] 3 4 [5 6 7] [[8] 9] 10]
[[8] 9]
```

So we need a program that will remove all but the outermost pair of brackets in a multi-level list. Here it is:

```
to reduce :alist
if wordp :alist [op :alist]
if emptyp :alist [op []]
if and wordp first :alist emptyp bf :alist [op :alist]
op (se reduce first :alist)(reduce bf :alist)
end
```

Try it on the list of lists above.

List manipulation permits us to create programs to do sorting, searching, replacing, and so on. You will see in PARTS TWO and THREE several examples of these using both recursion and repetition. Often, with list-processing, there is more than one way of arriving at the desired result, but one method may well be faster than another and less memory-expensive. If you find you've created a program that takes an age to complete its work, or fills up the memory in no time, try another algorithm. Just in case you haven't come across the word before, 'algorithm' is just a fancy way of saying 'method': a set of steps you use in working out the solution to a problem. The starting point and the finishing point are the same: the problem is the starting point, the answer is the finishing point. The algorithm is the bit in the middle; how you arrive at the answer to the problem. Unfortunately, the 'bit in the middle' is the hard part.

10.7 Removing Items From Lists

Here's an example of two programs written using two different methods, recursion and accumulation, but which both achieve the same objective, that is they both remove an element from a list; Dr LOGO has no primitive to do this. First the recursive method:

```
to take.out :item :list
local "temp
make "temp []
take.out.work :item :list
end
```

```
take.out.work :item :list
if emptyp :list [stop]
if not :item first :list
   [make "temp lput first :list :temp]
take.out.work :item :bf :list
end
```

And now using repetition. The indentations in this procedure are critical, although there need not be so many spaces. One in each case is sufficient.

```
to remove :item :list
(local "temp "w)
if memberp :item :list [make "w where] [stop]
if :w = 1 [make "list bf :list op :list]
   [repeat :w - 1
      [make "temp lput first :list :temp
       make "list bf :list]]
make "list bf :list
make "list se temp :list op :list
end
```

Looking at REMOVE it may seem a very complicated way of achieving the same thing that TAKE.OUT achieves relatively simply. But now try running the two programs using the same input list. The test list used to produce the following table of results contained 30 elements: a grocery list of items like 'bread, tea, sugar' etc. You may make the list much longer if you like: it won't alter the operation of the program, only the time it takes to do its work. Incidentally, the programs work appreciably faster with numbers rather than words. Try the two different programs with your own list and time them. The test results on the thirty-item grocery-list showed the following:

ITEM REMOVED	PROGRAM	SIZE (nodes)	WORKSPACE USED (nodes)	RUN TIME (seconds)
10th	TAKE.OUT	232	431	6
10th	REMOVE	256	102	0.5
20th	TAKE.OUT		456	7
20th	REMOVE		245	2.5
30th	TAKE.OUT		456	8
30th	REMOVE		490	4

Which just goes to show that the simplest and seemingly most obvious method is not always the best. REMOVE shows a speed advantage and a greater relative saving on memory space up to about 25 items. After that the speed advantage remains, but it gradually uses up more (temporary) memory. The primitive **where** returns the position in a list of an item following a **memberp** test. For example:

```
?memberp "g [d r a k g p w]
TRUE
?where
5
?
```

where only returns this value from the *latest* **memberp** test, but will continue to do so for as long as the particular program runs. **where** is extremely useful in sorting and searching programs. See MAXSORT and DATABASE, both in PART THREE, for examples of the use of **where**. This only works if the **memberp** test was successful: if it was not successful, **where** will output '0'.

10.8 Testing For Lists And Names

There is a primitive, **listp** (**list** **p**roperty), which tests an input to see whether it is a list or not. It is used in exactly the same way as **numberp**, **wordp** and **memberp**:

```
?make "alist [1 2 3]
?listp :alist
TRUE
?
```

There is yet another checking primitive available: **namep** (**name** **p**roperty). This checks to see whether a variable name already exists in the program. If it does, **namep** returns 'TRUE'. The input to **namep** must have a quote mark in front of it, as must all names. This is how it works:

```
?make "engine "diesel
?namep "engine
TRUE
?namep "diesel
FALSE
?
```

FALSE because 'diesel' is the *value* of the variable, not its *name*.

10.9 Extracting Chunks

Now for a useful primitive which can extract any piece of information from almost anything: **piece**. **piece** takes three inputs, the first two are numbers, and the third a data list. The first number is the position of the first item to be extracted, the second the position of the last item to be extracted, the third obviously is the list, or word, or number from which the section is to be taken. **piece** is more or less analogous to BASIC's MID$.

```
?make "animals [horse dog cow cat sheep pig donkey]
?piece 2 3 :animals
dog cow
?piece 4 7 :animals
cat sheep pig donkey
?piece 1 1 :animals
?horse
?last piece 5 5 :animals
p
?piece 2 4 683279
832
?piece 4 4 "animals
m
?
```

We can also use **piece** to test for the presence or absence of an item:

```
?equalp piece 6 6 :animals "pig
TRUE
?
```

It is important to note that **piece** extracts *items* from a *list*, and therefore the output will not be within square brackets. The difference between a list and an element of list is a difference of types, and this is one area where data 'typing' is rigid. You cannot compare a list with an element of a list, or a word, or a variable that contains a value that is not a list. These two may look the same, but they're as different as cats and dogs:

```
?if 6 = [6] [pr "true] [pr "false]
false
?
```

But:

```
?if (list 6) = [6] [pr "true] [pr "false]
true
?
```

10.10 Shuffling

Before we leave list-processing, there's an oddity we can use: **shuffle.** This takes one input, a list, and shuffles the contents randomly. You'll find it used in 'WARSHIP' in PART THREE. It could be used in a card game, dominoes, or whatever else you can think of where you want a list shuffled randomly. The useful thing about it is that you can assign the shuffled list to a variable, pick off elements from the beginning or the end as you want them, and hence you can keep a 'map' of your shuffled list (a screen map, or a card-hand map perhaps) to check whether a particular item has been used or not (a position, or a card). If you study 'WARSHIP', you'll see this in action. A point to notice, however, is that **shuffle** behaves like **random** and repeats itself from boot-up. Use RANSEED before you run your program with **shuffle** in it and **shuffle** will be nicely unpredictable.

And there we'll leave list-processing for now. As we shall see in the next chapter, it is closely allied to property-processing. In fact it is perfectly possible to build a database without using property-processing at all. But that's jumping the gun.

11

PROPERTIES AND DATABASES

11.1 Objects, Properties And Values

Although the names 'object', 'property', and 'value' are not LOGO primitives and have no actual meaning within the language, they are convenient labels and we shall be using them repeatedly in this chapter, so let's get to know them. Each *object* can have as many *properties* as you like, though each property can only have one *value*. For example, the object 'chair' could have a property 'upholstered', which might have the value 'blue'. It might have another property 'high-backed', which in turn might have the value 'winged'. Consider too that 'chair' might also be the property of an object 'furniture', and might have the value 'dining'. Confused? Probably!

For now just keep in your mind the sequence 'object - property - value'. Consider an object 'dog'. We know that a dog can have, apart from other things, a colour particular to that dog. So the object 'dog' can have a property 'colour', which in turn can have a value, say, 'brown'. Of course 'dog' can have many other properties: size, weight, breed, and so on. Each of these properties can have a multiplicity of values. Using the structure 'object - property - value' we can build up a whole database of information about dogs - or cats, or trains, or anything else we fancy.

11.2 The Property Processors

But we must first introduce some special property-processing primitives. **pprop** (**put prop**erty) puts a value into a property belonging to an object.

```
?pprop "dog "colour "brown
```

Object 'dog', property 'colour', value 'brown'. We could now add:

```
?pprop "dog "breed "Terrier
```

and:

```
?pprop "dog "name "Spot
```

If we now use another primitive **plist** (property **list**), we can retrieve all the properties and values relative to 'dog':

```
?plist "dog
[name Spot breed Terrier colour brown]
```

Not exactly a giant step for mankind, but it's a start. The primitive **pps** (**p**rint **p**ropertie**s**) outputs all the objects, properties and values present in the workspace all in one go:

```
?pps
dog's name is Spot
dog's breed is Terrier
dog's colour is brown
?
```

Which means that **pps** is a clever little fellow. It's put in the "'s" and the "is" all by itself. But its grammar isn't always terribly useful. Consider these:

```
?pprop "lettuces "are "Iceberg
?pprop "Iceberg "is "crisp
```

They seem to make sense. However:

```
?pps
Iceberg's is is crisp
lettuces's are is Iceberg
?
```

Not really English as she is spoke! **plist** does a little better:

```
?plist "lettuces
[are Iceberg]
?plist "Iceberg
[is crisp]
?
```

Rather more sensible. There's a moral here: make sure you know how your data will appear when you retrieve it. This determines how you enter it. Don't plunge in and build up a large database, and then find at the end of all your work that you don't like the way the answers are coming out. Keep testing each section of the program until you're sure it works, and produces the output in the way you like it before you move on.

11.3 Building A Database

In order to build a database we must first create a means of inputting data to it. We could do it all in command mode using **pprop**, but that would be as tedious as writing the wretched thing out in long-hand. Aren't computers supposed to take the hard work out of everything? Sometimes I'm not quite so sure, but we won't go into that just now.

Before we plunge in and start writing procedures we must decide exactly what are the things that we want our database to do. Writing out a list of our requirements at this stage will save us a great deal of hard work later on. It cannot be too strongly stated that a few minutes spent planning a program in advance can make the world of difference to the result. In a sense it is unfortunate that LOGO is a fairly unstructured language because it permits us to get away with sloppy programming. Against this is the freedom LOGO gives us to romp around a program and have fun. So we must try to strike a balance and try not to be too 'free', or we may find that a perfectly workable idea refuses to work in practice simply because it gets muddled up in the programming stage. A little sensible planning never hurt no-one! So here's our fairly modest list of database wants:

1. Accept new data.
2. Delete unwanted data.
3. Store data.
4. View data
5. Search for and find data.
6. Print results.

So that automatically gives us an opening menu:

```
to menu
local "inp
ct (pr [DATABASE: Add data=A] [] [Delete=D] [] [View=V] []
   [Store=S] [] [Find=F] [] [Quit=Q])
make "inp uc rc
if :inp = "A [add]
if :inp = "D [delete]
if :inp = "V [view]
if :inp = "S [store]
if :inp = "F [find]
if :inp = "Q [throw "TOPLEVEL]      ;exits to ? prompt
menu                                ;loops back
end
```

All perfectly straightforward. That long line of options is all one line, but you can break it with a <RETURN> when you type it in if you wish, so long as the continuation part is indented by at least one space. Or you could just let LOGO wrap it for you.

11.4 Adding Data

Here is the the 'add' procedure, together with its assistant 'adprop':

```
to add
(local "datalist "obj "prop "val)
ct pr [Enter OBJECT PROPERTY VALUE. Press RETURN for menu]
make "datalist rl
if :datalist = [] [menu]            ;a null entry calls 'menu'
if not count :datalist = 3
   [pr [Invalid entry] repeat 500 [] add]
make "obj first :datalist
make "prop item 2 :datalist
make "val last :datalist
adprop :obj :prop :val
end
```

The instruction 'repeat 500 []' merely wastes a bit of time so that the user has a chance to read the message before it disappears. If the pause is too long for you, reduce the number of repeats to 400, or even 300. If it's too short, increase the repeats. More on this in the next chapter.

Now we can enter the 'adprop' procedure, which actually does the work of building up the database:

```
to adprop :obj :prop :val
if memberp :val gprop :obj :prop
   [pr [Data already exists] repeat 500 [] add]
pprop :obj :prop se :val gprop :obj :prop
{pprop :val :prop se :obj gprop :val :prop}
add
end
```

The line in curly brackets {...} is optional, depending on whether you require the data to be entered in reverse as well as forwards. In certain database applications this is necessary: it's up to you. The reason we have used the form 'pprop :obj :prop se :val gprop :obj :prop', rather than the simple 'pprop :obj :prop :val' form, is that, when we retrieve data we want to see *all* the values of a property. What the slightly more complex form of entry does is it takes the values already input and adds the new value to the list.

11.5 Removing Items Of Data

There are only two ways we can get rid of data from the workspace. We cannot use **er** or **ern**, or even **erall**: none of these affect the properties we have entered using **pprop**. One way is to quit LOGO by typing 'bye' (the primitive **bye** – 'good-**bye**'), which wipes the workspace as clean as a whistle. Unfortunately we lose everything that is in the workspace in the process, which might not be what we want. We may wish to erase only one or two properties. The way we do that is to use the primitive **remprop** (**rem**ove **prop**erty). **remprop** takes two inputs, the first is an object, the second the property we wish to remove, or delete. If you look at this example you will see how it works in practice:

```
?pprop "dress "colour "yellow
?plist "dress
[colour yellow]
?remprop "dress "colour
?plist "dress
[]
?
```

We remove the property from the object, so naturally the property–*value* goes as well. Simple enough, but we would certainly not want the chore of doing this from the command line. We need a procedure, and here it is:

```
to delete
(local "inlist "one "two)
ct pps pr [] pr []
pr [DELETE: Enter OBJECT PROPERTY. Press RETURN for menu.]
make "inlist rl
if :inlist = [] [menu]
make "one first :inlist
make "two item 2 :inlist
remprop :one :two
{remprop gprop :one :two :two}      ;LOGO can sort this out!
delete
end
```

The full list of properties is printed first with the command **pps** so that we can see what we want to delete. The optional line {...} should only be included if reverse-storage has been adopted in 'adprop'. It's a little complicated, but it works.

11.6 Storing, Viewing And Finding

Having amassed a load of data in the workspace, we must now create a means of storing that information on disk:

```
to store
local "dbase
pr [Enter name to save database]
make "dbase lc rq
if :dbase = " [menu]
if memberp uc :dbase (dir) [pr [File exists. Overwrite? y\/n]
   if lc rc = "y [erasefile :dbase] [store]
erall save :dbase load "database menu
end
```

You can call your data list anything you like, but remember that the name must not have more than eight letters. In the last line, we are assuming that the procedures so far have been saved under the imaginitive name 'DATABASE'. We also require a method of viewing everything that is in the database. We can do this very simply:

```
to view
ct pr [Press RETURN for menu]
pr [] pps pr [] make "inp rc
if rc = " [ct menu]
end
```

But it would be very irritating if we had to search through a mass of data to find a particular item. The program should do this for us:

```
to find
(local "inp "fact)
ct ron
(pr [] [FIND: Enter 'O' for OBJECT, 'P' for PROPERTY] []) rof
make "inp lc rc if not memberp :inp "op [find]
if :inp = "o [pr [Enter OBJECT to find]] [pr [Enter PROPERTY to find]]
make "fact rq
if :inp = "p [if emptyp glist :fact [pr [Not found]]
   [listfact :fact glist :fact]]
if :inp = "o [if emptyp plist :fact [pr [Not found]]
   [make "fact plist :fact pr :fact]]
repeat 800 [] menu
end

to listfact :fact :proplist
if emptyp :proplist [repeat 800 [] menu]
(pr first :proplist :fact (list gprop first :proplist :fact))
listfact :fact bf :proplist
end
```

That'll do nicely. We're going to leave printing to paper at this stage; that deserves a chapter to itself. So there we are. A very simple database, stripped of most of the trimmings, but it will serve.

If we have a lot of data stored it may well shoot off the top of the screen before we can see it properly in 'delete' and 'view'. This can be solved very simply: to pause, press '<ALT> Z' or f1, and the property list will stop printing instantly, with a little message:

```
pausing... in view [.....]
view ?
```

And there the cursor will sit until you type 'co' and press <RETURN>. The list will then go on printing at the same frenetic rate as before. You can use this trick as often as you like. No matter how much data you have, you can stop it scrolling for as long as you like.

11.7 Saving Data In Reverse

A word now about saving data in a reversed form. Why should we save it both ways round? Take the earlier example we were using: you may want to know the names of all dogs that have brown coats, or, if the dog has a white coat with black spots, what breed is it? So long as the facts are stored both ways round, we can question the database any way we like. If data is stored only one way round, we may have problems, because we cannot question a value, only an object or a property. But of course reverse storage takes up twice as much space, so only use it if you really need it.

How you dress up the data output is up to you. We've already seen how **pps** inserts "'s" and "is", whereas **plist** simply presents us with a list of properties. However we could easily make the readout more presentable using a line like:

```
pprop :obj word :prop "'s word :val ",
```

The output using **plist** would now be something like:

```
plist "dog
[name's Spot, breed's Terrier, colour's brown]
```

Or we could use **se**:

```
pprop :obj :prop se "is :val
```

which gives:

```
plist "dog
[name [is Spot] breed [is Terrier] colour [is brown]]
```

The program 'REDUCE' could be used to remove the inner brackets, or we might use this:

```
to printdat :name
local "alist
make "alist plist :name
printout :alist
end
to printout :alist
if emptyp :alist [stop]
(type item 1 :alist [])
pr item 2 :alist
printout bf bf :alist
end
```

The possibilities for data storage, presentation and retrieval are many and varied. You need not feel that you are restricted to just three items - object, property, value. You can go on adding data to any object as many times as you like. Where you *are* restricted is in, say, a name and address database. You cannot have two person's names that are the same, since the program will think that all inputs to a particular name pertain to that one name, meaning one person. It is more than likely that there will be two different people with the same surname: this is a problem, because **pprop** will simply add data to the property list it already holds for that name. Suppose we enter the following data, using 'adprop', in our database:

```
pprop "Smith "firstname se "John gprop "Smith "firstname
```

and then use **plist**, we shall see:

```
[Smith firstname [John]]
```

But if we now enter another Smith's data, Fred Smith, who lives a hundred miles away:

```
pprop "Smith "firstname se "Fred gprop "Smith "firstname
```

we shall get the output from **plist**:

```
[Smith firstname [Fred John]]
```

pprop, knowing nothing of geography, assumes that the Smith referred to in the second entry is the same Smith as in the first one, and that we've merely added another firstname to his data. This makes writing a name and address database very complicated. It's not impossible, but it is very difficult. For this reason you will find a database in PART THREE (also imaginatively named DATABASE) which dispenses with **pprop** and uses lists instead, and which has the added advantage that data may be written in a natural manner. Instead of having to write:

```
Dalmatian colour white_with_black_spots
```

we may enter a more readable:

```
Dalmatian  colour  white with black spots
```

Furthermore it will accept multiple entries and distinguish between them, and perform multiple searches. It also has a proper label-printing facility, so it really is an all-singing all-dancing database! However for many database applications LOGO's dedicated property-handling operators are perfectly capable of coping, and you should certainly not dismiss them out of hand. They're fast and neat, and will answer well for many applications.

gprop is a very useful primitive, both in and out of databases. If we want to retrieve the information from an object-property pair, **gprop** is our man:

```
?gprop "Terrier "name
Spot
?
```

gprop whittles down the amount of information that is passed back to just that which we want, whereas **plist** is more profligate and may provide far more information than we require. Each application should be tailored to suit the particular demands of the database in question. **gprop** is also immensely useful outside databases, since it can reveal the properties and values of pretty-well everything. As we shall see it can unveil some of the innermost secrets of LOGO: most usefully of all the memory locations of primitives. This is the first step towards re-writing the LOGO system itself, but that exciting prospect is something that will have to wait its turn.

11.8 Loading The Database In Sections

Obviously the amount of data that can be stored in the workspace depends on how much space there is remaining after the database program itself has been loaded. Which may be not a lot. One way round this is to load only those procedures which are immediately needed by the program and to erase them from within the program after we've finished with them. Using the database program we have just constructed, we might do this sort of thing:

```
to menu
...
if :inp = "A [er "menu load "add add]
if :inp = "D [er "menu load "delete delete]
if :inp = "V [er "menu load "view view]
if :inp = "S [er "menu load "store store]
if :inp = "F [er "menu load "find find]
if :inp = "Q [stop]
...
```

The procedures 'add' and 'adprop' should have been saved as one file called 'add'. Then, when we move on to 'add', we must have a means of getting back to the menu. All we need is a slight alteration in 'add':

```
if :datalist = [] [er [add adprop] load "menu menu]
```

We can carry on this system of loading and erasing throughout the program. The penalty is that the program will be considerably slower to run, but we can speed things up a lot if we run it from the M: drive. The quickest way of doing this is using PIP.COM from CP/M before you run LOGO. Then when you boot up LOGO, all your files will be sitting there waiting for you in the M: drive. There is also a utility to be found in PART TWO called 'MOVF' which will move files from drive to drive from within LOGO, but it is considerably slower than PIP. If you have a lot of files to move, leave LOGO with bye, PIP the files across to M: and then re-enter LOGO by typing 'logo'.

There is another way of speeding up LOGO: by using an accelerator such as Cirtech's excellent SPRINTER, which, although it cannot speed up disk-drives, makes LOGO a great deal nippier in every other way. In fact it makes the PCW think it's a PC and the LOGO turtle think it's a greyhound!

12

INPUT AND OUTPUT

12.1 Screen Presentation: Messages

We've already seen many examples of screen output using **pr**, **type**, and **show**. We know that screen output can be directed to any part of the screen using **setcursor**. We can even output to the screen in reverse video, using the CP/M escape codes 'ESC p' and 'ESC q'. In LOGO these become:

```
type word char 27 "p   ;turns on reverse video
type word char 27 "q   ;turns off reverse video
```

These functions are best put into procedures, and you will find them in PART TWO, listed as 'RON' and 'ROF'. You'll also find that there is a problem that can occur with RON, which is also dealt with in PART TWO.

Not all output needs to be displayed on screen, indeed we often explicitly require output to be hidden. Screen messages such as '*procedurename* defined' can ruin the look of a program; variable values output from one part of the program to another need to be kept out of sight; error messages may need to be suppressed; and so on.

We've already touched on the subject of hiding 'such-and-such defined' messages. All we have to do is go into the **fs** screen state and no text (except error messages) will be output. So if we load a new procedure or procedures whilst the program is running, it will be done discreetly. Sometimes however we may wish a message to be displayed for a time and then extinguished. There are several ways this can be done:

1. Display the message, and then, after a given interval, erase it by going back to the beginning and typing an equal number of blanks over the message.
2. Display the message and subsequently clear the screen using **clean**, **cs**, or **ct**.
3. Display the message and then erase it using 'ESC M'.
4. Display the message and then write over it with a different message.
5. Display the message in a viewport (window) and then clear only the viewport.

The first is simple:

```
setcursor [35 10] type [Message displayed]
setcursor [35 10] repeat 17 [type []]
```

This is fine as far as it goes, but without some sort of delay, the message, especially if it is short, will become almost subliminal. The easiest delay loop is the one we saw in the last chapter:

repeat *N* []

where *N* controls the delay. *N*=500 gives a delay of about 2 seconds, which is long enough for a short message. If you want a longer delay, scale it up accordingly. If we don't particularly want to see the cursor dancing around the screen whilst these or other actions are being performed, we can use the command 'ESC f' to switch the cursor off, and 'ESC e' to switch it back on. In LOGO terms these are:

```
type word char 27 "f                ;turns the cursor off
type word char 27 "e                ;turns the cursor on
```

You don't need to turn the cursor off in the delay loop: it moves too fast to show anyway.

The second option, clearing the screen, is fine if there is nothing else displayed on the screen that we don't want erased. Option 3 uses the CP/M escape command 'ESC M', translated as:

```
type word char 27 "M
```

which causes the line on which the cursor currently rests to be erased. This command also causes all rows below the line to be scrolled up one line. You can if you wish counteract this effect by following the 'ESC M' instruction by 'ESC L', which inserts a line, scrolling all lines below it down one row. In other words all that appears to happen is that the line with the message in it disappears, and the rest of the text stays put.

Option 4 works very well providing the two messages are of roughly equal length: the second message, if shorter, can be padded out with spaces. If it's longer, then it doesn't matter.

The last option 5 is a little more complicated. There is a CP/M escape command to define a new viewport:

ESC 27 X *tr lc h w*

where *tr* is the top row, *lc* is the left column, *h* is the height, and *w* is the width. It takes a bit of special magic to translate into LOGO terms and it is rather complex, so I have put it in PART TWO as a program called 'VPORT', which sorts out all the problems.

12.2 Another Type Of Delay Loop

Naturally all these methods require a delay of some sort to be incorporated, so that the user will have time to read the message. The three user input primitives **rq**, **rl** and **rc** give us an automatic pause, since the program will not proceed until the user inputs some data. But there is another way in which we can control the length of time that a message is displayed: by use of the primitive **keyp** (**key** press). This is an oddity that has an inbuilt logic value of FALSE. However, when **keyp** is used with **if** to test its truth value, and any key is pressed, **keyp** becomes TRUE, and we already know that we can use a truth value to execute a list of instructions. In all but one respect, **keyp** is the same as BASIC's INKEY$. This is how we use **keyp**:

```
to while.wend
pr [Press a key]
if keyp [action]
while.wend
end

to action
pr [A key has been pressed]
end
```

Obviously this example does nothing useful – except to demonstrate how **keyp** is used. Whilst no key is pressed, **keyp** is value is FALSE and the 'while.wend' procedure loops round. As soon as a key is pressed, **keyp** becomes TRUE and the instruction in the brackets is executed. You don't have to use **keyp** in exactly this way, but it must be in a loop, since it must repeatedly be tested. If you don't want the keypress character to be printed, you will have to use the spacebar, or go into the **fs** state.

The one drawback to **keyp** – and it is a major one – is that once its truth value has been changed to TRUE, it will remain so until you return to **TOPLEVEL** (the ? prompt), when it will be reset to FALSE. That means you can only use it once in a program. There is a way round this: a pause, either written into the program or executed by pressing f1, will re-set **keyp**. When we enter the primitive **co** the program continues and **keyp** can be used again. Try this variation of 'while.wend':

```
to while.wend
type [Press any key] repeat 18 [type char 8]
if keyp [action]
while.wend
end

to action
pr [A key has been pressed]
pr [Press 'c + RETURN' to continue]
pause
end

to c
ct co
end
```

Start it with 'ct while.wend'. A stationary message (Press any key) appears. When you duly press a key, you get the second message. Finally, when you press 'c' followed by <RETURN>, the first message re-appears. Pressing <STOP> is the only way of breaking the loop! A useless program in itself, but it shows how **keyp** can be revived and used again. We can also use **keyp** very effectively in conjunction with a flashing screen message:

```
to flash.message
setcursor [37 15] pr [FLASHING MESSAGE]
if keyp [action]
repeat 300 []
ct fs repeat 300 []
ts flash.message
end
```

Line 3 looks for a keypress every time the procedure loops round. The delays can of course be altered to suit yourself. If the procedure 'action' contained a 'pause' before continuing, **keyp** could be reactivated for later use, as above.

12.3 Forms Of User Input

Although we've been using the input operators **rc**, **rq**, and **rl**, it won't hurt to recap them here. **rc** waits for one character to be entered, does not print that character to the screen and does not require <RETURN> to be pressed. If you want the character printed you must specifically command it with a 'type' instruction. **rq** reads a string of characters, prints the input to the screen as you type it in, but does not go into action until <RETURN> is pressed. **rl** does the same as **rq**, but puts the input into a list. It is always wise to put in error-traps with these input primitives, to prevent accidental keypresses crashing the program. For example, if it doesn't matter whether an upper or lower case character is input, use the form 'make "input uc rc', or 'make "input lc rc'. It is particularly important to error-trap inputs to **rc**, because it doesn't give one time for second thoughts.

12.4 Outputting To The Printer

When it comes to printing hard copy, LOGO is not the greatest. But with a little help from CP/M it can be made very workable indeed. LOGO only has two print commands: **copyon** and **copyoff**. But LOGO is a CP/M based program, which means we can use CP/M printing commands to a great extent. Let's start with simple basic printing from LOGO. Suppose we wish to print out a listing of a LOGO procedure called 'add', you would first load it into the workspace and then enter:

```
?copyon po "add copyoff
```

and press <RETURN>. Immediately the printer will spring to life and print out your listing in draft pica, with a line-width of 80 characters and a line-pitch of 6: these are the default settings. Unfortunately, too, **copyon** will cause the command 'copyon po "add copyoff' to be printed out as well. Altogether a very unsatisfactory state of affairs.

Fortunately there is a simple solution. The CP/M operating system contains a host of commands to alter type-size, page-length and width, print quality, etc. What we need to do is to write a simple SETLST file to set up the required parameters in CP/M and include the call to that file in our PROFILE.SUB. In APPENDIX IV you will find two suggested print files, one for listings and the other for label-printing. If you don't know how SETLST.COM works, you'll find full instructions in APPENDIX IV. There are some CP/M printing commands which will work from within LOGO, but they really aren't very satisfactory and often fall apart in the middle of printing a file, which is not very helpful. Still, if you want to try them out, they work in the form:

type word char 27 "*escapecode*

You'll find all the necessary escape codes in the Amstrad User Guide, unless you're a PcW owner that is! However, don't despair: you'll find all the necessary information in *this* book. Suppose you want to enter a particular word in italics (eg: the word 'stressed'), you would enter:

```
(type word char 27 4 "stressed word char 27 5)
```

ESC 4 turns on italic printing, ESC 5 turns it off. ESC is the way we write 'escape' in CP/M. In BASIC it's 'CHR$(27)'; in LOGO it's 'char 27'.

In this example we have ignored the actual printing commands **copyon** and **copyoff**. They would of course still need to be used. To prevent **copyon** and **copyoff** printing themselves out, all we have to do is to use the **fs** screen state to mask them:

```
?fs copyon ts po "add fs copyoff
?
```

Typing in the commands whilst in a graphics state prevents the text from printing to screen or printer, but the commands are still executed. If you make a typing error, it's hard to spot it in the dark, as it were! If you know you've done it, press <STOP> to abort the command. Even if you *don't* know it, you'll get an error message and the command will be aborted anyway.

The best way of printing hard copy is to write a simple program to handle the whole thing. Here it is, called 'PQ', with a few bells and whistles added. You'll also find it in PART TWO with even more bells on.

```
1  to pq
2  local "a
3  ts ts pr [Load continuous paper]
4  pr []
5  (type [Enter procedure to print, or 'all':] [])
6  make "a lc rq
7  if :a = "all [er "pq fs copyon ts poall fs copyoff ts stop]
8  if not memberp :a glist ".DEF
9  [fs copyoff ts pr [Procedure not found] stop]
10 [fs copyon ts po :a fs copyoff ts]
11 ct
12 end
```

The numbers down the left-hand side are only there for reference - don't type them in. Line 8 checks to see whether the named procedure is in the workspace. The system property **.DEF** is explained in CHAPTER 14. The procedure 'pq' itself is erased in line 7, if all the procedures are printed out, but is kept in the workspace if only a selected procedure is printed. Line 8 is an error-trap, in case the input procedure isn't present in the workspace. It is not strictly necessary to clear the screen before using **copyon**: only text appearing after the command has been issued will be printed. We've started off with a clear text screen ('ts ts') simply for the sake of neatness. PQ will only work properly if you have used the file SETPRINT.FIL from APPENDIX IV, or a similar printer file of your own.

It is also possible to press <PTR> and use the printer 'buttons' to alter the print quality, and to execute a form-feed or line-feed. You should check what line the printer is on when it's finished printing. It doesn't run on to the end of the page as in normal printing. You can easily get over this: just put in the command 'type char 12' just before **copyoff** and a form-feed will be executed. In the full version there is an error-trap built in which won't allow you to print out anything unless there is paper in the printer, an improvement which not a few word-processors might well emulate! How easy it is to forget and print out a letter onto the platen!

12.5 Printing Graphics

Printing graphical output is quite another problem. The simplest way (not available on the 9512) is a screen dump. However it is possible to purchase a public domain 'screen dump' program. To get a screen dump on those machines which have the built-in facility, press <EXTRA><PTR> and away you go. But screen dumps are very unsatisfactory. They are too small for many purposes and they print at the very left margin of the page. You can get over this last by gently manually pushing the print-head towards the middle of the paper to where you want printing to start before you execute the dump, but this is a palliative, not a solution. And if you do do it, take care, the print-head may be very hot! The worst drawback to screen-dumping (apart from getting through your ribbons at a rate of knots) is that you cannot export the output to another environment, such as a desk-top publishing program.

However, all is by no means lost. BASIC comes to the rescue. The PCW graphics extension, GSX, which is what we have to use if we want graphical output from a BASIC program, is a clumsy and difficult concept. However Mallard BASIC is an excellent program in other respects and can easily convert a LOGO picfile to MicroDesign2/3 or Stop Press formats, or print it out directly on paper in A4 size, using bit-image printing. Thus we can incorporate pictures we have drawn in LOGO in desk-top publishing output, or bind graphs into text documents printed from a word-processor, and so on. Both these conversion programs will be found listed in APPENDIX V. 9512 owners will still need a dot-matrix, ink-jet, or laser printer, however.

12.6 Extra Printer Files

Finally it is worth remembering that you can have as many CP/M printer files on your LOGO 'Start Of Day' disk as you like. To load a different one, leave LOGO with 'bye', type 'SETLST *printfilename*', and then re-load LOGO by typing 'logo'. You will of course lose everything in the workspace - save it first if you need it - but you will *not* lose anything from the M: drive.

13

PROGRAM DEBUGGING

13.1 Run-time Errors

So let us assume that you've written a program and you try to run it. If every program you write runs first time without a single error, you are either the luckiest programmer on earth, or you're a solid gold genius! For the rest of us, as we're probably going to spend as long debugging our programs as we spent writing them - or probably even longer - we might as well have all the help we can get. For a start LOGO has some extremely user-friendly error messages. Compare these two:

```
disk write error no data block. $$$
disk full
```

The first one is CP/M's version of LOGO's simple 'disk full' message. I know which one I prefer. APPENDIX III lists all LOGO's error messages, together with the action to take. When you get a run-time error report, you will not only be told what the error is, but also where it occurs. For example:

```
not enough inputs to loop in loop: loop
```

If you now type:

```
?ed "loop
```

(or even just 'ed', although this doesn't always work) you will be taken into the editor with the cursor positioned at, or quite often just after, the point where the error has occurred. Usually it will be a typing mistake, or, as in this case, a missing parameter. This kind of mistake is easy to spot and put right. If only life were as simple as that!

13.2 Tracing Program Execution

Most errors, the really baffling ones, are the ones that aren't really errors at all: the program bugs, the points at which the program doesn't behave as it should, often for no apparent reason. Fortunately we have a whole armoury of bug-spotters at our disposal. First **trace** , which literally traces the program through as it runs. We invoke it by typing 'trace' at the command prompt, then run the program and watch closely. It moves fairly slowly, but we shall see how we can slow it up even more. Let's have a look at its output, using the program GUESS from CHAPTER 6. First let's remind ourselves of the program:

```
to proc.one
(local "num "guess "goes)
make "num random 100
type [Guess the hidden number, 0 to 99, in 6 goes:]
make "guess rq
make "goes 1
proc.two :num :guess :goes
end

to proc.two :num :attempt :goes
if :attempt > :num [pr [Too big] proc.four :num :goes]
if :attempt < :num [pr [Too small] proc.four :num :goes]
if :attempt = :num [proc.three :num :attempt :goes]
end

to proc.three :num :try :goes
(pr [You guessed:] [] :try "in :goes "goes)
(pr [You win!!!])
proc.one
end

to proc.four :num :goes
local "newguess
if :goes = 6
   [(pr [You've had your 6 goes...you lose! Number was] :num) stop]
(type [Try again:] [])
make "newguess rq
proc.two :num :newguess :goes + 1
end
```

Now we'll run it and put a trace on it. Here's what you might see if you ran the program once through:

```
?trace
?proc.one
[1]  Evaluating proc.one
[1]  making "num 60
[1]  making "goes 1
Guess the hidden number, 0 to 99, in 6 goes:
45                                  ;user has typed 45
[1]  making "guess 45
[2]  Evaluating proc.two
[2]  goes is 1
[2]  attempt is 45
[2]  num is 60
Too small                           ;program output
[3]  Evaluating proc.four
[3]  goes is 1
[3]  num is 60
Try again: 66                       ;user enters 66
[3]  making "newguess 66
[4]  Evaluating proc.two
[4]  goes is two
```

```
[4]  attempt is 66
[4]  num is 60
Too big                              ;program output
[5]  Evaluating proc.four
[5]  goes is 2
[5]  num is 60
Try again: 60                        ;user enters 60
[5]  making "newguess 60
[6]  Evaluating proc.two
[6]  goes is 3
[6]  attempt is 60
[6]  num is 60
[7]  Evaluating proc.three
[7]  goes is 3
[7]  try is 60
[7]  num is 60
You guessed:  60 in 3 goes           ;program output
You win!!!
...
```

...and so on. The numbers in the square brackets are put there by **trace** and indicate the depth of the calls, not the numbers of the procedures. Level [0] (which you will never see) is **TOPLEVEL** - the ? prompt. Where there's no number, the line is text that is output to the screen. The real value of **trace** is in its ability to interrogate local variables and extract their values, which would not normally be possible. It also shows us the program path, and exactly where it goes astray, if it does. And as it reveals the depth of calls, we can readily see where memory or stack space might be saved.

Switch **trace** off with **notrace**. Both commands need a line to themselves. Don't try to put any other instructions on the same line after them, or you will probably get an error message. Sometimes **trace** 'sticks': type <RETURN> and it will continue on its merry way. But make sure first that it isn't just waiting for user input.

trace shows us the interim results of computations within the program, and most importantly it allows us to check up on the wrong-doings of local variables. For example, if we had this line in a procedure and the variables were all local:

```
...
make "a 4 make "b 6 make "a :a * :b
...
```

trace might show:

```
[4]  making a 4
[4]  making b 6
[4]  making a 2
```

which allows us to check that the calculations within the program are being correctly carried out. **trace** follows the program right the way through (slowing it up considerably in the process), but an error causes it to dump you back to **TOPLEVEL** in the normal way. Pressing f1 will make the program pause; **co** will let it continue. It is interesting and valuable to note that, during a pause, you may go into edit mode and edit the program as much as you like. When you leave the editor, you will still be inside the program, and still in the pause state. This makes it possible to alter a program whilst it's running. Quite clever.

13.3 Watching Program Execution

Used wisely **trace** will sort out most of your ordinary run-time errors, but sometimes, even at the reduced rate that **trace** ambles along, it still runs ahead too quickly to spot every nuance. This is where **watch** comes in. **watch** takes one input, the name of a procedure, a list of procedures, or none. To put a neighbourhood watch on a procedure called 'test', we would enter:

```
?watch "test?
```

When we run the named procedure, the first line of instructions is printed to the screen and the procedure then pauses. Press <RETURN> and the first instruction in the line will be carried out and again the procedure pauses. This goes on through the procedure until the procedure ends, whereupon **watch** ceases to act on any other part of the program. Unless, that is, we have put a watch on another procedure within the program. We may 'watch' as many procedures in the program as we like, but each one must be noted separately before the program is run. Alternatively, to 'watch' the entire program, just enter 'watch' without any input.

watch doesn't print out variable values and the like as does **trace**, but we can use **trace** and **watch** together, and although this is painfully slow, it lets us examine the running of the program from the inside and in minute detail; an immensely instructive exercise.

To get rid of **watch**, use the primitive **nowatch**. Once again put it on a line by itself - **watch** and **nowatch** are just as antisocial in this respect as **trace** and **notrace**.

13.4 Pausing In A Program

We have yet another aid to debugging, in the form of the primitive **pause**. This may be written into your program at any point and will automatically pause the execution at that point, in the same way that f1 does. What you can do at these points is make the program yield up any information you want; variable values, procedure calls, etc. Put in a 'type :variable', or whatever, at the appropriate point just before the pause and you can examine how things are going. Or wait for the pause to happen and then examine the values, or enter the editor and make changes to the program. In other words you have total control over the program whilst it's running.

Once you have got the hang of **trace**, **watch** and **pause**, you will find them extremely useful. You can try out different versions of a procedure or program and evaluate the workings step by step, and hence improve your programming skills out of all recognition. Make it a rule, with every new program you write, to run **trace** on it, and use the results to find better ways of achieving your objectives. There are almost invariably better ways to be found if you look hard enough. In particular you should take note of the depth of calls. Any program which has to make deep calls uses up more memory and more stack-space than a program that sticks around levels 1 and 2. If you find you're running into depths of 10 or 11 you'll almost certainly find you're in some sort of trouble: either the program's slow, or it's eating up memory like a ravening wolf.

13.5 Throwing And Catching

Now for some rather more sophisticated debugging tools. Firstly a double act which we have already glimpsed: **catch** and **throw**. Strictly speaking these are not debugging tools, but jump instructions, but used in a special way they can help us no end. Used in the normal way they enable us to jump from the middle of one procedure to the middle of another. But given certain labels they can be made into error–traps. It is important to note however that the **catch** and **throw** must be in the same program path. In other words a **throw** will only return control to a **catch** if the procedure in which the **throw** sits is reached as a result of the **catch** instruction.

Consider the following:

```
to proc.1
pr 1
catch "here [proc.2]
pr 4
throw "there
end

to proc.2
pr 2
catch "there [proc.3]
pr 5
end

to proc.3
pr 3
throw "here
end
```

Try to follow the program path. **catch** has a label, a name – any one word name you like – which the corresponding **throw** command also takes. When the program reaches the **catch**, it executes the instruction list on the same line as the **catch** label. When, as a result of the instructions being carried out, it subsequently meets the matching **throw**, it jumps back (or forward) to the command immediately following the **catch** label. Sounds more complicated than it really is in practice. If you type in the above program and run **trace** on it, the path will be traced out for you. **trace** and **watch** show you exactly which way the program goes. The legend 'evaluating *procedure–name*' in **trace** shows you which procedure has been called.

So how do **catch** and **throw** help us with debugging? There are two special inputs we can use with **catch**: **error** and **TRUE**. If we use 'TRUE' as the **catch** label, 'catch "TRUE' will intercept any 'throw' no matter what the 'throw label' is. If we use the label 'error', 'catch "error' will intercept any action the system would take in dealing with the error, which allows us to deal with the error ourselves. It does in fact prevent error messages being displayed.

If you insert either of these special **catch** labels (temporarily) at points in the program where you think things are going awry, you will usually be able to find even the most elusive of bugs. What so often happens is that you don't notice that a variable is changing its value when it shouldn't, or *vice versa*. The reason for this kind of malfunction is a bad algorithm – and that is one of the hardest faults to trace.

The first thing we have to do is to use an odd primitive, **ERRACT** (**ERR**or **ACT**ion). Normally **ERRACT** has a truth value of FALSE. But enter:

```
?make "ERRACT "TRUE
```

and it not only prevents error reports, but it inserts a pause as well. Here is an example of how it works, assuming that **ERRACT** has been made TRUE:

```
to debug
catch "error [action]
pr [An error has been found]
end
```

```
to action
make :a ascii rc
pr :a
end
```

In this mini-program, which I've deliberately kept simple, there is an error in the line 'make :a ascii rc'. This should of course refer to the variable *name* and read 'make "a ascii rc'.If we run it this is what will happen:

```
?debug
pausing... in action: :a
action?
```

In other words no error message has been printed, the program has merely paused. If you now enter 'co' the program will go to the instruction following the 'catch': in this case it will print the message and stop, but normally, providing there were further instructions, the program would continue on its merry way - and most probably crash! As a matter of interest rather more than usefulness, you can use the 'catch "error' statement to show the full error description, including the error number, so long as **ERRACT** is still TRUE. Enter this procedure, which we'll call 'show.err':

```
to show.err
catch "error [action]
op error
end
```

Now run 'show.err' and it will output:

```
pausing... in action: :a
action?co
[41 [pr doesn't like :a as input] action [:a] catch [:a]]
```

When you've finished with **ERRACT**, enter 'make "ERRACT "FALSE', or better still enter 'ern "ERRACT', and you'll be returned to the *status quo ante*.

13.6 A New Operating Level

It is possible to use 'catch "error' in a mini-program which will return the main program to level [1] if there is an error, instead of level [0]. Tack the following procedure onto any program you like - except a program which already has a 'catch "error' statement in it. You will find your program operating at level [1], with a new prompt, '#', replacing the ? prompt. This is really only a bit of fun, a spot of LOGO conjuring, but it demonstrates yet another way in which **catch** can be used.

```
to level.one
(local "err "input)
catch "error [work]
make "err error
if first :err = 35 [catch "error [pr first bf :err
show run :input]]
[pr first bf :err]
level.one
end
```

```
to work
type "#
make "input rl
run :input
work
end
```

To return to **TOPLEVEL**, press <STOP>. Here's an example of 'level.one' in action:

```
?level.one
#4 + 3
7
#type addition
#
Stop pressed!
?
```

As you can see there is an error in the fourth line 'type addition'. There should be a quote mark before the word 'addition'. The program does not report an error message and we can only return to **TOPLEVEL** with <STOP>.

13.7 Hidden Bugs

Intelligent use of all the above debugging tools should sort out most of your problems, but don't forget that the most difficult, elusive and infuriating bugs of all are the ones you never test for. Suppose we write a database program that can handle, say, 100 records. We test it for the first record, the second, the third, the tenth, the fiftieth ...and finally for the hundredth. It works perfectly every time. So we declare our program bug-free. But suppose buried somewhere in the program is an instruction limiting field line-length:

```
...
if :r = 36 [make "r 35]
...
```

where :r is supposed to be a local variable limiting the number of characters in a line to 35. Only we forgot to declare it as a local, and we have a *global* variable :r which represents the record number. Now when we try to access record number 36 (one we haven't tested) with the command:

```
make "r 36
```

we shall find ourselves dumped into record number 35. In other words we can never access record 36! Quite an annoying little bug. This is a somewhat far-fetched example, but it serves to make the point that some bugs will only show up if *every* action of which the program is capable is tested. In many programs - most in fact - this is clearly an impossibility. One thing we can absolutely guarantee is that the end-user will instantly stumble across bugs that the programmer has spent hours, days, or even months, testing for, and has happily concluded do not exist. But that's programming for you.

All you can do is test, test, and test again. Then give it to one or two computer-literate friends to try out. Or better still, computer-*ill*iterate friends. They're more likely to find your bugs, because they'll do the unexpected. After all, you wouldn't expect anyone to disobey a simple screen instruction would you? They will you know. A perfectly straightforward instruction like 'press any key to continue'. Now *we* all know that this doesn't actually mean what it says. *We* all know it means press any key *except*, probably, <STOP>, or <EXIT>, or a dozen others, depending on the program. But we shouldn't take it for granted that everyone knows this. Either we must tell them, or we must put in an error-trap. We could say 'press space-bar to continue', and put in this trap:

```
if not :input = char 32 [instruction to loop back]
```

That would do it.

13.8 Faulty Algorithms

Finally one more type of bug that can go totally unnoticed and one that we mentioned briefly earlier: a faulty algorithm. This can easily happen with a mathematical program, where we have worked out all the formulae on paper and all is well. We therefore assume that the LOGO program is also producing correct results, when it may not be. It is especially important in cases like this to bring in an outside source to cross-check the results. For example, a LOGO program to produce square-roots should be checked against a pocket-calculator. So why use a program when we can use a calculator? Because the square-root operation may only be a small part of the main program, and we hardly want to stop the program every time it asks for a square-root so that we can get the result from a calculator. And once we know that the program works, we can dispense with the checking.

Debugging can be fun, but only if you tackle it methodically, thoroughly, and above all calmly. If you do get completely bogged down, give up! I mean it. Don't sit there for hours biting your finger-nails down to your elbows: put the program away for an hour, a day, even a week. Then come back to it fresh. Chances are the answer's been staring you in the face all the time - you've just got too close to it to see it. A rest, I promise you, works wonders.

14

MANIPULATING THE MEMORY

14.1 Direct Memory Addressing

It is possible to include machine code in LOGO programs: in practice this is a limited facility (but see APPENDIX IX). However there are some operators which allow us to mess about with memory quite effectively, which we may call 'dot' commands, because they all begin with a full-stop.

.examine .deposit .in .out

These are the memory and port addressing commands. **.examine** is entirely equivalent to BASIC's PEEK command. It takes one input, a memory address, and returns the byte value stored at that address. **.deposit**, which is entirely equivalent to BASIC's POKE, takes two inputs, the first a memory address and the second a byte value which it inserts at that address.

All very fine and dandy, but unless you know what's where, that's not a lot of help. There are many examples of the use of **.examine** and **.deposit** in PARTS TWO and THREE, and see also APPENDIX IX.

The commands **.in** and **.out** perform the same for the CP/M ports as **.examine** and **.deposit** do for the memory addresses. They are entirely equivalent to BASIC's INP and OUT. For example:

.out 242 3	returns to CP/M
.out 245 0..255	displays various patterns
.out 245 91	returns to normal screen from the patterns
.out 246 1..254	moves the screen display up or down 1 pixel
.out 246 0 or 255	restores vertical display
.out 247 25	flashes display off and on
.out 247 128 *et seq*	flashes reversed screen on and off
.out 248 8	blanks the screen display
.out 248 7	restores the screen display
.out 248 9	turns on default drive motor
.out 248 10	turns off default drive motor
.out 248 11	turns on the bleep (continuous)
.out 248 12	turns off the bleep
.out 248 1	reboots LOGO

There are many others, mostly in the range 240..248, and a lot of them, particularly in the 240..241 range, crash the program if you blunder around unguided. **.in** returns the byte values at the various ports, but again you need to be careful. Program FLASH in PART TWO gives an example of the use of **.out**, and ALARM in PART THREE uses **.examine** and **.deposit**. PQ in PART TWO uses the **.in** command. The REFERENCE section gives more details of all these commands.

The vertical screen controller '.out 246 *N*' moves the screen display up or down a number of pixels by the difference between consecutive inputs. For example, '.out 246 1' followed by '.out 246 16' scrolls the display 15 pixels down. The following short program will scroll a display:

```
to scroll
local "n
(type word char 27 char 102) ct
setcursor [38 0] type [SCROLLING MESSAGE]
make "n 0
scroll.work :n
end

to scroll.work :n
repeat 500 [if :n < 1 [make "n 254]
   .out 246 :n make "n :n - 2]
.out 246 255 (type word char 27 char 101)
end
```

Start it off by entering 'scroll'. The number of repeats is up to you, as is the message. If you want the message to scroll the other way round, change the condition and the increment in 'scroll.work' to:

```
...
[if :n > 254 [make :n 0]
   .out 246 :n make "n :n + 2]
...
```

The rate of scroll is controlled by the increment to :n, which can be any number you like up to 255, which last effectively makes the display stand still. You can easily write a program to scroll a display up and down alternately. Works just as well with graphics, which is one way of animating a screen display.

14.2 The System Properties

Now for the seven system properties, some more useful than others. Once again notice that they all begin with a full-stop. **.PRM** (**PRI**mitive location) is the memory-location property of a primitive and returns the address at which the instructions pertaining to that primitive are stored. With the assistance of CP/M's debugger, SID, or a similar tool, you can then read the machine-code instructions relative to that primitive. You can also alter them, but beware: a crash is often the result of such hacking. It isn't easy to read someone else's machine-code! The CP/M program SAVE, which takes memory snapshots, is a handy tool here, as is DUMP, but again that is beyond the scope of this book (but see APPENDIX IX). It is worth mentioning, however, that you need to add 100 hex to the LOGO location if you are reading it in SID. For example, 'gprop "keyp ".PRM' returns 7710 decimal, which is 1E1E hex. But you will find the machine code for **keyp** at 1F1E in SID; that is 1E1E + 0100 = 1F1E. You can verify the truth of this by noting the nine bytes starting at 1F1E in SID, going back to LOGO and using **.examine** to look at the nine memory locations starting at 7710d (1E1Eh). These are the machine code data for **keyp**. The reason for this offset is that LOGO measures its locations as if the system starts at 0000h, whereas SID loads programs in at 0100h and measures from there.

All the memory locations in LOGO are given in decimal, which is a blessing in one way and a curse in another, since SID, DUMP, SAVE, etc, work in hexadecimal. Use programs 'DH' and 'HD' from PART TWO to perform the necessary conversions to and from hexadecimal. This is how **.PRM** works:

```
?gprop "edf ".PRM
9505
?
```

which is the (decimal) memory address of where **edf** lives.

Typing 'glist ".PRM' will reveal a list of all the primitives and system properties that Dr LOGO supports. But there is something much more useful that you can do with **.PRM**. Suppose you decide you don't like typing 'setcursor' every time you want to set the cursor position. After all 'setc' is quicker, easier and less prone to typing errors. So this is how we change the primitive **setcursor** to a new primitive 'setc':

```
?pprop "setc ".PRM gprop "setcursor ".PRM
```

and from now on **setc** has become a cursor-setting primitive. But supposing we have some programs already written which use **setcursor**, do we have to rewrite them? The answer is no, you can use either **setc** or **setcursor**: both will have precisely the same effect. True, you will have used a little precious memory space, but only a few nodes.

There is a special program in PART TWO called 'STARTUP' which redefines **setcursor** and **defaultd** (which I personally *always* mis-spell!). It does many other things as well.

.DEF (**DEF**inition property) is the definition-property of a procedure.

```
glist ".DEF
```

returns a list of all the procedures in the workspace.

```
gprop "procedurename ".DEF
```

returns the procedure definition as a list. It also prints the procedure's parameters as a list. If there are no parameters it prints an empty list. The primitive **text** produces exactly the same result. 'glist ".DEF' is useful, since it allows us to manipulate the list of procedures in the workspace during the course of a program, like this:

```
...
if memberp "procedure glist ".DEF [action]
...
```

We could not use **pots** in this way: an error message would result, because **pots** doesn't just print the names of the procedures, it puts 'to' in front.

.APV (Associated Property Value), as we've already seen, returns the value held by a global variable:

```
?make "a 89
?gprop "a ".APV
89
?
```

Using the primitive **thing** produces exactly the same result:

```
?make "b "feather
?thing "b
feather
?
```

We can use levels of **thing**. For example:

```
thing thing thing :a
```

is possible, so long as :a has values to that depth. You can find out all about **thing** by looking it up in the REFERENCE section.

'glist ".APV' will output a list of all the global variables, and there's one more way of examining a variable:

```
?plist "a
[.APV 89]
?plist "b
[.APV feather]
?
```

14.3 Formatting

.FMT returns various values to do with formatting, which are a little complicated, so we'll look at them bit by bit. Formatting in LOGO terms means procedures having indents, remarks and removed-lines. Suppose we have a procedure called 'example' which has been written like this:

```
to example
   pr [Indented line]  ;indent here
   make "inp rq
      if :inp = "b [type char 7]  ;sounds the beep
      if :inp = "c [repeat 3 [type char 7]]
end
```

This procedure is not supposed to do anything special: it's the formatting we're interested in. We will assume it's sitting in the workspace all by itself, just to keep things reasonably simple. Now we enter:

```
?glist ".FMT
[example]
?
```

This tells us that there is a procedure in the workspace which is formatted in some way. Bear in mind that if we had more procedures in the workspace we would most probably get a longer list. Next we use:

```
?gprop "example ".FMT
[[0 .SPC . 3] [5 .ENL ;indent here] [5 .SPC . 3] [8 .SPC . 6] [17 .ENL . !
;sounds the beep] [17 .SPC . 6]]
?
```

The wrapping is done by LOGO by inserting an exclamation mark, and a line-feed and carriage-return at the end of the physical line. Note that these are all second-level lists; we'll see why in a moment. Let's look at the information piece by piece. In the second line '0' is a word-count from the beginning of the procedure (the definition line is not included in these word-counts) to where the first indent starts. **.SPC** means 'spaces', so the figure following '.SPC' is the number of spaces at the specified location. We can also see that there are 3 more spaces at word-count 5, and 6 more spaces at word-count 8. Finally '17 .SPC . 6' tells us that there are 6 more spaces at word-count 17. A 'word' in this context means an item separated by spaces either side of it. It also means a bracket (round or square) even if it isn't separated by spaces. If you look at this count of the 'words' and spaces in 'example' you'll soon get the idea:

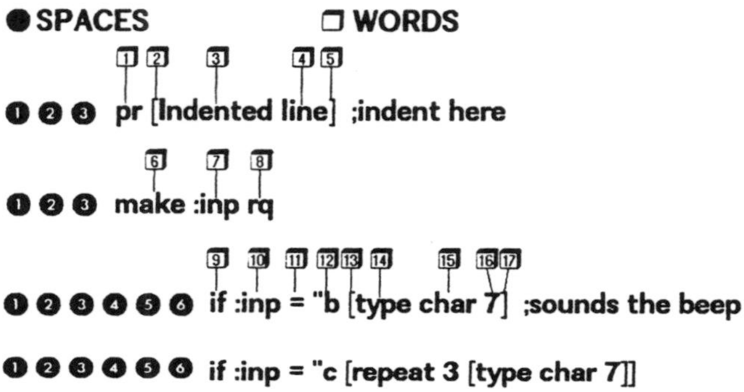

Figure 14.1 How the word- and space-counts are determined in the procedure 'example'

Now to .ENL. It indicates the ExtensioN to the Line in the form of a remark. As we already know, remarks may be entered at the ends of lines by preceding them with a semi-colon, even the definition line, but not the 'end' line, which makes sense: the end is the end, after all. .ENL again gives us a word-count, this time to the position of the remark (remarks words are not included in the word-counts). It also prints out the remarks.

Now let us suppose we decide that we want temporarily to remove the line 'if :inp = "c...' etc – perhaps because while we are testing the program the incessant beeping gets on our nerves. More practically and with a more complex program, we may wish to chop out the frills whilst we test the bare bones. There is a simple way to keep the line in the procedure, but render it inactive: put a semi-colon at the beginning of the line, like this:

```
;      if :inp = "c [repeat 3 [type char 7]]
```

Now when we enter:

```
?gprop "example ".FMT
```

we get yet another piece of information on formatting:

```
[[0 .SPC . 3] [5 .ENL . ;indent here] [5 .SPC . 3] [8 .SPC .6][17 !
.ENL . ;sounds the beep] [17 .REM . ;      if :inp =! "bbb [repeat 3 [typ!
e char 7]]]]
```

The first number in the **.REM** list is the word-count to the semi-colon that removes the line ('.REM' stands for **REM**oved line), and then the line that has been removed is printed. Finally we can use the big net, **plist**, and catch the lot:

```
?plist "example
[.DEF [[] [pr [Indented line] make "inp rq if :inp = "b [type char 7] if!
 :inp = "bbb [repeat 3 [type char 7]]]] .FMT [[0 .SPC . 3] [5 .ENL . ;in!
dent here] [5 .SPC . 3] [8 .SPC . 6] [17 .ENL . ;sounds the beep] [17 .R!
EM . ;     if :inp  = "c [repeat 3 [type char 7]]]]
?
```

Which just about says all there is to say about that procedure. As a matter of interest the lists go to a depth of five, with the '.DEF' list being the first-level list. **.FMT** prints a *list* of **.SPC**, **.ENL**, and **.REM** *lists*. The exclamation marks are, as usual, entered by LOGO to indicate wrapping of lines.

14.4 Removing Formatting

All this may be very interesting, but what does it actually do for us? Consider a case where we have a large program and we're running out of space and would like to know where we can save some. Now, there may be upwards of twenty procedures in the program: do we really want to have to load each one into the editor to examine them for wasted space? Hardly. We may, very sensibly, have larded our program with remarks whilst we were writing it, and we may well want to keep these remarks intact in one (saved) version of the program, whilst removing them from the working version.

Also we may have locked a few lines out here and there with semi-colons and we may well have forgotten exactly where they are. So we use **.FMT** to look at then for us, going through the sequence 'glist..., gprop..., plist...' as necessary. We can then use another primitive with sweeping powers: **noformat**. By entering 'noformat' we completely eliminate formatting, removed-lines and remarks throughout all procedures in the workspace. A pretty dangerous thing to do without checking first with **.FMT**. Look at this program fragment. First before using deep-cleaning **noformat**:

```
...
if (and and :a = 6 :b > :a not :a = :c)
   [action1]  ;:c is count of items in :alist
;  [action2]  ;print results of comparison
...
```

Now after using 'noformat':

```
...
if (and and :a = 6 :b > :a not :a = :c) [action1]
...
```

What **noformat** has done for us is to make one line of the instructions and taken out the removed-line altogether. Admittedly it has saved us memory-space by removing remarks and indent spaces, but in this case it could also have wrecked the procedure into the bargain. So the answer is, use **noformat** with great care. However it's worth considering that if we run **noformat** on procedure 'example' above, we shall see a saving of 74 nodes. Throughout a long and complex program we may well be able to save a lot of memory-space by this method.

14.5 The Definition Operators

So much for the 'dot' commands. There are a couple of other oddities we haven't covered yet. First **define**, which takes two inputs, the first a name, the second a list of instructions. It then promptly turns the lot into a full-blooded working procedure. For an idea of how it works, look at the REFERENCE section and POLYGONS in PART THREE. **define** is an oddball, but you may find uses for it.

Now to one we can certainly make use of: **REDEFP** (**REDEF**ine **P**rimitive). It is another of those primitives that has an inbuilt truth value. It normally has the value **FALSE**, but if we enter:

```
?make "REDEFP "TRUE
```

it enables us to redefine primitives. There are several primitives which are not implemented in the PCW version of Dr LOGO, and they each take up about 10 nodes of workspace. In addition there may well be some we feel we can happily do without. In SPACER in PART TWO you will see how we can reclaim the space taken up by these variables using **REDEFP**. Here's a brief example which assumes the work-space is empty:

```
?recycle nodes
3633
?to wait
wait is a primitive          ;error message
?make "REDEFP "TRUE
?to wait
>end
wait defined
?er "wait
?ern "REDEFP
?recycle nodes
3643
?
```

What we have done here is to cancel the validity of **wait** as a primitive by turning it into a procedure. As we can see in the example, we cannot normally use a primitive name as a procedure name, but when we make **REDEFP** TRUE that rule no longer applies. So we turn the primitive into a procedure and then erase it – it does nothing anyway. We have lost the primitive **wait** – which also did nothing – and gained 10 nodes in the process. To tidy things up we must then erase the variable we have created called "REDEFP (you can look at it with **pons**). We could cancel **REDEFP** by entering 'make "REDEFP "FALSE', but there seems little point in hanging onto it. All it will do is take up the space we have just created!

In APPENDIX IX you will find programs for memory-scanning and full details of storing machine-code data.

15

HINTS AND TIPS

This is a general section covering some of the things that didn't find their way into the rest of the TUTORIAL section.

1. When you are drawing in the graphics screen, everything moves much faster with the turtle hidden, but sometimes the turtle can be used to effect, not as a drawing tool, but as a pointer, as in SCRNCHAR, or, as in WARSHIP, as a shell-burst. You'll find both these programs in PART THREE.

2. Use **fill** with great care. The area to be filled must be completely enclosed, and the the pen must be in the opposite state to the pixel on which the turtle rests (**pd** or **pe**), whether the turtle is visible or not. Even a one pixel gap in the line surrounding the area to be filled will allow **fill** to escape and flood the entire screen, which takes ten to fifteen minutes! The only way to stop it is to reset the computer. Always save your workspace and/or picture before using **fill** in your program for the first time. You can then easily reset with <SHIFT><EXTRA><EXIT> and re-boot LOGO. Exclude the **fill** instruction line with a semi-colon (;) until you are sure the area is properly enclosed.

3. You cannot merge picfiles in any way. The latest one loaded completely wipes anything on the screen. However to load a full screen picfile, you must be in a full-screen state. Loading a picfile in a split-screen state causes the graphics part of the screen to be filled, but not the text part. This can be very useful, especially if combined with **setsplit**, since it allows you to use text input with previously-saved graphics. You might well use this facility with a text-and-graphics adventure game. Consider that you can have interactive graphics, as well as interactive text.

4. If you load a procedure and there is already a procedure of the same name in the workspace, the new one will completely overwrite the old one. The same applies to global variables which may come in with the new procedure. They overwrite variables of the same name that are already in the workspace.

5. Using **edf** in no way disturbs the workspace, so that it may be used to examine procedures before they are loaded and to check them out. You can then make any necessary alterations before loading the procedures into the workspace.

6. Jumping around a program may be done in a number of ways:

   (a) A call to another procedure — Use the procedure name.
   (b) Return to the calling procedure — Use **stop** or **op**.
   (c) Jump from within one procedure to within another procedure
   Use **catch** and **throw** (but see PART FOUR for limitations).
   (d) Jump from one part of a procedure to another part
   Use **label** and **go**.
   (e) Return to the start of the current procedure
   Use recursion.

   When a program is saved, any global variables present (including their current values) are saved to disk, along with all the other contents of the workspace, including properties. Variables may be examined in the editor – they will appear tacked on at the end of the program when **edall** is used. **poall** will print out the global variables and their values as well as the procedures. Beware! Properties do not appear in the edit screen, nor does **erall** erase them.

8. The operator **dir** may be used in two ways other than as a straight command. First it will accept a filename as a parameter and return an answer dependent on whether the file is present on the disk or not. Like this:

```
?dir "loop
[LOOP]                    ;the file is present
?dir "turpos
[]                        ;the file is not present
?
```

   dir will also accept the ? wildcard:

```
?dir "l???
[LOOP LINE]               ;all 4-letter files beginning with 'L'
?
```

   Naturally enough, **dirpic** works in exactly the same way. **erasefile** and **erasepic** both accept the ? wildcard, but use with care! The '*' wildcard will not work with LOGO.

9. It frequently happens, when you are writing a program, that the procedures get into an illogical order. It is advantageous, as we have already mentioned, to put the procedures that are most used nearest to the top of the list. There's a very easy way of altering the order. Suppose we have a program with three procedures: 'to start', 'to work', and 'to print', and we would like them in that order. They have unfortunately got muddled up and are now in the order:

```
to print
to start
to work
```

   The procedure we want at the top is 'start', so type 'ed "start', change the name to 'start2' and exit from the editor. 'start2' will be defined and will be, apart from its name, identical to 'start'. If there is room for all the procedures in the editor, use **edall**. Now type 'pots':

```
to print
to start
to work
to start2
```

Now type 'er "start ed "work'. In the editor, do the same as you did with 'start' - tack a '2' onto its name and exit. Then type 'er "work'. Finally repeat the process with 'print'. You will now have three procedures in the workspace:

```
to start2
to work2
to print2
```

Put each in turn back into the editor - 'start2' first, then 'work2', then 'print2' - deleting the '2' in each case. You will now have:

```
to start2
to work2
to print2
to start
to work
to print
```

Finish off by typing:

```
?er [start2 work2 print2] recycle
?
```

and you have re-ordered your program.

10. If you find the LOGO editor too small to take a whole program you can use any word-processor that is capable of outputting an ASCII file. Protext has a program mode which is ideal: save the file using *filename*.LOG. LocoScript 1 and 2 are equally acceptable. Save using the ASCII, again tacking on the .LOG suffix. Using a word-processor with block moves is a perfectly acceptable way of re-ordering the procedures in a program. Make sure the left margin is at 0 when you begin.

11. In command mode, <RETURN> may be pressed when the cursor is anywhere in the line, it doesn't have to be at the end. <COPY> and <PASTE> will repeat the last command typed.

12. In edit mode, if you delete a line with <ALT><DEL->>, <COPY> or <PASTE> will bring the line back. Very useful if you have a number of similar lines to repeat. Type in the first one, delete it with <ALT><DEL->>, press <COPY> to undelete it, move down a line and press <COPY> again to repeat the line. Keep copying the line as many times as you need and then edit as necessary. This is often much quicker than typing out similar lines several times. The same trick works in definition mode.

13. When using the primitive **if**, the list of instructions must either be on the same line as the **if** statement, or they must be indented by *at least one space* on the following line. Similarly an optional second list of instructions should also be indented. The following will not work and will throw up an error message:

```
...
if :value1 > :value2
[make "value1 fput :value1 :temp]
...
```

But this will work perfectly:

```
...
if :value1 > :value2
 [make "value1 fput :value1 :temp]
...
```

That one space makes all the difference.

14. Before saving a program to disk, always check with **pots**, **pons**, and **pps**, to make sure that you're not saving a lot of rubbish with your program. Get rid of anything that shouldn't be there, use **recycle**, and then save your program.

15. Although global variables show up in the edit screen, they cannot be erased from the workspace simply by erasing them in the editor. They will still exist and the only way of getting rid of them is by using **ern** or **erall**.

16. Always run **trace** on a new program to examine where the program goes, particularly watching for depths of calls. You will often be able to save memory and enhance speed by making small changes to the way your program is written and avoiding unnecessarily deep calls..

17. If you want a couple of seconds pause in a program to allow the user time to read a message, put in a **recycle** command at the appropriate spot. This not only gives you a convenient pause, but also clears out garbage at the same time.

18. Load CP/M and with the system disk in place type 'basic rped'. Up will come the RPED editor. Put your LOGO start-of-day disk in A: and press f1 to edit an existing file. Enter KEYS.DRL in the box, press <RETURN> twice and add this line to the end of the file:

    ```
    22 N     "^'34'"  DOUBLE-QUOTE     - 1/2 key
    ```

    Press <EXIT> twice and from now on pressing the 1/2 key in LOGO will type a double-quote (") (one of the most-used keys) without pressing <SHIFT>. Add this line in KEYS.CPM:

    ```
    22 N     "^'169'"
    ```

    to return the 1/2 key to normal.

And now for the commercial break...

19. If you want to speed up LOGO, fit Cirtech's Sprinter to your PCW. It gives LOGO a real kick up the pants - and does the same for pretty-well every other program too. The results will astonish you.

20. There is a very useful program which will translate LOGO picfiles to other formats and *vice versa* (as well as doing lots of other clever things) called 'PCW Presenter' from DGC Software.

21. For superb print-outs of LOGO pictures, MicroDesign3 is an absolute must. However, drawing freehand pictures is much easier in LOGO than MicroDesign, especially if you use DESIGNER from PART THREE.

22. For further hints and tips on LOGO and general information on all things PCW, there are two excellent monthly magazines available which you should not be without: 'PCW USER' and 'PCW PLUS'. They also give you the opportunity, through readers' letters, etc, to pass on your own accumulated wisdom to the rest of us, for which all us PCW'ers will be truly grateful!

Well, that just about brings us to the end of the tutorial, but by no means to the end of what we may learn about LOGO. Careful study of the programs in PARTS TWO and THREE will give you more insights into programming in LOGO than pages of explanation can achieve. You will find many programs and procedures that can be adapted, used, and doubtless improved upon, for your own purposes. And if you forget what a particular primitive does, or what its syntax is, PART FOUR has all the details. And if you can't find the answer *there*, then there are ten APPENDICES covering just about everything else.

But what you really need to do most of all is to try things out for yourself. In the end there is no substitute for what is usually called the 'hands-on experience'. It might sound vaguely suggestive, but there's no doubt about its value.

In conclusion, let me add a personal note. I use LOGO a lot. I find it a very enjoyable language to play around with, and a particularly easy way of trying out new ideas. Unfortunately for me, when I learned LOGO I had no manual to follow, so I had to hack it around and poke at its innards to see how it worked. But I still found it a relatively simple language to understand and for the most part very user-friendly. And LOGO is by no means confined to the PCW. There are implementations for virtually every type of computer you can think of.

It is by no means a dead-end language. Don't think for one moment that, because it is slow and has certain limitations, that it is of no practical use. Nothing could be further from the truth. However, the real benefit you will gain from learning to program in LOGO is that it will teach you a great deal about the art of programming in general, and that knowledge can be carried over to any other language you may care to learn.

LOGO is fun. So go have some fun!

PART TWO

LIBRARY PROGRAMS

Catalogue

These programs may be used as they stand, but many of them may be adapted and used in your own programs. The programs should be listed and saved to a 'library' disc, which can be added to from time to time, and called up when required.

PROGRAM NAME: **ABS**
FUNCTION: Outputs the absolute value of the input number.

```
to abs :n
if :n < 0 [op -:n] [op :n]
end
```

PROGRAM NAME: **ADLET**
FUNCTION: Takes an input string of characters and returns the ASCII value of each character, together with a total of all the ASCII values.

```
to adlet
(local "temp "let "cou "tot)
make "temp 0 make "tot 0 type char 10
(type [ENTER LETTERS TO ADD:] [])
make "let rq make "cou count :let
if :let = " [recycle op "] adloop 1 :cou 1
(type [TOTAL:] []) pr :tot adlet
end

to adloop :f :t :st
if :f > :t [stop]
make "temp ascii item :f :let make "tot :tot + :temp
if :temp = 32 [make "tot :tot - 32]
if not :temp = 32 [(type :temp [])] [(type ". [])]
adloop + :f :st :t :st
end
```

NOTE: This program can easily be adapted to allow comparisons between whole words rather than just the first character of the word, permitting proper indexing of sorted lists.

PROGRAM NAME: **ASC**
FUNCTION: Returns the ASCII value of any input character.

```
to asc
local "a
make "a ascii rc pr :a
asc
end
```

NOTE: May be used to obtain the ASCII value of any keypress.

PROGRAM NAME: **BCD_DEC**
FUNCTION: Converts binary-coded decimal numbers (BCD) to decimal.

```
to bcd.dec
(local "inp "ans "y)
pr [BCD >>>>> DEC]                          ;chevrons are <EXTRA><#>
make "y item 2 cursor make "inp rq
if :inp = " [throw "TOPLEVEL]      ;press <RETURN> to exit
make "ans ((quotient :inp 16) * 10) + (remainder :inp 16)
setcursor se 12 :y show :ans bcd.dec
end
```

PROGRAM NAME: **BIN_DEC**
FUNCTION: Binary to decimal. Maximum input 524287 decimal.

```
to bin.dec
(local "n "ans "y "accum)
pr [BIN >>>>>>> DEC]                        ;chevrons are <EXTRA><#>
make "ans 0 make "y item 2 cursor make "accum 1
make "n rq if :n = " [throw "TOPLEVEL]      ;press <RETURN> to exit
op bin.dec.work :n :ans :accum
end

to bin.dec.work :n :ans :accum
if emptyp :n [setcursor se 14 :y show :ans bin.dec]
if last :n = 1 [make "ans :ans + :accum]
op bin.dec.work (bl :n) :ans (:accum * 2)
end
```

NOTE: The input in binary is 1111111111111111, which is 16 1's and probably quite enough for most purposes! The value of the rightmost (least significant bit) is 0 or 1, the next is 0 or 2, and so on doubling the value of each bit moving to the left, until the rightmost (most significant byte) is 0 or 32768. The least significant bit and the most significant bit are often abbreviated to LSB and MSB.

PROGRAM NAME: **CENTRE**
FUNCTION: Takes a word or sentence, centres it on the present row.

```
to centre :sentence
(local "length "x "y)
make "length (count :sentence)
make "x (44 - round (:length / 2))
make "y (item 2 cursor)
setcursor se 0 :y repeat :length [type []]
setcursor se :x :y
pr :sentence
end
```

NOTE: This procedure may be used in a program in much the same way that a word-processor code to centre a line might be used. For example: 'setcursor [0 14] centre [This is the centre of the row]' would print out the message to centre screen in row 14.

PROGRAM NAME: **COF**
FUNCTION: Turns the cursor blob off.

```
to cof
(type word char 27 "f)
end
```

PROGRAM NAME: **CON**
FUNCTION: Turns the cursor blob on.

```
to con
(type word char 27 "e)
end
```

PROGRAM NAME: **CURPOS**
FUNCTION: Translates a turtle position in the graphics screen to a corresponding cursor position in the text screen. Enables cursor movement, through the cursor keys, and text-writing.

```
1    to curpos
2    (local "cx "cy "inp)
3    make "cx item 1 tf make "cx round (:cx + 357) / 8
4    make "cy item 2 tf make "cy round (:cy - 255) / 17
5    fs ts label "X
6    setcursor se :cx :cy
7    make "inp rc
8    if :inp = char 175 [fs stop]
9    if :inp = char 222 [curwrite]
10   if :inp = char 240 [make "cy :cy + 1]
11   if :inp = char 250 [make "cx :cx + 1]
12   if :inp = char 242 [make "cy :cy - 1]
13   if :inp = char 254 [make "cx :cx - 1]
14   go "X
15   end

16   to curwrite
17   local "a make "a rq
18   if :a = " [stop]
19   end
```

NOTE: Line 8 is <EXTRA><!>. Line 9 is <EXTRA><+>.

PROGRAM NAME: **DBIN**
FUNCTION: Decimal to binary. Maximum input 32767.

```
to dbin :decnum
if :decnum = 0 [op "]
op word dbin (quotient :decnum 2) (remainder :decnum 2)
end
```

PROGRAM NAME: **DEC_BCD**
FUNCTION: Decimal to Binary-Coded Decimal (BCD).

```
to dec.bcd
(local "inp "ans "y)
pr [DEC >>>>> BCD]                          ;chevrons are <EXTRA><#>
make "y item 2 cursor make "inp rq
   if :inp = " [throw "TOPLEVEL]            ;press <RETURN> to exit
make "ans ((quotient :inp 10) * 16) + (remainder :inp 10)
setcursor se 10 :y show :ans dec.bcd
end
```

PROGRAM NAME: **DEC_BIN**
FUNCTION: Decimal to binary.

```
to dec.bin
(local "inp "ans "factor)
pr [DEC >>>>>>> BIN]                        ;chevrons are <EXTRA><#>
make "inp rq if :inp = " [throw "TOPLEVEL]
make "ans [] make "factor 128
dec.bin.work :inp :ans :factor
end

to dec.bin.work :inp :ans :factor
local "n
if :factor = 1 [result :ans :inp :factor]
make "n quotient :inp :factor
if not :n = 0 [make "ans lput 1 :ans] [make "ans lput 0 :ans]
make "inp remainder :inp :factor
dec.bin.work :inp :ans :factor / 2
end

to result :ans :inp :factor
make "ans lput remainder :inp 2 :ans
pr :ans
dec.bin
end
```

NOTE: Maximum entry 65535 = 111111111111111 (15 bytes).

PROGRAM NAME: **DEPTH**
FUNCTION: Measures the depth of lists in a multi-level list.

```
to depth inlist
if wordp :inlist [op 0]
if emptyp :inlist [op 1]
if (and emptyp bf :inlist wordp first :inlist) [op 1]
op max (1 + depth first :inlist) (depth bf :inlist)
end
```

```
to max :n1 :n2
if :n1 > :n2 [op :n1]
op :n2
end

make "inlist [a [[[b] c] d] e [[e] f] [] [] [[g] h]]
```

NOTE: The example list may be used to try out DEPTH.

PROGRAM NAME: **DH**
FUNCTION: Converts decimal values to their hexadecimal equivalents. Accepts inputs up to 524287 (7FFFF hex)).

```
to dh
(local "n "q "r "y "ans)
pr [DEC >>>>> HEX] label "Y make "y item 2 cursor
if :y > 28 [ct ts type :n setcursor [10 0] pr :ans dh]
make "n 0 make "ans " make "n rq
if :n = " [recycle throw "TOPLEVEL]
label "X make "q int (:n / 16) make "r :n - (:q * 16)
if :r > 9 [make "r item :r - 9 [A B C D E F]]
make "ans fput :r :ans
if and :q < 16 :q > 9 [make "q item :q - 9 [A B C D E F]
    make "ans fput :q :ans setcursor se 10 :y
    show :ans go "Y]
if :q < 10 [make "ans fput :q :ans setcursor se 10 :y
    show :ans go "Y]
make "n :q
go "X
end
```

NOTE: The chevron characters (French quotes, or *Guillmets*) are obtained with <EXTRA><#>. If **quotient** and **remainder** are used instead of the more complicated forms 'int (: / 16)' and ':n - (:q * 16))' the maximum input is 32767.

PROGRAM NAME: **FACT**
FUNCTION: Outputs the factorial of the input positive integer.

```
to fact :m
op fact.work :m 1
end

to fact.work :n :accum
if :n = 0 [op :accum]
op fact.work (:n - 1) (:accum * :n)
end
```

NOTE: Factorials are expressed thus: if N=0 then N!=1, if N>0 then N!=N*(N-1)!. (N! expresses the factorial of a positive integer N).

PROGRAM NAME: FIB
FUNCTION: Outputs the Fibonacci number of the input number. It will accept inputs up to 89; over that there is insufficient LOGO stack space to compute the result.

```
to fib :m
op fib.work :m 0 1
end

to fib.work :n :acc :current
if :n = 0 [op :acc]
op fib.work (:n - 1) (:acc + :current) (:acc)
end
```

NOTE: Fibonacci numbers are defined thus:
if N=0 then FIB N is 0,
if N=1 then FIB N is 1,
if N>1 then FIB N=FIB(N-1) + FIB(N-2).

PROGRAM NAME: **FLASH**
FUNCTION: Prints a flashing message to the screen. Can be stopped by pressing any key. The message may be altered to suit. The time delays may also be altered to suit. This program flashes the whole screen, not just the message. It is possible to write a program to flash just the message, using spaces to overwrite the message and then writing it again, or using ESC A and ESC M (see APPENDIX IV). See also the SCROLL program in PART THREE.

```
to flash
ts setcursor [40 15]
type [FLASHING MESSAGE] fs repeat 50 [type []]
.out 248 8 repeat 20 [pr []]
if keyp [.out 248 7 ct ts throw "TOPLEVEL]
.out 248 7
flash
end
```

PROGRAM NAME: **GRAPHSCR**
FUNCTION: Plots the extremities of the graphics screen and draws a line joining up those extremities.

```
to graphscr
cs ct fs pu ht setpos [-360 263] pd
repeat 2 [rt 90 fd 719 rt 90 fd 528]
end
```

NOTE: This procedure might profitably be used to draw a border in DESIGNER (PART THREE). To draw a thicker line use parameters for the start co-ords and the line units, and decrease the X and Y co-ordinates as many times as you like using recursion.

PROGRAM NAME: **HD**
FUNCTION: Converts hexadecimal values to decimal. Accepts inputs up to &HFFFF (65535 dec).

```
to hd
(local "a "b "c "d "n "y "co "ans)
pr [HEX >>>>> DEC]                              ;chevrons are <EXTRA><#>
label "C make "y item 2 cursor
if :y > 28 [ct fs ts type :n setcursor [10 0] show :ans dec]
make "n uc rq if :n = "
   [recycle throw "TOPLEVEL] make "co count :n
if item :co :n > 9 [make "a ascii item :co :n make "a :a - 55]
   [make "a item :co :n]
if :co = 1 [go "A]
if and :co > 1 item :co - 1 :n > 9
   [make "b ascii item :co - 1 :n make "b :b - 55]
   [make "b item :co - 1 :n] if :co = 2 [go "A]
if and :co > 2 item :co - 2 :n > 9
   [make "c ascii item :co - 2 :n make "c :c - 55]
   [make "c item :co - 2 :n] if :co = 3 [go "A]
  if and :co = 4 item :co - 3 :n > 9
   [make "d ascii item :co - 3 :n make "d :d - 55]
   [make "d item :co - 3 :n]
label "A if :co = 1 [make "ans :a go "B]
make "b :b * 16 if :co = 2 [make "ans :b + :a go "B]
make "c :c * 256 if :co = 3 [make "ans :c + :b + :a go "B]
make "d :d * 4096 if :co = 4 [make "ans :d + :c + :b + :a go "B]
label "B setcursor se 10 :y show :ans go "C
end
```

NOTE: In spite of its apparent complexity this program works quite quickly. It could be extended to accept greater inputs.

PROGRAM NAME: **LOOP**
FUNCTION: Provides a looping procedure. Variable :st is the starting number, :en is the ending number, :step is the step value either + or −, allowing loops to be either incremental or decremental.

```
to loop :st :en :step
action :st
if :st = :en [stop]
loop :st + :step :en :step
end

to action :st
make "a :st (type :a char 32)
end
```

NOTE: The procedure 'action' is purely there as an example of how LOOP works. This program produces a 'for...next' loop and can easily be re-written to produce 'while...wend' or 'repeat...until' loops.

PROGRAM NAME: **MAXLIST**
FUNCTION: Outputs the highest number of an input list.

```
to maxlist :numlist
if count :numlist = 2 [op max first :numlist last :numlist]
op max first :numlist maxlist bf :numlist
end

to max :n1 :n2
if :n1 > :n2 [op :n1]
op :n2
end
```

NOTE: Procedure 'max' may be utilised with other programs.

PROGRAM NAME: **MOVF**
FUNCTION: Moves files from one drive to another. The workspace must be empty before using MOVF.

```
to movf
(local "d "inp)
make "d defaultd type defaultd pr [MOVF]
pr [> FROM FILENAME TO] (type "> []) make "inp rl
if :inp = [] [er "movf recycle throw "TOPLEVEL]
setd word first :inp ":
load "item 2 :inp
setd word last :inp ":
er "movf
save item 2 :inp
setd :d
erall recycle load "movf movf
end
```

NOTE: Entries must be made in the form 'a *filename* m'. It is not necessary to enter quote-marks or colons. The chevron characters > are obtained with <EXTRA><#>.

PROGRAM NAME: **MID**
FUNCTION: Works out the necessary start position of the cursor for the input string to be centered on a line. Prints the column for text to commence in row 0. *cf* CENTRE.

```
to mid
type [sentence?] make "sentence rq
make "length (count :sentence)
setcursor se (45 - round (:length / 2)) 0
show cursor
end
```

PROGRAM NAME: **POWER**
FUNCTION: Raises a number :num to a power :exp.

```
to power :num :exp
local "ans
make "ans :num
repeat :exp - 1 [make "ans :num * :ans]
op :ans
end
```

PROGRAM NAME: **PQ**
FUNCTION: Prints procedures to paper.

```
to pq
local "a
ct label "P if not = .in 253 220
   [type [Load continuous paper, press RETURN]
   if not rc = char 13 [ct go "P]
ct (type [Enter procedure to print, or 'all':] [])
make "a rq if :a = "all [er "pq fs copyon ts poall fs copyoff stop]
if not memberp :a glist ".DEF
   [fs copyoff ts pr [Procedure not found] stop]
fs copyon ts po :a fs copyoff ts ct
end
```

NOTE: The CP/M program SETPRINT.FIL should be run with SETLST.COM before using PQ. See APPENDIX IV. **po** and **poall** give 'paged' output. Press <RETURN> to continue when print-out pauses. **.in 253** only returns 220 if paper is loaded in the printer.

PROGRAM NAME: **PV**
FUNCTION: Prints a list vertically commencing in column 0.

```
to pv :list
if emptyp :list [stop]
pr first :list
pv bf :list
end
```

PROGRAM NAME: **RANSEED**
FUNCTION: Sets a random seed for the primitive **random**. It takes the seconds count from the internal CP/M clock as the number of random calls, thus giving an unpredictable seed.

```
to ranseed
repeat .examine 64504 [if random 2 = 2 []]
end
```

PROGRAM NAME: **RANDLIST**
FUNCTION: Outputs a random list of numbers between :fi and :la, the first and last of a sequence of numbers.

```
to randlist
(local "fi "la "list)
cs ct fs ht ts make "list []
setcursor [0 0] randlist2
end

to randlist2
(pr [Enter first number, press RETURN:] [])
make "fi rq if :fi = "
   [er [randlist randlist2 newlist results init]
   throw "TOPLEVEL]
(pr [Enter last number, press RETURN:] [])
make "la rq
pr " pr [Random list being generated. PLEASE WAIT] pr "
init :fi :la :list
end

to init :fi :la :list
make "list lput :fi :list
if equalp :fi :la [newlist :list]
init :fi + 1 :la :list
end

to newlist :list
local "ch
make "ch 0 make "list shuffle :list make "ranlst :list
results :list :ch
end

to results :list :ch
local "a
if emptyp :list [pr [] pr [] pr [List stored as :ranlst]
   pr [Press RETURN to erase prog & quit, or PLEASE WAIT]
   pr [] recycle randlist2]
if :ch > 12 [pr " make "ch 0] (type first :list [])
results bf :list :ch + 1
end
```

PROGRAM NAME: **REMOVE**
FUNCTION: Removes an item from a list.

```
to remove :item :list
(local "temp "w)
if memberp :item :list [make "w where]
if :w = 1 [make "list bf :list op :list]
   [repeat :w - 1
      [make "temp lput first :list :temp make "list bf :list]]
make "list bf :list
make "list se :temp :list op :list
end
```

PROGRAM NAME: **RESTC**
FUNCTION: Restores the cursor to the latest position saved by SAVEC (*qv*).

```
to restc
(type char 27 "k)
end
```

PROGRAM NAME: **REVOF**
FUNCTION: Restores screen colours to normal after a REVON instruction. Entirely equivalent to Palette 0 1.

```
to revof
(type (word char 27 "b6 char 27 "c0))
end
```

PROGRAM NAME: **REVON**
FUNCTION: Reverses screen colours. Background becomes green/white, print becomes black. Entirely equivalent to Palette 1 0.

```
to revon
(type (word char 27 "b0 char 27 "c6))
end
```

NOTE: There is no mistake in 'c6': it should theoretically be 'c63', but the 3 proves to be superfluous and will print out if included. The same stricture applies to REVOF.

PROGRAM NAME: **ROF**
FUNCTION: Turns off reverse video.

```
to rof
type word char 27 "q type char 8
end
```

PROGRAM NAME: **RON**
FUNCTION: Turns on reverse video.

```
to ron
type word char 27 "p type char 8
end
```

NOTE: RON and ROF sometimes cause a space shift and a phantom repeat of the input character when used with **rc**, **rq**, and **rl**. The solution is to follow the instructions with a backspace ('type char 8') as has been done here.

PROGRAM NAME: **REDUCE**
FUNCTION: Reduces a multi-level list to a one-level list.

```
to reduce numlist
if wordp :numlist [op :numlist]
if emptyp :numlist [op []]
if (and (wordp first :numlist) (emptyp bf :numlist))
   [op :numlist]
op (se reduce first :numlist reduce bf :numlist)
end
```

PROGRAM NAME: **REVERSE**
FUNCTION: Reverses the order of the contents of a list.

```
to reverse :alist
local "temp
make "temp []
repeat count :alist [make "temp fput first :alist :temp
   make "alist bf :alist]
op :temp
end
```

NOTE: In long lists using **fput** rather than **lput** is considerably quicker, to the point where, with very long lists, using **lput** causes the stack buffer to fill up and the program to halt.

PROGRAM NAME: **SAVEC**
FUNCTION: Saves the current cursor position in memory. RESTC (*qv*) restores the cursor to the latest SAVEC position.

```
to savec
(type word char 27 "j)
end
```

PROGRAM NAME: **SQRT**
FUNCTION: Outputs the square-root of the input number.

```
to sqrt :num
local "root
make "root :num / 2
repeat 64 [if abs (:root - :num / :sq) < :root * 5.E-15 [op :root]
   [make "root (:root + :num / :root) / 2]]
op :root
end

to abs :n
if :n < 0 [op -:n] [op :n]
end
```

PROGRAM NAME: **STARTUP**

FUNCTION: Sets up the workspace. <#><RETURN> will now show the default drive. A new primitive 'setc' as an alternative to **setcursor** is created. Optionally, 'spacer' may be called to enlarge the workspace. On exit it clears the workspace except for UPD. Any file called STARTUP will load automatically when LOGO is booted. Press <s><RETURN> to run STARTUP.

```
to s
local "dd
;{spacer}
ts ts ron (type [] [DEFAULT DRIVE?] []) rof
make "dd uc word rc ": type :dd setd :dd
type word char 27 0
pprop "# ".PRM gprop "defaultd ".PRM
pprop "setc ".PRM gprop "setcursor ".PRM
pr [SETPRINT.FIL loaded:]
pr [To print procedures, load file 'pq'] pr "
pr [side margins at 9 and 93]
pr [bottom margin 5]
pr [continuous printing]
pr [Elite type, High Quality]
pr [PL 66] pr "
pr [Press "£ to show DEFAULT drive, or use defaultd]
pr [Use 'setc' or 'setcursor']
pr [Type upd FILENAME to update file] pr "
(pr [Type ! to QUIT] [])
dircol :dd
end

to dircol :dd
local "a
(pr [Drive is:] :dd)
ron (type [] [For directory, enter Drive:] []) rof
make "a rc if :a = "!
   [er [ron rof setup dircol dircol.work print.col]
   recycle throw "TOPLEVEL]
setd word :a ": type char 8
(pr [DIRECTORY OF DRIVE] word uc :a ":)

dircol.work :a :dd
dircol :dd
end

to dircol.work :dr :dd
(local "x "y "list "co "yy)
setd word :dr ": make "list (dir)
make "co int (1 + (count :list) / 8)
make "x item 1 cursor make "y item 2 cursor
if emptyp :list [pr [No files found] pr [] setd :dd stop]
setc [0 30] repeat :co + 1 [type char 10]
make "y (:y - :co) setc se :x :y make "yy :y + :co + 1
print.col :list :x :y :dd :co :yy
end
```

```
to print.col :list :x :y :dd :co :yy
type word char 27 "f
repeat ((count :list) / :co) + 1
   [repeat :co
      [if emptyp :list [setc se 0 :yy type word char 27 "e stop]
      pr first :list make "list bf :list
      make "y :y + 1 setc se :x :y]
      make "x :x + 11 make "y :y - :co setc se :x :y]
end

to upd :file
erasefile :file save :file
end

to ron
type word char 27 "p type char 8
end

to rof
type word char 27 "q type char 8
end

to spacer
(local "prims "len "procs)
ct setcursor [40 27] pr "SPACEMAKER
setcursor [38 28] pr [...please wait]
fs ht pu setpos [100 0] seth 0 pd
make "procs [] make "len 210 pd make "REDEFP "TRUE
make "prims (list "pal "setpal "wait "tones "setpen "towards
   "setbg "noformat "dot "dotc "rerandom ".contents
   ".examine ".deposit ".in ".out "paddle "changef "setpc
   "equalp "buttonp)
space.work :prims :procs :len
er [pal setpal wait tones setpen towards setbg noformat dot dotc
rerandom .contents .examine .deposit .in .out paddle
changef setpc equalp buttonp run.procs space.def space.work
spacer]
ern "REDEFP recycle ts ts stop
end

to space.work :prims :procs :len
local "name
if emptyp :prims [run.procs :procs :len stop]
make "name first :prims make "procs lput first :prims :procs
space.def :name
space.work bf :prims :procs :len
end

to space.def :name
local "alist
make "alist (list "fd ":len "rt 90)
make "alist (list "repeat 4 :alist)
make "alist list [len] :alist
define :name :alist
stop
end
```

```
94   to run.procs :proclist :len
95   if emptyp :proclist [stop]
96   make "len :len - 10 pu bk 10 lt 90 fd 10 rt 90 pd
97   run (se first :proclist :len)
98   run.procs bf :proclist :len
99   end
```

NOTE: In line 3 the optional call {spacer} should be omitted if you do not wish to redefine the primitives. Also omit the 'spacer', 'space.work', 'space.def' and 'run.procs'. If 'spacer' is to be used, remove the braces and the semi-colon. Lines 9 to 15 should be omitted if SETPRINT.FIL has not been used. In line 25, the drive letter is all that needs to be entered: no quote-mark, no colon, do not press <RETURN>. In lines 68..71 any of the primitives listed may be omitted if desired, but they must also be deleted from lines 73..76. Lines 86 *et seq* define the unwanted primitives as procedures, hence they are no longer recognised as primitives. A pretty pattern will be drawn to the screen by 'run.procs'. Use STARTUP as a start of day program, in conjunction with SETPRINT.FIL (see APPENDIX IV). SPACER increases the workspace by about 200 nodes. Any other primitives may be included. 'Make' the list by typing: 'make "prims glist ".PRM' and delete those primitives that you want to keep. Note that any file called 'startup' will be automatically loaded by LOGO on booting up.

PROGRAM NAME: **STOF**
FUNCTION: Disables the status line.

```
to stof
(type word char 27 0)
end
```

PROGRAM NAME: **STON**
FUNCTION: Enables the status line.

```
to ston
(type word char 27 1)
end
```

PROGRAM NAME: **TRIG**
FUNCTION: Outputs the tangent, cotangent, secant, or cosecant of the input.

```
to tan :num
op sin :num / cos :num
end
```

```
to cot :ang
op 1 / ((sin :ang) / (cos :ang))
end

to sec :ang
op 1 / cos :ang
end

to cosec :ang
op 1 / sin :ang
end
```

PROGRAM NAME: **TURPOS**
FUNCTION: Translates a cursor position in the text screen to a corresponding turtle position in the graphics screen. Enables turtle movement, and line drawing.

```
to turpos
(local "tx "ty "inp)
fs make "tx item 1 cursor make "tx (:tx * 8) - 368
make "ty item 2 cursor make "ty -:ty * 17 + 256
fs ht pu label "X setpos se :tx :ty st
make "inp rc
if :inp = char 190 [ht fs stop]
if :inp = char 222 [pd]
if :inp = char 94 [pu]
if :inp = char 240 [make "ty :ty + 8]
if :inp = char 250 [make "tx :tx + 8]
if :inp = char 242 [make "ty :ty - 8]
if :inp = char 254 [make "tx :tx - 8]
go "X
end
```

NOTE: <EXTRA><+> is **pd**, <EXTRA><u> is **pu**. <EXTRA><r> returns to **ts** state. The turtle is set to the cursor position so that if vertical and horizontal lines are drawn upwards and to the right from the turtle position, they will precisely enclose the character at the cursor position. To adjust this setting, alter the figures at the end of lines 3 and 4. Char 190 is <EXTRA><r>, char 222 is <EXTRA><+>, and char 94 is <EXTRA><u>.

PROGRAM NAME: **ULOF**
FUNCTION: Turns off underline.

```
to ulof
(type word char 27 "u)
end
```

PROGRAM NAME: **ULON**
FUNCTION: Turns on underline. Subsequent underlining is shown on screen.

```
to ulon
(type word char 27 "r)
end
```

PROGRAM NAME: **UPD**
FUNCTION: Updates a previously saved file.

```
to upd :fil
erasefile :fil save :fil
end
```

NOTE: Enter in the form 'upd "filename'.

PROGRAM NAME: **VPORT**
FUNCTION: Sets a new text viewport. :tr is the top row, :lc the left column, :h the height in rows, :w the width in columns.

```
to vport :tr :lc :h :w
(type (word char 27 "X char :tr + 31 char :lc + 31 char :h + 31
      char :w + 31))
ts ts
end
```

NOTE: There is no mistake in the offsets: LOGO requires all offsets to be 31 to give correct viewports. 'ts ts' clears the new viewport and takes the cursor to the top left. Cursor co-ordinates start from [0 0] in the top left corner of the new viewport. Commands such as **cs** and **ct** will affect only the new viewport. To return to the full screen, enter: 'vport 0 0 31 90'.

PROGRAM NAME: **WHILE**
FUNCTION: A while-wend looping program. The variable :condition contains a test for the continuation of the loop. The variable :action contains the action to be called if the condition outputs FALSE.

```
to while :condition :action
if not run :condition [stop]
run :action
while :condition :action
end
```

NOTE: The condition may be used either way, to produce a TRUE or FALSE output, and the line 'if not :condition' changed to 'if :condition'.

PROGRAM NAME: **WINDOWS**
FUNCTION: A quick method of reversing the video of blocks of any size, which can then be written to or drawn on.

```
1    to ron
2    (type word char 27 "p char 8)
3    end

4    to rof
5    (type word char 27 "q char 8)
6    end

7    to windows
8    (local "x "y "tl "br)
9    make "tl [] make "br []
10   ts ct pr [Position the cursor with the cursor keys]
11   repeat 30 [(type [] char 8)]
12   pr [Press 't' for top left of reverse video window]
13   repeat 30 [(type [] char 8)]
14   pr [Press 'b' for bottom right]
15   repeat 40 [(type [] char 8)]
16   ct setcursor [45 15]
17   make "x item 1 cursor make "y item 2 cursor
18   windows.help :x :y :tl :br
19   end

20   to windows.help :x :y :tl :br
21   local "inp
22   setcursor se :x :y label "W
23   make "inp rc
24   if :inp = char 250 [make "x :x + 1]
25   if :inp = char 254 [make "x :x - 1]
26   if :inp = char 242 [make "y :y + 1]
27   if :inp = char 240 [make "y :y - 1]
28   if :inp = "t [make "tl cursor]
29   if :inp = "b [make "br cursor
30      if :br > :tl [go "W] [windows.work :x :y :tl :br]]
31   windows.help :x :y :tl :br
32   end

33   to windows.work :x :y :tl :br
34   (local "repc1 "repr1 "repc2 "repr2 "repc "repr)
35   make "repc1 item 1 :br make "repc2 item 1 :tl
36   make "repc :repc1 - :repc2
37   make "repr1 item 2 :br make "repr2 item 2 :tl
38   make "repr :repr1 - :repr2
39   setc se :repc2 :repr2 ron
40   repeat :repr + 1 [setc se :repc2 :repr2
41   repeat :repc + 1 [type char 32] make "repr2 :repr2 + 1]
42   rof
43   end
```

NOTE: In lines 12 and 14, the top left position must be on the same line as, or higher than, the bottom left position, and in the same column as, or to the right of, the bottom right position. If this is not true, the procedure jumps back and waits for fresh input. The top left must be set before the bottom right. This program would need to be used with a write or draw program. Once the reverse video block or blocks have been drawn, the WINDOWS procedures can be erased.

PROGRAM NAME: Z
FUNCTION: Lists the procedures in the workspace vertically and numbered. Selected groups of procedures may be erased by entering numbers only. Run by entering 'z'.

```
to z
(local "st "en "list)
make "list [] y
type [ERASE FROM \(nos.\):\*] type char 32
make "st rq
if :st = " [recycle op "]
repeat 3 [type char 9] type [...TO:\*] type char 32
make "en rq
if :st = " [recycle op "]
if :st = 1 [er piece :st :en :list recycle op "]
er piece :st :en :list
z
end

to y
local "x
make "x 1
make "list glist ".DEF
label "A
if not "z = item 1 :list
   [make "list lput item 1 :list :list
   make "list bf :list go "A]
x :list
end

to x :list
if emptyp :list [stop]
pr se :x first :list
if :x = 3 [pr "\-\-\-]
make "x :x + 1
x bf :list
end
```

NOTE: A vertical numbered list of all the procedures in the workspace is printed to screen. Procedures may be erased by entering the numbers of the first and last to be erased at the prompts. If only one procedure is to be erased, type in the same number twice. Leave the three program procedures 'z', 'x' and 'y' until last, then erase them by entering '1' and '3'. <RETURN> exits from the program at any time without erasing the program itself. This is a useful utility to have in the workspace whilst developing a program.

PART THREE

WORKING PROGRAMS

Catalogue

Here's a few I prepared earlier as they say. They are all complete LOGO programs, which may however be tailored to your own needs. Programs will benefit from running from the M: drive if there is any intermediate loading and saving to be done during their execution. This particularly applies to DATABASE, SCRNGRID & WARSHIP. Most of the programs are run simply by typing the name of the first procedure. Where there is any departure from this practice it is stated. Do *not* type in the line numbers: they are only simply for reference and to make it easier to keep track in long programs.

PROGRAM NAME: **ALARM**
DESCRIPTION: Alarm clock. May be set for any time up to 24 hours. The bleep will sound continuously when the time has elapsed. Press any key to stop. Run by typing 'prime'.

```
to prime
 (local "t "h "m)
 cs ht ts ts make "amin 0
 pr [ALARM y\/n ?] if rc = "y [setalarm] [make "set "off]
 pr " pr [SET TIME\/JUMP TO CLOCK s\/j ?]
 if not rc = "s [time]
 pr " pr [TME NOW (hh mm) ?]
 pr [(Press RETURN when seconds\=59\):]
 make "t rl
 make "h first :t make "m last :t
 make "h (quotient :h 10) * 16 + remainder :h 10
 make "m (quotient :m 10) * 16 + remainder :m 10
 .deposit 64502 :h
 .deposit 64503 :m
 .deposit 64504 0
 ct time
 end

 to setalarm
 pr [ALARM TIME (hh mm\) ?]
 make "al rl make "ahr first :al make "amin last :al
 make "al (word :ahr ": :amin)
 make "set "on
 end

 to time
 (local "hrs "mins "secs)
 cs ht if :set = "on [frame] [frame2]
 ts cof setcursor [43 13] type "TIME
 if :set = "on [setcursor [35 17] (type [Alarm set for:] :al)
    setcursor [37 18] type [any key to stop.]]
 repeat 30000 [make "hrs .examine 64502
    make "mins .examine 64503
    make "secs .examine 64504
    make "secs (quotient :secs 16) * 10 + remainder :secs 16
    make "mins (quotient :mins 16) * 10 + remainder :mins 16
    make "hrs (quotient :hrs 16) * 10 + remainder :hrs 16
    if and :set = "on :amin = :mins [switch :hrs]
    setcursor [37 15]
    (type :hrs [] ": [] :mins [] ": [] :secs [] [] [])]
 end
```

```
40  to cof
41  (type word char 27 char 102)
42  end

43  to switch :hrs
44  if :ahr = :hrs [.out 248 11] [stop]
45  if keyp [.out 248 12 make "set "off time]
46  end

47  to frame
48  fs pu setpos [-120 -75] pd
49  repeat 2 [fd 130 rt 90 fd 240 rt 90]
50  end

51  to frame2
52  fs pu setpos [-120 -25] pd
53  repeat 2 [fd 80 rt 90 fd 240 rt 90]
54  end

55  to con
56  (type word char 27 char 101)
57  end
```

NOTE: ALARM does a garbage collection every now and then - you'll see it pause for a second here and there, or jump on a second - but when it continues it also updates the time correctly. The seconds read-out isn't 100% accurate, due to the lack of synchronisation between the looping and the actual seconds count, but it is accurate over a period of one minute. If you really expected an upwards of £400 computer to do as well as a £2 digital from the garage round the corner, you obviously didn't read Modern Technology at the University of Life! You only need to set the time once at the start of each session, after that you can run ALARM anywhen you like (use the jump to clock option) and it will tell you the right time. In line 6, you give the program a second to access the time, set it, and nip down to TIME and start it running. The formulae in lines 9 and 10 are there because of the peculiar way CP/M stores the hours, minutes and seconds. These are in the form:

REAL TIME	HELD AS
0..9	0..9
10..19	16..25
20..29	32..41
30..39	48..57
40..49	64..73
50..59	80..89

It's all to do with the time being held inside the computer as binary-coded decimal. In lines 13..15, the hours, minutes and seconds are set. In line 30, a ridiculously high repeat is set, so that there is no danger of the clock's mainspring running down. The three addresses are then searched for the time values, which are duly re-converted to real-time and the time displayed. Just a reminder that LOGO requires all its inputs and outputs to be in decimal. Use HD and DH from PART TWO to do the calculations for you. Also note that LOGO uses many of the same CP/M memory addresses as BASIC, so any PEEKS and POKES you happen to know you can quite possibly use in LOGO. For example: 64500 & 64501 hold the date values in BCD. A simple program will re-set the date and display it.

PROGRAM NAME: **BARGRAPH**
DESCRIPTION: A program to draw a shadowed three-dimensional bargraph of a given data set of up to twelve entries. The graph may also be written to, and may be saved to disc as a LOGO picfile.

```
to graph
ts ts pr [Enter name to save graph to disc:]
make "graph rq
label "A pr [Enter Y\-range: high, Y\-div]
make "yr rl if not count :yr = 2 [go "A]
label "B pr [Enter X caption\-list:]
make "inlist rl pr [Enter PLOT values]
make "valist rl
if not equalp count :inlist count :valist [go "B]
make "xh count :inlist
make "yh first :yr make "ydiv item 2 :yr
make "ymark :ydiv make "xdiv quotient 600 :xh
make "ydiv :yh / :ydiv make "yr :ydiv
make "ydiv quotient 400 :ydiv
cs fs ht xaxis yaxis make "check 0
repeat :xh [plot] pu make "check 0
repeat :xh [shade] pu write
end

to xaxis
fs make "check 0
pu setpos [-290 -210] pd seth 90 fd :xdiv / 2
repeat :xh [xline] setx 350
end

to xline
pu sety -245 make "check :check + 1
curpos item :check :inlist sety -210 pd fd :xdiv
end

to yaxis
pu setpos [-290 -210] pd seth 0 make "check 0
repeat :yr [yline] sety 250 pu stop
end

to yline
fd :ydiv pu setx -342 make "check :check + :ymark
curpos :check setx -310 pd setx -290
end
```

```
36 to curpos :input
37 (local "cx "cy)
38 make "cx item 1 tf make "cx round (:cx + 357) / 8
39 make "cy item 2 tf make "cy round (:cy - 255) / 17
40 fs ts setcursor se :cx :cy
41 pr :input fs
42 end

43 to plot
44 fs make "check :check + 1
45 make "yplot round 400 / :yh * (item :check :valist) - 210
46 if :check = 1 [make "xplot (:xdiv / 2) - 300]
47     [make "xplot (:check * :xdiv) - 300 - (:xdiv / 2)]
48 setpos se :xplot -210 pd sety :yplot top
49 setx (:xplot + 20) sety -210 pu setpos se :a :b
50 pd sety -210 pu setpos se :xplot (:yplot + 25)
51 curpos (item :check :valist)
52 end

53 to shade
54 fs make "check :check + 1
55 make "yplot round 400 / :yh * (item :check :valist) - 206
56 if :check = 1 [make "xplot :xdiv / 2 - 300]
57     [make "xplot (:check * :xdiv) - 300 - (:xdiv / 2)]
58 setpos se :xplot + 23 -206 pd fill pu
59 end

60 to write
61 (local "a "b "x "y)
62 ts setcursor [45 15]
63 make "x item 1 cursor make "y item 2 cursor
64 label "W setcursor se :x :y make "a rc
65 if :a = char 186 [fs savepic :graph ts ts throw "TOPLEVEL] ;EXTRA s
66 if ascii :a < 186 [type :a make "b rq]
67 if :a = char 240 [make "y :y - 1]
68 if :a = char 242 [make "y :y + 1]
69 if :a = char 250 [make "x :x + 1]
70 if :a = char 254 [make "x :x - 1]
71 go "W
72 end

73 to top
74 seth 50 fd 10 rt 40 fd 20
75 make "a item 1 tf make "b item 2 tf
76 seth 230 fd 10 seth 0 setpos se :xplot :yplot
77 end
```

NOTE: In line 4, 'high' must be a number above the greatest number in the data set. The 'Y-div' is the marked division of the Y axis. For example an entry of '200 50' would make the Y axis 200 divisions high, marked off every 50 divisions. In line 6, the 'X caption-list' may have up to 12 divisions, and these will be spaced out evenly along the X axis. Each caption should not be more than about 5 characters long if 12 sets are used, or they will run into each other. The 'PLOT values' in line 7 are the data values. If the PLOT values and the X caption-list are not equal in number, the PLOT values will not be accepted. In line 65, the save option is selected with <EXTRA><s>. The graph will be saved to the default drive under the name entered in line 2. The cursor may be moved with the cursor keys. Any characters typed will be printed to the screen. Fix by pressing <RETURN>, erase with the space-bar and then press <RETURN> to 'fix' the spaces.

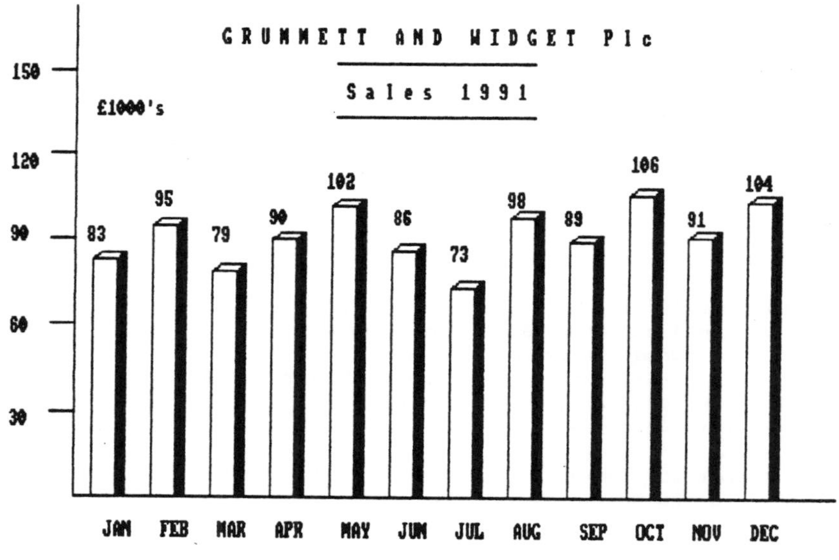

Figure III.1 Three-dimensional graph drawn using BARGRAPH

PROGRAM NAME: **BAR3GRPH**

DESCRIPTION: A program to draw a bargraph of three given data sets of up to twelve entries each. The graph may be written to, and may be saved to disc as a LOGO picfile. Optionally the bars may be filled.

```
to graph
ts ts pr [Enter name to save graph to disc:]
make "graph rq label "A pr [Enter Y\-range: high, Y\-div]
make "yr rl if not count :yr = 2 [go "A]
pr [Enter X captionlist:] make "inlist rl
make "num 0 repeat 3 [plotval]
graph.work
end

to plotval
make "num :num + 1
(pr [Enter DATA\-SET] :num [VALUES:])
make word "valist :num rl
end

to graph.work
make "xh count :inlist
make "xl -300 make "yh first :yr make "ydiv item 2 :yr
make "ymark :ydiv make "xdiv quotient 600 :xh
make "ydiv :yh / :ydiv make "yr :ydiv
make "ydiv quotient 360 :ydiv
cs fs xaxis yaxis make "check 0 setx -330
make "valist :valist1 make "factor 300
repeat :xh [plot] pu make "check 0
make "valist :valist2 make "factor 290
repeat :xh [plot] pu make "check 0
make "valist :valist3 make "factor 280
repeat :xh [plot] pu write
end

to xaxis
fs make "check 0 pu setpos [-290 -210] pd
seth 90 fd :xdiv repeat :xh [xline] setx 350
end

to xline pu sety -245
make "check :check + 1
curpos item :check :inlist
sety -210 pd fd :xdiv
end

to yaxis
pu setpos [-290 -210] pd seth 0 make "check 0
repeat :yh [yline] sety 250 pu stop
end

to yline
fd :ydiv pu setx -342 make "check :check + :ymark
curpos :check setx -310 pd setx -290
end
```

```
45  to plot
46  fs make "check :check + 1
47  make "yplot round 360 / :yh * (item :check :valist) - 210
48  make "xplot (:check * :xdiv) - :factor
49  setpos se :xplot -210 pd
50  setpos se :xplot :yplot
51  setx (:xplot + 10) sety -210
52  end

53  to curpos :input
54  (local "cx "cy "inp)
55  make "cx item 1 tf make "cx round (:cx + 345) / 8
56  make "cy item 2 tf make "cy round (:cy - 255) / 17
57  fs ts setcursor se :cx :cy pr :input fs
58  end

59  to write
60  (local "a "b "x "y)
61  ts setcursor [45 15]
62  make "x item 1 cursor make "y item 2 cursor
63  label "W setcursor se :x :y make "a rc
64  if :a = char 186 [fs savepic :graph throw "TOPLEVEL]   ;EXTRA s
65  if ascii :a < 190 [type :a make "b rq]
66  if :a = char 240 [make "y :y - 1]
67  if :a = char 242 [make "y :y + 1]
68  if :a = char 250 [make "x :x + 1]
69  if :a = char 254 [make "x :x - 1] go "W
70  end
```

NOTE: In this case the 'high' input in line 3 must be higher than the highest entry of any of the data sets.In line 65, the save option is activated by pressing <EXTRA><s>. The file will be saved under the name given in line 2.

PROGRAM NAME: **BAR3FILG**
DESCRIPTION: Additional procedure 'shade', and an alternative procedure 'graph.work', which together permit the filling of the bars in the three-bar graph.

```
to shade
fs make "check :check + 1
make "xplot (:check * :xdiv) - :factor
setpos se :xplot + 5 -206 pu fd 10 pd fill pu
end

to graph.work
make "xh count :inlist make "xl -300
make "yh first :yr make "ydiv item 2 :yr
make "ymark :ydiv make "xdiv quotient 600 :xh
make "ydiv :yh / :ydiv make "yr :ydiv
make "ydiv quotient 360 :ydiv cs fs xaxis yaxis
make "check 0 setx -330
make "valist :valist1 make "factor 300
repeat :xh [plot] pu make "check 0
```

```
make "valist :valist2 make "factor 290
repeat :xh [plot] pu make "check 0
make "valist :valist3 make "factor 280
repeat :xh [plot] pu
make "check 0 setx -330 make "factor 300 repeat :xh [shade] pu
make "check 0 make "factor 290 repeat :xh [shade] pu
make "check 0 make "factor 280 repeat :xh [shade] pu
write
end
```

NOTE: The procedure 'graph.work' must be erased from a copy of BAR3GRPH and the new procedures 'graph.work' and 'shade' added to give BAR3FILG.

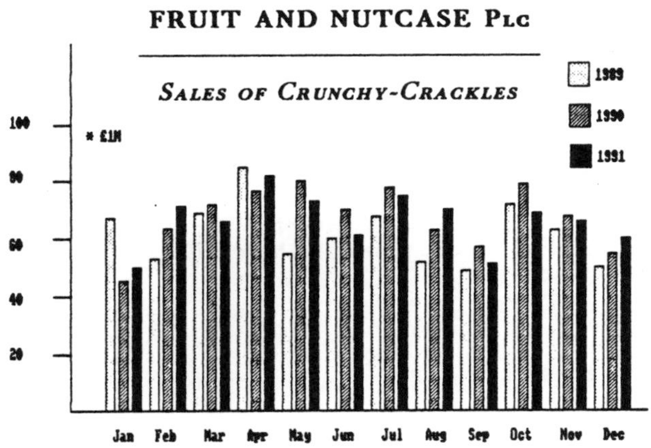

Figure III.2 Three data-set bargraph drawn using BAR3GRPH and then enhanced in MICRODESIGN to give a variety of shades. To draw an accurate graph took only seconds in LOGO, but the sophistication of shading in a MICRODESIGN is much greater than procedure 'shade' can achieve.

PROGRAM NAME: **CLOCK**

DESCRIPTION: A fun stop-watch. A moving second hand shows analogue time, with a digital read-out when stopped. Options to start from zero and re-start from elapsed time. The clock is not terribly accurate, but is a good demonstration of simple moving graphics.

```
to clock
(local "a "co)
setsplit 3 make "co 0
cs ct home pu ht circle 165 recycle
(pr [Press "S" to start clock, spacebar to stop]
make "a lc rc if :a = "s [start :co]
end

to circle :rad
ht pu fd :rad rt 90 pd
fd :rad / 11.5 rt 10
repeat 35 [fd :rad / 5.75 rt 10]
fd :rad / 11.5 rt 90 pu fd :rad rt 180 numbers
end

to numbers
fs ts setcursor [44 7] type "60
setcursor [62 15] type 15
setcursor [44 23] type 30
setcursor [26 15] type 45 fs ss stop
end

to start :co
drawline
if keyp [(pr :co "seconds) make "co2 :co
   (pr [Press "R" + \<RETURN\> to re\-start.] []
   [Press "C" + \<RETURN\> to continue]) throw "TOPLEVEL]
eraseline rt 6 start :co + 1
end

to drawline
repeat 2 [pd fd 95 bk 95]
end

to eraseline
repeat 2 [pe fd 95 bk 95 pu]
end

to r
make "co2 0 seth 0 start 0
end

to c
start :co2
end
```

NOTE: Type 'clock' to draw the clock face, and follow the prompts.

PROGRAM NAME: **DATABASE**

DESCRIPTION: Name and address database. Facilities include adding, deleting and searching records on any field. Field lengths are not fixed. Label printing is available from within the program. Up to 26 separate files are possible, consisting of at least 20 records per file, making a database of over 500 records. This could easily be increased with slight adjustments to the program. There are three modules: ADDR_DAT, FIND_DAT, and STOR_DAT, which should be typed in and saved separately. They, and the accompanying datafiles, must all be on the default drive. Select the default before starting the program. To start, type: 'load "dataddr add'. The program loads the other modules as required. The indents must be obeyed.

MODULE NAME: **ADDR_DAT**

```
to add
(local "inp "rn)
ct ts ts make "rn 0 make "flag 0 ron
(pr [] [Enter DATAFILE to load: A, B, etc] [] [NEW datafile: #] []
   [MENU: &] [] [CLEAR ALL DATA: $] [])
rof pr " make "inp lc rc ct
if :inp > "& [pr [Please wait...]
   make "inp (word :inp "_ "_ "_ "_ "dat)
   if memberp uc :inp (dir) [fs ht load :inp ts]
   [(pr [File] uc :inp [not found]) recycle add]]

if :inp = "# [make "data []]
if :inp = "& [if not namep "data [make "data []] menu :rn]
if :inp = "$ [if namep "data
   [ern "data] make "data [] make "rn 0 make "flag 0]
menu :rn
end

to add.rec :rn
local "inp
if not emptyp :data [make "rn first last :data]
make "rn :rn + 1

ct ts type char 8 ron
(pr [] [Enter data ...Empty field: press RETURN ...Menu: &] []) rof
if :rn > 10 [pr [Storing data. Please wait...]
   er [add add.rec menu view er.rec del.rec]
   fs load "stor_dat ts ct store]
pr [] type [Surname] setcursor [15 2] make "inp rl pr "
if first :inp = "& [menu :rn]
make "data lput :inp :data
type [First name:] setcursor [15 4] make "inp rl pr "
make "data lput :inp :data
type [House name:] setcursor [15 6] make "inp rl pr "
make "data lput :inp :data
type [Street name:] setcursor [15 8] make "inp rl pr "
make "data lput :inp :data
type [Town:] setcursor [15 10] make "inp rl pr "
make "data lput :inp :data
```

```
type [Cnty + pstcd:] setcursor [15 12] make "inp rl pr "
make "data lput :inp :data
make "data lput (list :rn) :data
add.rec :rn
end

to menu :rn
(local "ch "in "vdat)
ct if namep "data [make "ch (count :data) / 7] [make "ch 0]
ron (pr [] [Add rec: A] [] [View recs: V] [] [Delete rec: D] []
   [Total recs: T] [] [Load: L] [] [Save: S] [] [Find: F] []) rof pr "
make "in uc rc
if :in = "A [add.rec :rn]
if :in = "V [make "vdat :data view :vdat]
if :in = "D [del.rec :rn]
if :in = "T [(type [Total records held: ...] :ch) recycle]
if :in = "L [ct add]
if :in = "S [pr [Please wait] fs
   er [add menu add.rec del.rec er.rec view]
   recycle load "stor_dat store]
if :in = "F [type [Please Wait] fs
   er [add menu add.rec del.rec er.rec view]
   recycle load "find_dat search]
menu :rn
end

to del.rec :rn
local "inp
if not :data = []
   [ron (pr [] [RECORD NUMBER to DELETE:] []) rof type char 8]
   [pr [No files] recycle]
make "inp rq
if not memberp (list :inp) :data [pr [File not found] recycle menu :rn]
er.rec :rn :inp
end

to er.rec :rn :elem
(local "temp "w)
if memberp (list :elem) :data [make "w where]
if :w = 7 [make "data bf bf bf bf bf bf bf :data menu :rn]
   [repeat :w - 7
      [make "temp lput first :data :temp make "data bf :data]]
make "data bf bf bf bf bf bf bf :data
make "data se :temp :data
menu :rn
end

to view :vdata
if emptyp :vdata [ron (type []
   [No more files] []) recycle (type [Press SPACE for menu.]) rof
   if rc = char 32 [menu :rn :st :en]]
pr piece 1 7 :vdata
view bf bf bf bf bf bf bf :vdata
end
```

```
86  to ron
87  type word char 27 "p type char 8
88  end

89  to rof
90  type word char 27 "q type char 8
91  end
```

NOTE: In lines 4..6, data files may be given names in the range a..z. NEW datafiles will be given the name entered. To append data, a file must first be loaded. 'View records' accesses all the records in the file. The record number always remains the same for the record to which it is attached, even if some records are deleted. 'Total' is the only way of counting the number of records in a file. In lines 72, 75 and 84 there are 7 bf's.

MODULE NAME: **FIND_DAT**

```
to ron
type word char 27 "p type char 8
end

to rof
type word char 27 "q type char 8
end

to search
local "inp
ts ct ron (pr [] [ENTER DATABASE TO LOAD, A, B, etc.] [] []
   [Search resident data..#] [] [] [Return to ADD..&] []) rof pr "
make "inp lc rc
if :inp = "# [if :flag = 1
   [pr [LOAD DATA] repeat 500 [] search] [search.work]]
if :inp = "&
   [pr [Please wait...] fs
   if memberp "subdata glist ".APV [ern "subdata]
   er [search search.work search.sort
   pair display print print.work re.search]
   load "addr_dat ts ct add]
pr [Please wait...] fs make "inp (word :inp "_ "_ "_ "_ "dat)
load :inp make "flag 0
ts search.work
end

to search.sort :key :find
local "w
make "subdata :data
if memberp :find :subdata [make "w where]
   [if :flag = 1 [pr [Re\-load Datafile]] [pr [Data not found]]
   repeat 500 [] search]
pair :key :w :find
end
```

```
to pair :key :w :find
(local "co "temp "ww)
ct ts make "co 1 make "temp []
make "ww :w if :key = 1 []
if :key = 2 [make "w :w - 1]
if :key = 3 [make "w :w - 2]
if :key = 4 [make "w :w - 3]
if :key = 5 [make "w :w - 4]
if :key = 6 [make "w :w - 5]
if :key = 7 [make "w :w - 6]
if :key > 7 [search.work] ;error-trap
display :ww :w :co :temp :find :key
end

to display :ww :field :co :temp :find :key
local "a
if :co = 8 [repeat 500 [] pr [] pr [] ron
   (pr [] [Search..S] [] [] [Re\-search..R] [] [] [Print..P] []) rof
   pr [] make "a uc rc
   if :a = "P [print :co :temp]
   if :a = "R [re.search :ww :find :key]
   if :a = "S [search]]
pr item :field :subdata make "temp lput item :field :subdata :temp
display :ww :field + 1 :co + 1 :temp :find :key
end

to search.work
(local "key "find)
ct ts pr [Keys.....Fields:] pr "
pr [key 1 ...Surname]
pr [key 2 ...Firstname]
pr [key 3 ...Housename]
pr [key 4 ...Street]
pr [key 5 ...Town]
pr [key 6 ...Cty + pstc]
pr [key 7 ...Record num] pr []
ron (type [] [Enter key to search:] []) rof setcursor [25 10]
make "key rc pr :key pr "
ron (type [] [Enter search string:] []) rof setcursor [25 12]
make "find rl make "flag 0
search.sort :key :find
search.work
end

to print :co :temp
local "li
make "li 9
print.work :temp :li
end

to print.work :temp :li
(local "check "ptd) make "check 1
make "ptd 2 fs ht copyon
(pr first bf :temp first :temp)
   make "ptd :ptd + 1 make "check :check + 1
repeat 4 [if item :ptd :temp = [] [(type [] char 8)]
```

```
84      [pr item :ptd :temp make "check :check + 1]
85     make "ptd :ptd + 1 if :ptd = 7 [type char 12
86         fs copyoff ts]]
87   repeat 500 [] search
88   end

89   to re.search :ww :find :key
90   pr [Searching. Please wait...] make "flag 1
91   if (:ww + 7) > count :subdata
92      [pr [Out of data.] repeat 500 [] make "flag 0 search]
93   repeat 7 + :ww - :key [make "subdata bf :subdata]
94   search.sort :key :find
95   end
```

NOTE: This is a stand-alone module, and does not require ADDR_DAT to be loaded first. Line 12 checks for data present in the workspace. Variable :flag is 0 if data is present, 1 if no data. Data files and database modules can be PIPped to M: using: 'PIP m:=a:????dat.log' before loading LOGO. At the end of the session, leave LOGO with 'bye' and PIP just the datafiles back to disk using: 'PIP a:=m:????dat.log'. In line 67, the 'key' to enter is the field number. In line 68, the 'search string' is the line to search for. The figure in line 75 of 'print' sets the number of lines between the top of one label and the top of the next at 6 lpi. The default is 9, but this may be changed to any appropriate number. A left-offset must be set in CP/M. NLQ or draft may be selected from the printer status line. See APPENDIX IV for label-printing file.

MODULE NAME: **STOR_DAT**

```
1    to store
2    (local "rep "fil)
3    ts ct label "F
4    ron (pr [] [ENTER file letter to SAVE, A, B, etc.] []
5       [Abandon & return to MENU: &] []) rof
6    pr [Files saved are:] pr []
7    pr dir "?____dat pr []                  ;4 underline characters
8    make "fil uc rc pr [Please wait...]
9    if :fil = "& [er "store fs load "addr_dat ts ct add]
10   make "fil (word :fil "_ "_ "_ "dat)
11   if not memberp uc :fil (dir)
12      [er "store ern "flag save :fil ern "data
13         fs load "addr_dat ts ct add] [go "F]
14   end
```

NOTE: Line 11 checks the directory to ensure that you don't use a filename that has already been used. When the file has been saved, module ADDR_DAT is re-loaded and 'add' run. Files should be saved with single letter names, A, B, C, etc: the module adds the rest of the information and erases itself before saving just the data. It also erases the data after it has been saved in line 12, although you may prefer to keep the data present in the workspace. If so, simply remove the command 'ern "data' in line 12.

ACTION	KEY	INPUTS			
DESIGN					
hide turtle	h				
show turtle	t				
home turtle	<EXTRA><+>				
pen down	d				
pen up	u				
pen erase	e				
pen XOR	x				
forward 100	F				
forward 50	f				
forward 1	<EXTRA><f>				
jump forward	j	*units*	<RETURN>		
turn to right	r	*angle*	<RETURN>		
turn to left	l	*angle*	<RETURN>		
reverse heading	v				
arc right	a	*radius*	<RETURN>	*angle*	<RETURN>
arc left	<EXTRA><a>	*radius*	<RETURN>	*angle*	<RETURN>
circle	C	*radius*	<RETURN>	*pen-state*	<RETURN>
ellipse	E	*length*	<RETURN>		
rectangle	R	*side 1*	<RETURN>	*side 2*	<RETURN>
triangle	T	*side*	<RETURN>		
fill	!				
zap (erase)	z				
scale	m				
no scale	n				
write	w				
move u d l r	CURSORS				
save picture	*				
update picture	U				
recycle	§ (section marker)				
WRITE					
return to design	<EXTRA><d>				
recycle	§ (section marker)				

Figure III.3 Menu of key-presses for DESIGNER. The commands are printed to the bottom three lines of the screen as they are entered and are cleared automatically when a picfile is saved

PROGRAM NAME: **DESIGNER**

DESCRIPTION: A full-feature drawing program, with line, circle, ellipse, arc, triangle and rectangle facilities. Fill, erase and write options. Save, update, and load from within the program.

```
to start
setsplit 3 ct cs fs st make "fn "01 ss design
end

to redraw
local "a
cs ct ht setsplit 3 ts ts (type [ENTER FILEPIC NAME TO LOAD:] [] [])
make "a rq cs fs loadpic :a make "fn piece 7 8 :a design
end

to design
(local "a "rad "ang "len "hi "wi "sid "pen)
fs ss pu st label "A make "a rc pr :a
if :a = "h [ht]
if :a = "t [st]
if :a = "u [pu]
if :a = "d [pd]
if :a = "e [pe]
if :a = "x [px]
if :a = "r [make "ang rq right :ang]
if :a = "l [make "ang rq left :ang]
if :a = char 176 [fd 1]                            ;<EXTRA><f>
if :a = "f [fd 10]
if :a = "F [fd 50]
if :a = "j [make "len rq jump :len]
if :a = "v [rt 180]
if :a = char 222 [pr "HOME home]                   ;<EXTRA><+>
if :a = "! [pr "FILL fill]
if :a = "m [pd scale]
if :a = "n [pe scale]
if :a = "C [pr [CIRCLE rad pen]
   make "rad rq make "pen rq circle :rad :pen]
if :a = "a [pr [ARCRIGHT rad arc]
   make "rad rq make "ang rq arcr :rad :ang]
if :a = char 160 [pr [ARCLEFT rad arc]
   make "rad rq make "ang rq arcl :rad :ang]
if :a = "E [pr [ELLIPSE len] make "len rq ellipse :len]
if :a = "R [pr [RECTANGLE side1 side2]
   make "hi rq make "wi rq rect :hi :wi]
if :a = "T [pr [TRIANGLE side] make "sid rq triangle :sid]
if :a = char 240 [seth 0]
if :a = char 250 [seth 90]
if :a = char 242 [seth 180]
if :a = char 254 [seth 270]
if :a = "w [write]
if :a = "\* [pr "SAVING saved]
if :a = "U [pr "UPDATING update]
if :a = "z [zap]
if :a = char 189 [pr "RECYCLE ht recycle st]       ;<EXTRA><y>
go "A
end
```

```
to scale
(local "h "x "y)
make "h item 3 tf make "x item 1 tf make "y item 2 tf
fs ht pu setpos [-355 260] seth 180 pd
fd 20 lt 90 fd 10 bk 10 rt 90
repeat 4 [fd 50 lt 90 fd 5 bk 5 rt 90 fd 50 lt 90 fd 10 bk 10 rt 90]
fd 50 lt 90 fd 5 bk 5 rt 90 fd 50 lt 90
repeat 7 [fd 50 lt 90 fd 6 bk 6 rt 90 fd 50 lt 90 fd 12 bk 12 rt 90]
fd 20 pu seth :h setpos se :x :y st
end
to circle :rad :pen
if not numberp :rad [stop]
if not memberp :pen "udex [stop]
pu fd :rad rt 90
if :pen = "u [pu] if :pen = "d [pd] if :pen = "e [pe] if :pen = "x [px]
fd :rad / 11.5 rt 10
repeat 35 [fd :rad / 5.75 rt 10]
fd :rad / 11.5 rt 90 pu fd :rad rt 180
end

to triangle :sid
if not numberp :sid [fs design]
repeat 3 [fd :sid rt 120]
end

to arcr :rad :ang
if not numberp :rad [stop]
if not numberp :ang [stop]
repeat (:ang / 10) [fd :rad / 5.75 rt 10]
end

to arcl :rad :ang
if not numberp :rad [stop]
if not numberp :ang [stop]
repeat (:ang / 10) [fd :rad / 5.75 lt 10]
end

to ellipse :len
(local "fact1 "fact2 "fact3)
if not numberp :len [stop]
rt 5 make "fact1 1.2 make "fact2 0.5 make "fact3 0.2
repeat 2 [arcr (:len * :fact1) 30 arcr (:len * :fact2) 45
   arcr (:len * :fact3)
   45 arcr (:len * :fact2) 45 arcr (:len * :fact1) 30]
lt 5
end

to right :ang
if not numberp :ang [stop]
rt :ang
end

to left :ang
if not numberp :ang [stop]
lt :ang
end
```

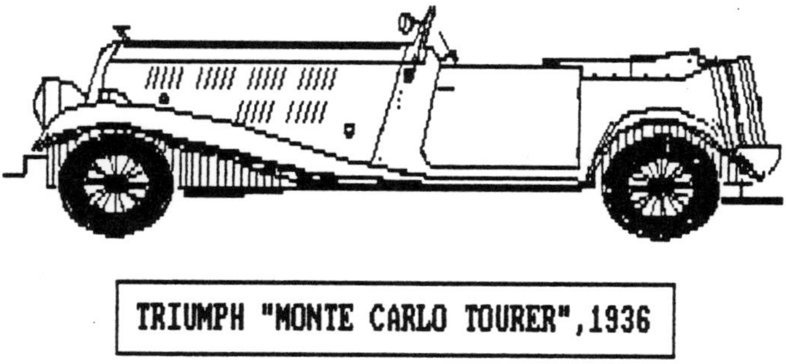

Figure III.4 DESIGNER drawing exported to MicroDesign3 and printed unretouched. The BASIC listing LOGOSCRN.BAS from APPENDIX V was used to perform the necessary data conversion. A full A4 size print-out may be made direct from the LOGO picfile using LOGOPRNT.BAS, also in APPENDIX V

```
to zap
local "h make "h item 3 tf
ht pe seth 90 repeat 2
   [fd 10 lt 90 fd 2 lt 90 fd 10 rt 90 fd 2 rt 90]
fd 10 lt 90 fd 2 lt 90 fd 10 pu st seth :h st
end
to jump :len
if not numberp :len [stop]
fd :len
end

to rect :hi :wi
if or not numberp :hi not numberp :wi [fs design]
repeat 2 [fd :hi rt 90 fd :wi rt 90]
end

to write
(local "a "b "j "k)
ht ts make "j 45 make "k 14
label "B setcursor se :j :k make "a rc
if :a = char 167 [fs st design]                     ;<EXTRA><d>
if :a = char 189 [fs recycle ss]                    ;<EXTRA><y>
if ascii :a < 127 [type :a make "b rq]
if :a = char 240 [make "k :k - 1]
if :a = char 242 [make "k :k + 1]
if :a = char 250 [make "j :j + 1]
if :a = char 254 [make "j :j - 1]
go "B
end
```

```
123  to saved
124  (local "list "temp)
125  make "temp []
126  make "list (dirpic "design??)
127  if emptyp :list [savepic word "design :fn stop]
128  if count :list = 1 [make "fn piece 7 8 first :list] [high :list :temp]
129  make "fn :fn + 1
130  if :fn < 10 [make "fn word 0 :fn]
131  clear savepic word "design :fn fs ss
132  end

133  to update
134  (local "list "temp)
135  make "list (dirpic "design??) clear
136  if emptyp :list [savepic word "design :fn stop]
137  if count :list > 1 [make "temp [] high :list :temp]
138  erasepic word "design :fn savepic word "design :fn fs ss
139  end

140  to high :list :temp
141  if emptyp :list [stop]
142  if and count :list = 1 count :temp = 1
143     [if item 1 :list > item 1 :temp
144        [make "fn piece 7 8 first :list stop]
145        [make "fn piece 7 8 first :temp stop]]

146  if count :list = 1
147     [make "temp fput item 1 :list :temp make "list :temp make "temp []]
148  if first :list > first bf :list
149     [if not memberp first :list :temp
                [make "temp lput first :list :temp]]
150  high bf :list :temp
151  end

152  to clear
153  ct fs stop
154  end
```

NOTE: In 'redraw', a previously saved file may be loaded, to allow further work to be done. The program may be started with either 'start' or 'redraw'. In line 7, 'setsplit 3' confines any error messages to the bottom lines, so that they cannot accidentally spoil the picture. It also permits commands entered by the user to be displayed. This area is cleared automatically before files are saved. In line 31 char 160 is <EXTRA><a>. Lines 126 and 135 only check 'design' files, and take no account of space on the disk: this should be checked before running DESIGNER. Lines 128 and 137 call 'high' and lines 140 *et seq* determine the highest 'design' file on the disk. The appropriate file number is then set. Use the menu and instructions in Figure III.3. You may run out of editor space whilst typing in 'design' (the machine will beep and refuse to accept further entries). If so, shorten words like 'RECTANGLE' and 'ELLIPSE' to 'RECT' and 'ELPSE' and you will find it fits.

PROGRAM NAME: **DUMP**
DESCRIPTION: Dumps the hex byte held at the input memory location and the following 255 bytes, plus ASCII print-out.

```
to dump :addr
(local "hexadd "num "hexnum "alist)
repeat 8 [make "alist [] make "hexadd hex :addr
   (type :hexadd char 32)
   repeat 16 [type char 9 make "num .examine :addr
   make "hexnum hex :num
   type :hexnum make "addr :addr + 1
   make "alist lput :num :alist]
   asc :alist type char 10]
end

to hex :n
(local "q "r "y "ans)
make "ans "
label "X make "q quotient :n 16 make "r remainder :n 16
if :r > 9 [make "r item :r - 9 [A B C D E F]]
make "ans fput :r :ans
if and :q < 16 :q > 9 [make "q item :q - 9 [A B C D E F]
   make "ans fput :q :ans op :ans]
if :q < 10 [make "ans fput :q :ans op :ans]
make "n :q
go "X
end

to asc :alist
local "ch
type char 9 repeat 16
    [make "ch first :alist
    if or :ch > 127 :ch < 32 [type ".] [type char :ch]
    make "alist bf :alist]
end
```

NOTE: The program is slow, but it does have the advantage of working from within LOGO. Also there is no need to add 100 hex offset as with SID. Since all LOGO's memory locations are in decimal, DUMP is easier to use than SID. The input must be in decimal (100h=256d).

PROGRAM NAME: **HILBERT**
DESCRIPTION: Graphics drawing program to draw a Hilbert curve, an algorithm devised by the German mathematician David Hilbert. Try 'start' values of 10 10.

```
to start
(local "h "parity)
make "parity 1
ts (type [Enter SIZE space LEVEL return:] [])
make "h rl cs ct fs ht pu setpos [300 -265] pd recycle
hilbert first :h item 2 :h :parity
end
```

```
to hilbert :size :level :parity
if :level = 0 [stop]
lt :parity * 90
hilbert :size :level - 1 -:parity
fd :size rt :parity * 90
hilbert :size :level - 1 :parity
fd :size hilbert :size :level - 1 :parity
rt :parity * 90 fd :size
hilbert :size :level - 1 -:parity
lt :parity * 90
end
```

NOTE: This is of no use, but it does fill the screen nicely!

PROGRAM NAME: **HISTOGRM**

DESCRIPTION: Program to draw a histogram of any number of input values. Scaling is automatic. The title is centred. Bars are filled and labelled. A write facility is also included.

```
to histo
(local "title "inlist)
ts ts
pr [Enter FILEPIC name to save to disc:]
make "hgram rq
pr [Enter TITLE:]
make "title rq
pr [Enter DATA LIST:]
make "inlist rl
plot :inlist :title
fs captions
end

to plot :inlist :title
(local "xplot "yplot)
ct ts
centre :title
make "yplot 4
make "xplot maxlist :inlist
make "xplot 50 / :xplot
plot.work :inlist :xplot :yplot
end

to plot.work :inlist :xplot :yplot
if emptyp :inlist [stop]
setcursor se 0 :yplot
ron repeat (:xplot * first :inlist) [type char 32] rof
setcursor se 60 :yplot type first :inlist
plot.work bf :inlist :xplot :yplot + 2
end

to centre :sentence
(local "length "x "y)
make "length (count :sentence)
make "x (44 - round (:length / 2))
```

```
make "y (item 2 cursor) - 1
setcursor se 0 :y repeat :length [type []]
setcursor se :x 0
type :sentence
end

to ron
type word char 27 "p type char 8
end

to rof
type word char 27 "q type char 8
end

to maxlist :inlist
if count :inlist = 2 [op max first :inlist last :inlist]
op max first :inlist maxlist bf :inlist
end

to max :n1 :n2
if :n1 > :n2 [op :n1]
op :n2
end
```

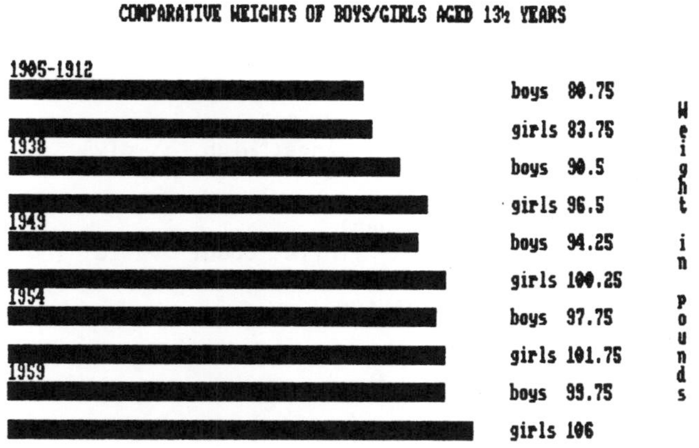

Figure III.5 Histogram, or horizontal bargraph, produced with the program HISTOGRM. The captions are added using the 'write' procedure

```
52  to captions
53  (local "a "b "x "y)
54  ts setcursor [45 2]
55  make "x item 1 cursor make "y item 2 cursor
56  label "W setcursor se :x :y
57  make "a rc
58  if :a = char 186 [fs savepic :hgram ern :hgram throw "TOPLEVEL]
59  if ascii :a < 190 [type :a make "b rq]
60  if :a = char 240 [make "y :y - 1]
61  if :a = char 242 [make "y :y + 1]
62  if :a = char 250 [make "x :x + 1]
63  if :a = char 254 [make "x :x - 1]
64  go "W
65  end
```

NOTE: In lines 4 and 6, the filename and the graph name need not be the same. In line 4, the FILEPIC name must be no longer than 8 letters. In line 8, the only limit on the number of items in the datalist is the page- or screen-length. In line 26, each data value is printed at the right of its bar. Use the space-bar in the write facility (procedure 'captions') to erase if not required. In line 27, ':yplot + 2' sets a one line gap between bars. This may be adjusted to suit. In line 58, <EXTRA><s> saves to disc.

PROGRAM NAME: **LINEGRPH**
DESCRIPTION: A program to produce a line graph from a given data-set. The number of inputs is limited only by the page-width.

```
to graph
ts ts pr [Enter name to save graph to disk:]
make "graph rq label "A pr [Enter Y\-range: High, Y\-div]
make "yr rl if not count :yr = 2 [go "A]
label "B pr [Enter X caption\-list:]
make "inlist rl pr [Enter PLOT values]
make "valist rl if not equalp count :inlist count :valist [go "B]
make "xh count :inlist make "xl -300
make "yh first :yr make "ydiv last :yr
make "ymark :ydiv make "yr :yh
make "xdiv quotient 600 :xh
make "ydiv :yr / :ydiv make "yr :ydiv
make "ydiv quotient 400 :ydiv
cs fs xaxis yaxis make "check 0 repeat :xh [plot] pu write
end

to xaxis
fs make "check 0 pu setpos [-290 -210] pd
seth 90 repeat :xh [xline] setx 350
end

to yaxis
pu setpos [-290 -210] pd seth 0 make "check 0
repeat :yr [yline] sety 250 pu stop
end
```

```
to xline
pd fd :xdiv sety -245 pu make "check :check + 1
curpos item :check :inlist sety -210 pd
end

to yline
fd :ydiv pu setx -342 make "check :check + :ymark
curpos :check setx -310 pd setx -290
end

to curpos :input
(local "cx "cy "inp)
make "cx item 1 tf make "cx round (:cx + 357) / 8
make "cy item 2 tf make "cy round (:cy - 255) / 17
fs ts setcursor se :cx :cy pr :input fs
end

to plot
fs make "check :check + 1
make "yplot (round 400 / :yh) * (item :check :valist) - 200
make "xplot (:check * :xdiv) - 290 setpos se :xplot :yplot pd
end

to write
(local "a "b "x "y)
ts setcursor [45 15] make "x item 1 cursor make "y item 2 cursor
label "W setcursor se :x :y make "a rc
if :a = char 186 [fs savepic :graph throw "TOPLEVEL]    ;<EXTRA><s>
if ascii :a < 190 [type :a make "b rq]
if :a = char 240 [make "y :y - 1]
if :a = char 242 [make "y :y + 1]
if :a = char 250 [make "x :x + 1]
if :a = char 254 [make "x :x - 1]
go "W
end
```

PROGRAM NAME: **LISSAJOU**

DESCRIPTION: Figure drawing program to draw Lissajou figures. Enter 'start' to begin and try: '11 20 21 40 1', '5 10 11 20 1,' '12 9 10 1 1', '5 5 6 30 3', '2 9 10 15 3'.

```
to start
local "a
(type [LISSAJOU FIGURES. Enter five numbers:] []
make "a rl cs ct fs ht pd recycle
lissajou first :a item 2 :a item 3 :a item 4 :a last :a
end

to lissajou :a :b :c :d :inc
fs ht cs pu liss 0
end
```

```
to liss :ang
setpos se (120 * cos (:a * :ang + :b))
   (80 * cos (:c * :ang + :d)) pd liss :ang + :inc
end
```

PROGRAM NAME: **MAXSORT**

DESCRIPTION: A sorting program for words or numbers. Takes a random list as input and outputs a sorted alphabetic or numeric list in ascending order. It uses **where** and 'maxlist' to pick out the highest element of a list, and 'remove' to put each highest element into a new, sorted, list.

```
1   to sort :list
2   local "newlist
3   ts ts make "newlist []
4   make "newlist sort.work :list
5   (pr [Sorted list is:] :newlist)
6   end

7   to sort.work :list
8   local "it
9   repeat (count :list) - 1
10     [make "it maxlist :list make "list remove :it :list]
11  make "newlist fput first :list :newlist
12  op :newlist
13  end

14  to maxlist :alist
15  if count :alist = 2 [op max first :alist last :alist stop]
16  op max first :alist maxlist bf :alist
17  end

18  to max :it1 :it2
19  if :it1 > :it2 [op :it1]
20  op :it2
21  end

22  to remove :item :list
23  (local "temp "w)
24  if memberp :item :list [make "w where]
25  if :w = 1 [make "newlist fput first :list :newlist
26     make "list bf :list op :list]
27     [repeat :w - 1
28        [make "temp fput first :list :temp make "list bf :list]]
29  make "newlist fput first :list :newlist make "list bf :list
30  make "list se :temp :list op :list
31  end
```

NOTE: In line 1, :list may be entered from another program. The highest item in the list is output using 'max' to compare two adjacent elements. In line 25, **where** points out the position in the list of the high element, which is then removed from the list and put into :newlist. The main advantage of this program over TREESORT is that it uses repetition, which is less memory-hungry than recursion.

PROGRAM NAME: **MOSAIC**

DESCRIPTION: A graphics drawing program that draws a random mosaic pattern. Try 'start' and '10 10' to kick it off.

```
to start
(local "inp "size "level)
pr [Enter SIZE, LEVEL, press return]
make "inp rl make "size first :inp make "level last :inp
fs cs ht pu seth 180 setpos [-150 0] pd
left :size :level
end

to left :size :level
if :level = 0 [fd :size stop]
left :size :level - 1 lt 90 right :size :level - 1
end

to right :size :level
if :level = 0 [fd :size stop]
left :size :level - 1 rt 90 right :size :level - 1
end
```

PROGRAM NAME: **PERSPECT**

DESCRIPTION: Perspective-drawing program. Five boxes are drawn showing different perspectives of the same figure.

```
to start
(local "right "left "y)
make "y -260
ct cs fs ht make "right [rpoint 500 200] make "left [lpoint -400 0]
repeat 5 [draw1 0 :y 40 60 100 :right :left make "y :y + 120]
end

to lpoint :lx :ly
seth towards list :lx :ly
end

to rpoint :rx :ry
seth towards list :rx :ry
end

to draw1 :x :y :hi :LEN1 :LEN2 :right :left
(local "y1 "y2 "y3 "y4 "y5 "ang1 "ang2 "LEN3 "x1 "x2 "x3 "x5)
fs pu setpos se :x :y pd
sety :y + :hi
run :right fd :LEN1 make "x1 item 1 tf make "y1 item 2 tf
pu setpos se :x :y pd
run :right make "ang1 90 - (item 3 tf)
make "LEN1 (:x1 - :x) / cos :ang1
fd :LEN1 make "x3 item 1 tf make "y3 item 2 tf
sety :y1 pu setpos se :x :y + :hi pd
run :left fd :LEN2 make "x2 item 1 tf make "y2 item 2 tf
pu setpos se :x :y pd
run :left make "ang2 (item 3 tf) - 270
```

```
make "LEN3 (abs (:x2 - :x)) / cos :ang2
fd :LEN3 make "x5 first tf make "y5 item 2 tf
sety :y2 pu setpos se :x1 :y1
draw2 :LEN2 :right :left :x2 :x3 :x5 :y1 :y2 :y3 :y5 :hi :y
shade :x :y
end

to draw2 :LEN2 :right :left :x2 :x3 :x5 :y1 :y2 :y3 :y5 :hi :y
(local "LEN3 "LEN4 "x4 "y4 "x6 "y6 "ang3)
if :y < 0 [pd] [pu]
run :left make "ang3 (item 3 tf) - 270
make "LEN3 :LEN2 * (:y1 - :y3) / :hi
fd :LEN3 make "x4 item 1 tf make "y4 item 2 tf
setpos se :x2 :y2 pu
draw3 :y1 :y2 :y3 :y5 :x3 :x4 :x5 :hi :y
end

to abs :n
if :n < 0 [op -:n] [op :n]
end
```

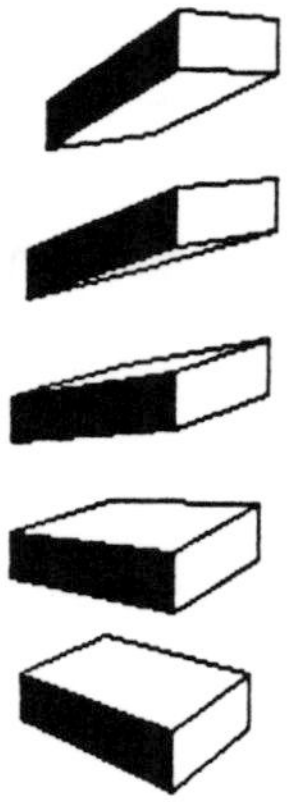

Figure III.6 Perspective views of a box viewed from different angles

```
to draw3 :y1 :y2 :y3 :y5 :x3 :x4 :x5 :hi :y
setpos se :x4 :y4
make "LEN4 (abs :y1 - :y3) * (abs :y2 - :y5) / :hi
if :y > 0 [pd] [pu]
seth 180 pu fd :LEN4 if :y > 0 [pd]
make "x6 item 1 tf make "y6 item 2 tf setpos se :x5 :y5
pu setpos se :x6 :y6 if :y > 0 [pd] setpos se :x3 :y3 pu
end

to shade :x :y
pu setpos se :x :y
seth 350 fd 5 pd fill pu
end
```

NOTE: This will not produce a true perspective drawing, since the vertical lines have been drawn parallel for simplicity's sake. However it would take another book to deal with all the vagaries of true perspective drawing! This program is offered as a starting point: building on this it is possible to write a program to draw three-dimensional objects in true perspective. Figure III.6 shows the boxes drawn by the program. (*cf* PERSPCT2).

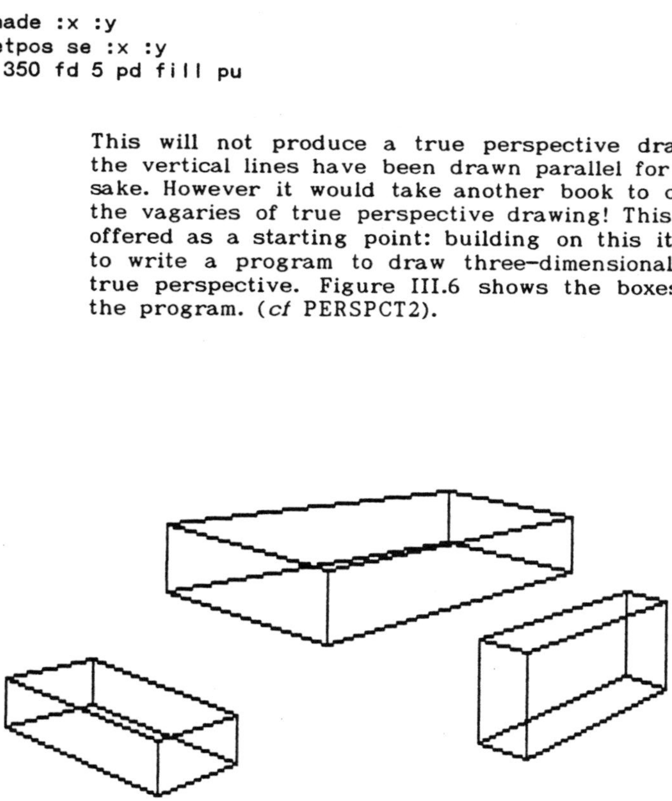

Figure III.7 The three boxes drawn from PERSPCT2. Variations of 'start' will give different shapes and aspects

PROGRAM NAME: **PERSPCT2**
DESCRIPTION: Substitute these two procedures for the equivalent procedures in PERSPECT to draw three transparent boxes.

```
to start
(local "right "left)
cs fs ht make "right [rpoint 600 200] make "left [lpoint -1000 350]
draw1 -100 -100 35 50 100 :right :left
draw1 0 0 50 150 100 :right :left
draw1 120 -75 70 90 30 :right :left
end

to draw2 :LEN2 :right :left :x2 :x3 :x5 :y1 :y2 :y3 :y5 :hi :y
(local "LEN3 "LEN4 "x4 "y4 "x6 "y6 "ang3)
run :left make "ang3 (item 3 tf) - 270
make "LEN3 :LEN2 * (:y1 - :y3) / :hi
pd fd :LEN3 make "x4 item 1 tf make "y4 item 2 tf
setpos se :x2 :y2 pu
setpos se :x4 :y4
make "LEN4 (abs :y1 - :y3) * (abs :y2 - :y5) / :hi
pd seth 180 fd :LEN4 make "x6 item 1 tf make "y6 item 2 tf
setpos se :x5 :y5 pu setpos se :x6 :y6 pd setpos se :x3 :y3 pu
end
```

PROGRAM NAME: **PIECHART**
DESCRIPTION: Program to draw a pie-chart from a data-set. All data values are printed to their slice. Write and save options.

```
to pie
local "rad
make "rad 200 setsplit 2 ss pr [Enter name to save to disc:]
make "piepic rq ct pu ht home
fd :rad rt 90 pd fd :rad / 11.5 rt 10
repeat 35 [fd :rad / 5.75 rt 10]
fd :rad / 11.5 pu rt 90 fd :rad rt 180 plot
end

to plot
(local "tot "total "ang "inlist "sector "check)
make "tot 0 pr [Enter DATA values:] make "inlist rl
make "total sum :inlist :tot make "check 1 pd
repeat count :inlist
   [make "sector 360 / :total
   make "ang :sector * item :check :inlist
   fd :rad pu fd 20 curpos :check :inlist bk :rad + 20
   bk :rad + 20 pd rt :ang make "check :check + 1]
ct fs write
end

to sum :inlist :tot
repeat count :inlist [make "tot :tot + first :inlist
   make "inlist bf :inlist]
op :tot
end
```

```
to curpos :check :inlist
(local "cx "cy "inp)
make "cx item 1 tf make "cx round (:cx + 345) / 8
make "cy item 2 tf make "cy round (:cy - 255) / 17
fs ts setcursor se :cx :cy pr item :check :inlist fs stop
end

to curwrite
local "a make "a rq if :a = " [stop]
end

to write
(local "a "b "x "y)
fs ts make "x 45 make "y 15
label "B setcursor se :x :y make "a rc
if :a = char 186 [fs savepic :piepic setsplit 10 throw "TOPLEVEL]
if ascii :a < 190 [type :a make "b rq]
if :a = char 240 [make "y :y - 1]
if :a = char 242 [make "y :y + 1]
if :a = char 250 [make "x :x + 1]
if :a = char 254 [make "x :x - 1]
go "B
end
```

NOTE: In line 3, the radius may be altered to a maximum of about 300. In line 4, error messages are confined to the bottom two lines of the screen. In line 16, DATA values may be of any size and theoretically the number of values in the set is umlimited. However for clarity probably about 25 is a reasonable maximum. Values are written to sectors in line 23. If this facility is not required, omit line 23 and procedure 'curpos'. In line 48, <EXTRA><s> saves the picfile to disk. There is no check made to see if there is already a file of that name on the disk, although this could be written in. However error messages in the bottom two lines of the screen can be erased with ct, fs entered and a new 'save "picfilename' command issued.

PROGRAM NAME: **POLYGONS**

DESCRIPTION: An automatic figure-drawing program which defines ten procedures to draw three- to twelve- plane figures. The procedures are then erased by the program.

```
o polygons
etsplit 12 ht cs ss ct seth 270 pu setpos [50 -50] pd
ake "st 3 make "len 80 procedures :st draw 3
ake "planes 12 erase :planes
rn [st len name inlist angle planes]
nd

o procedures :planes
f :planes = 13 [stop]
ake "angle 360 / :planes make "name lput :planes "planes
ake "inlist (list "fd :len "rt) make "inlist lput :angle :inlist
```

```
make "inlist (list "repeat :planes :inlist)
make "inlist list [len] :inlist
define :name :inlist procedures :planes + 1
end

to draw :planes
if :planes = 13 [stop]
make "name lput :planes "planes
(pr [Number of planes] [] :planes [])
run se :name :len draw :planes + 1
end

to erase :planes
if :planes = 2 [type [Drawing procedures erased] stop]
er word " lput :planes "planes
erase :planes - 1
end
```

NOTE: Procedure 'procedures' writes the definitions of the figure–drawing procedures and **define** is then used to turn the lists into procedures. The **ss** is used to permit text and graphics to be printed virtually at the same time.

PROGRAM NAME: **SCREENGRID**

DESCRIPTION: Draws an 8 X 8 grid on screen. The turtle acts as a pointer and can be moved to any square using the cursor keys. Squares may be filled and new screen characters drawn. The program will then total the data for use in Protext, Mini Office and BASIC to draw new screen characters. Module PRNTCHAR will then be loaded. Save each module separately under its name. Load SCRNCHAR and run with 'grid'.

MODULE NAME: **SCRNCHAR**

```
to grid
(local "div "nx "ny)
fs ht cs ts ts type [Please wait...]
fs recycle cs pu home make "div 20
make "nx 4 make "ny 4 draw.grid :div :nx :ny posit
end

to draw.grid :div :nx :ny
(local "n1)
ht fs make "n1 :nx vgrid :n1 :div :ny make "n1 :ny hgrid :n1 :div :nx
end

to vgrid :n1 :div :ny
pd if :n1 < 0 [stop]
draw.line :n1 * :div :ny * :div :n1 * :div -:ny * :div
draw.line -:n1 * :div :ny * :div -:n1 * :div -:ny * :div
vgrid :n1 - 1 :div :ny
end
```

```
to draw.line :x1 :y1 :x2 :y2
pu line :x1 :y1 pd line :x2 :y2 pu
end

to line :xw :yw
setpos (list :xw :yw)
end

to hgrid :n1 :div :nx
pd if :n1 < 0 [stop]
draw.line :nx * :div :n1 * :div -:nx * :div :n1 * :div
draw.line :nx * :div -:n1 * :div -:nx * :div -:n1 * :div
hgrid :n1 - 1 :div :nx
end

to posit
(local "tx "ty "inp)
fs ts setcursor [25 3]
(type [Mark...m] [] [] [] [Erase...e] [] [] [] [Total...EXTRA t])
setcursor [39 5] type [SCREEN DATA] fs
pu setpos [-70 70] make "tx item 1 tf make "ty item 2 tf
st pu label "X setpos se :tx :ty make "inp rc
if :inp = char 191 [ht fs init]                ;<EXTRA><t>
if :inp = "m [pd fill pu]
if :inp = "e [erase]
if :inp = char 240 [make "ty :ty + 20]
if :inp = char 250 [make "tx :tx + 20]
if :inp = char 242 [make "ty :ty - 20]
if :inp = char 254 [make "tx :tx - 20]
if :tx > 70 [make "tx 70] if :tx < -70 [make "tx -70]
if :ty > 70 [make "ty 70] if :ty < -70 [make "ty -70]
go "X
end

to erase
ht fd 8 rt 90 pe fd 9 rt 90 fd 15 rt 90 fd 17 rt 90
fd 15 rt 90 fd 8 lt 90 pu bk 8 pe fill pu st
end

to init
(local "tx "ty "tot "x)
make "tot 0 make "x 27 make "data [] setpos [-70 70]
make "tx item 1 tf make "ty item 2 tf
total :tx :ty :tot :x
end

to total :tx :ty :tot :x
local "c
st pu make "c 128 setpos se :tx :ty
repeat 8 [if dotc se :tx :ty = 1 [make "tot :tot + :c]
    make "tx :tx + 20 make "c :c / 2 setpos se :tx :ty]
make "ty :ty - 20 ts setcursor se :x 6 type :tot
make "data lput :tot :data make "x :x + 5 fs
if :ty < -70 [savedata :data]
make "tot 0 make "tx -70 total :tx :ty :tot :x
end
```

```
to savedata :data
local "file
er [total posit grid hgrid vgrid draw.grid
    erase init savedata line draw.line] fs ts
setcursor [0 0] (type [Filename to save \(max 7 letters\):] [])
make "file rq setcursor [0 0] type [Please wait...]
repeat 28 [type char 32]
fs save word "s :file ern "data
fs ts setcursor [0 0] (type [Print character data? y / n] [])
if rc = "y [setcursor [0 0] type [Please wait...]
    repeat 13 [type char 32] fs load "prntchar grid]
erall throw "TOPLEVEL
end
```

NOTE: The data will be saved to disk automatically as 's*filename*'. It may then be used with the SYMBOL command in Protext to produce a new screen character, or with ESC L *n1 n2* in BASIC. The grid produces the data for 8-bit graphics which is fine for screen use. Similarly the second module, PRNTCHAR also outputs 8-bit data, but with a little adaptation the PRNTCHAR grid can be made to produce 16, 24, or 48-bit graphics, which, with a suitable printer, can print higher definition characters.

MODULE NAME: **PRNTCHAR**
DESCRIPTION: Additional procedures that will draw a 12 by 8 screen grid. Permits the drawing of a corresponding printer character to SCRNCHAR. Totals will be made automatically and the data saved to disk as 'p*filename*'. Use >OC command in Protext, <ALT><X> in Mini Office and ESC L *n1 n2* in BASIC. Some of these procedures will overwite procedures of the same name in SCRNCHAR.

```
to grid
(local "div "nx "ny)
fs recycle fs pu home make "div 20 make "nx 6 make "ny 4
draw.grid :div :nx :ny posit
end

to posit
(local "tx "ty "inp)
fs ts setcursor [0 0] repeat 14 [type char 32] setcursor [25 3]
(type [Mark...m] [] [] [] [Erase...e] [] [] [] [Total...EXTRA t])
setcursor [40 7] type [PRINT DATA] fs
pu setpos [-110 70] make "tx item 1 tf make "ty item 2 tf
st pu label "X setpos se :tx :ty make "inp rc
if :inp = char 191 [ht fs init]              ;<EXTRA><t>
if :inp = "m [pd fill]
if :inp = "e [erase]
if :inp = char 240 [make "ty :ty + 20]
if :inp = char 250 [make "tx :tx + 20]
if :inp = char 242 [make "ty :ty - 20]
if :inp = char 254 [make "tx :tx - 20]
if :tx > 110 [make "tx 110] if :tx < -110 [make "tx -110]
if :ty > 70 [make "tx 70] if :ty < -70 [make "tx -70] go "X
end
```

```
to init
(local "tx "ty "tot "x)
make "tot 0 make "x 15 make "pdata []
setpos [-110 70]
make "tx item 1 tf make "ty item 2 tf
total :tx :ty :tot :x
end

to total :tx :ty :tot :x
local "c
st pu make "c 128 setpos se :tx :ty
repeat 8 [if dotc se :tx :ty = 1
   [make "tot :tot + :c]
   make "ty :ty - 20 make "c :c / 2
   setpos se :tx :ty]
make "tx :tx + 20 ts setcursor se :x 8 type :tot
make "pdata lput :tot :pdata make "x :x + 5 fs
if :tx > 110 [savedata :pdata]
make "tot 0 make "ty 70
total :tx :ty :tot :x
end

to savedata :pdata
local "file
er [total posit grid hgrid vgrid draw.grid
   init savedata erase line draw.line] fs ts
setcursor [0 0] (type [Filename to save \(max 7 letters\):] [])
make "file rq fs save word "p :file ern "pdata throw "TOPLEVEL
end
```

PROGRAM NAME: **SINEWAVE**
DESCRIPTION: Graph-drawing program to plot a graph of sines from 0°..360°.

```
to sine
ct cs ts setcursor [36 3] type [GRAPH OF SINES]
fs ht pu
setpos [-350 230] pd
lines
pu graph 0 pu titles 0
end

to lines
sety -230 setx 350 pu
end

to graph :ang
(local "x "y)
if :ang > 360 [stop]
make "x 1.9 * :ang - 365
make "y 200 * sin :ang
setpos se :x :y pd
graph :ang + 10
end
```

```
to titles :ang
(local "x "y)
if :ang > 360 [stop]
make "x 1.9 * :ang - 365
make "y 200 * sin :ang
setpos se :x :y
if = remainder (abs :ang / 10) 3 0 [curpos word :ang "°]
titles :ang + 10
end

to abs :num
if :num < 0 [op -:num] [op :num]
end
to curpos :input
(local "cx "cy "inp)
make "cx item 1 tf make "cx round (:cx + 357) / 8
make "cy item 2 tf make "cy round (:cy - 255) / 17
fs ts setcursor se :cx :cy
type :input fs
end
```

NOTE: For a graph of cosines, substitute **cos** for **sin** in 'graph' and 'titles', and change the caption in 'sine'. For neatness the name of procedure 'sine' to 'cosine'. It would be perfectly possible to re-write the program to allow for any ratio to be displayed (tangent, secant, etc), dependant on user choice.

PROGRAM NAME: **SNOWFLAK**

DESCRIPTION: Another fun drawing program that draws a Koch snowflake figure. Try 'start' and ' 300 4' to begin with. It takes some time to complete.

```
to start
(local "inp "length "limit)
pr [Enter LENGTH, LIMIT, press return]
make "inp rl
make "length first :inp make "limit last :inp
fs ht cs pu setpos [-100 -100] seth 0 pd
snowflake :length :limit
end

to snowflake :length :limit
repeat 3 [line :length rt 120]
end

to line :length
if :length < :limit [fd :length stop]
line :length / 3 lt 60
line length / 3 rt 120
line :length / 3 lt 60
line :length / 3
end
```

PROGRAM NAME: **STAR**
DESCRIPTION: Another figure-drawing program, this time various star-like structures. Try 'start' and '4 5 50', '8 3 60', '3 7 50', and then with **wrap** '8 3 1000'.

```
to start
local "list
cs ct pu setpos [-50 -100]
(type [STAR. Enter three numbers:] [])
make "list rl ct fs ht pd recycle
star first :list item 2 :list item 3 :list
end

to star :f :ang :size
fd :size * sin (:f * (item 3 tf))
rt :ang
star :f :ang :size
end
```

PROGRAM NAME: **TREESORT**
DESCRIPTION: A sorting program for words or numbers. Takes a random list as input and outputs a sorted alphabetic or numeric list in ascending order.

```
to sort
(local "inlist "wlist)
pr [Input words to sort]
pr [Press RETURN to finish]
make "inlist rl
make "wlist []
check.lst :inlist
pr :wlist
end

to check.lst :inlist
local "word
if emptyp :inlist [stop]
make "elem first :inlist
make "wlist sort.work :wlist
check.lst bf :inlist
end

to sort.work :wlist
if emptyp :wlist [op (list [] :elem [])]
if :elem > item 2 :wlist
   [op (list first :wlist item 2 :wlist sort.work last :wlist)]
   [op (list sort.work first :wlist item 2 :wlist last :wlist)]
end
```

NOTE: This is a sorting method based on a tree-sort algorithm. It is hardly swift, but it can manage to sort a 24 element list in perfect alphabetical order - that is 'Jane Jim John June' will be correctly indexed - in about 45 secs. The snag is that it outputs a list of lists. So line 8 may be changed to: 'pr (reduce :wlist)' and procedure 'reduce' added to give intelligible output.

```
to reduce :wlist
if wordp :wlist [op :wlist]
if emptyp :wlist [op []]
if (and (wordp first :wlist) (emptyp bf :wlist)) [op :wlist]
op (se (reduce first :wlist) (reduce bf :wlist))
end
```

NOTE: MAXSORT will sort more items than TREESORT, but it is a little slower. LOGO is not good at sorting! Unfortunately there is no equivalent to BASIC's SWAP command, so even a humble bubble sort is difficult to write in LOGO.

PROGRAM NAME: **WARSHIP**
DESCRIPTION: A version of the old paper-and-pencil game of Battleships, with shells exploding and ships sinking. The computer is hard to beat! Save the modules separately.

MODULE NAME: **W**

```
to w
cs ct ht ts setcursor [31 14] type [WARSHIP LOADING, PLEASE WAIT]
fs erall load "warship war
end
```

MODULE NAME: **WARSHIP**
The program loads the module automatically from default.

```
to war                                  ;writes the prompt to deploy.
fs recycle cs ts make "dep (list "B "C "D "S)
setcursor [15 25] type [DEPLOY SHIPS (B,C,D,S)]
make "h 0 make "k 0 fs sea
end

to sea                                  ;draws the two 'seas'
pu setpos [-300 262] seth 90
pd repeat 2 [fd 294 rt 90 fd 310 rt 90]
pu fd 300 pd repeat 2 [fd 294 rt 90 fd 310 rt 90] pu
deploy
end

to deploy                               ;positioning of your ships
(local "a "c "d)
make "c -272 make "d 213 fs label "X
seth 0 setpos se :c :d st make "a rc
if :a = char 240 [make "d :d + 51]
if :a = char 242 [make "d :d - 51]
if :a = char 254 [make "c :c - 48]
if :a = char 250 [make "c :c + 48]
if :c < -272 [make "c -272] if :c > -32 [make "c -32]
if :d > 213 [make "d 213] if :d < -42 [make "d -42]
if :dep = [] [ht link]
```

```
if :a = "S [if not memberp :a :dep [go "X] [delete submarine]]
if :a = "D [if not memberp :a :dep [go "X] [delete destroyer]]
if :a = "C [if not memberp :a :dep [go "X] [delete cruiser]]
if :a = "B [if not memberp :a :dep [go "X] [delete battleship]]
go "X
end

to delete                                ;deletes item from list to
local "temp                              ;  prevent double entry.
make "temp [] cut :a :dep make "dep :temp stop
end

to cut :a :dep
if emptyp :dep [stop]
if not :a = first :dep [make "temp lput first :dep :temp]
cut :a bf :dep
end
```

NOTE: CHECK THE FOLLOWING FOUR SHIP-DRAWING PROCEDURES ARE CORRECT BEFORE TYPING IN THE 'FILL' COMMANDS!

```
to submarine                             ;draws your submarine
fs ht if :c > -32 [make "c -32]
setpos se :c :d make "T (list se :c :d)
seth 90 bk 22 pd
fd 44 lt 135 fd 6 lt 45 fd 8 rt 90
fd 15 bk 7 lt 90 fd 6 lt 90
fd 8 rt 90 fd 23 lt 45 fd 6
pu lt 135 fd 31 lt 90 fd 3 pd fill pu
end

to destroyer                             ;draws your destroyer
fs ht if :c > -80 [make "c -80]
setpos se :c :d make "des1 se :c :d make "des2 se :c + 48 :d
make "TT (list :des1 :des2)
seth 90 bk 18 pd
fd 80 lt 45 fd 10 lt 135 fd 16 rt 90
fd 6 rt 90 fd 6 bk 14 rt 90
fd 6 rt 90 fd 12 rt 90 fd 24
bk 12 lt 90 fd 4 lt 90 fd 6 rt 90
fd 8 rt 80 fd 8 lt 80 fd 6 lt 100
fd 10 rt 100 fd 8 lt 90 fd 6 rt 90
fd 25 lt 90 fd 5 bk 3
pu lt 90 fd 40 pd fill pu
end

to cruiser                               ;draws your cruiser
fs ht if :c > -128 [make "c -128]
setpos se :c :d make "cru1 se :c :d make "cru2 se :c + 48 :d
make "cru3 se :c + 96 :d
make "TTT (list :cru1 :cru2 :cru3)
seth 90 bk 5 pd
fd 102 lt 45 fd 10 lt 135 fd 18 rt 90
fd 6 rt 90 fd 6 bk 14 rt 90
fd 6 rt 90 fd 12 rt 90 fd 26
bk 12 lt 90 fd 4 lt 90 fd 6 rt 90 fd 8
```

```
repeat 2 [rt 80 fd 8 lt 80 fd 6 lt 100 fd 8 rt 100 fd 6]
lt 90 fd 8 rt 90 fd 10 rt 90
fd 6 lt 90 fd 14 bk 6 lt 90
fd 6 rt 90 fd 17 lt 90 fd 7 bk 4
pu lt 90 fd 50 pd fill pu
end

to battleship                                ;draws your battleship
fs ht if :c > -176 [make "c -176]
setpos se :c :d make "bat1 se :c :d make "bat2 se :c + 48 :d
make "bat3 se :c + 96 :d make "bat4 se :c + 144 :d
make "TTTT (list :bat1 :bat2 :bat3 :bat4)
seth 90 bk 5 pd
fd 146 lt 45 fd 12 lt 135 fd 24 rt 90
fd 8 rt 90 fd 8 bk 18 rt 90
fd 8 rt 90 fd 18 rt 90 fd 26 bk 10 lt 90
fd 6 lt 90 fd 6 rt 90 fd 8
repeat 3 [rt 80 fd 12 lt 80 fd 8 lt 100 fd 12 rt 100 fd 6]

lt 90 fd 10 rt 90 fd 16 rt 90 fd 8
lt 90 fd 18 bk 8 lt 90 fd 8 rt 90 fd 20
lt 90 fd 7 bk 3 pu lt 90 fd 70 pd fill pu
end

to link                                      ;erase used procs, load next.
ts setcursor [15 25] type [PREPARE FOR BATTLE....]
fs er [sea battleship cruiser destroyer submarine deploy
   war cut delete link] ern "dep recycle load "enemy locbat
end
```

MODULE NAME: **ENEMY**
Save the rest of the program as 'enemy' on the same disk as 'warship'. The program will load it automatically.

```
to shell                                     ;selects your shots, fires,
local "a                                     ;  calls 'hit' if you do.
fs ts label "A setcursor se :c :d make "a rc
if :a = char 240 [make "d :d - 3]
if :a = char 242 [make "d :d + 3]
if :a = char 254 [make "c :c - 6]
if :a = char 250 [make "c :c + 6]
if :a = "f [(type char 7 char 46) go "AA]
go "A label "AA
if equalp se :c :d :L [type "S hit]
if memberp se :c :d :LL [type "D hit]
if memberp se :c :d :LLL [type "C hit]
if memberp se :c :d :LLLL [type "B hit]
fs compshell bf :map
end

to hit                                       ;marks your hits & scores.
fs ts setcursor se :c :d (type char 7 char 42)
make "h :h + 1 setcursor [38 25] type :h
if :h = 10 [setcursor [15 25] pr [ENEMY FLEET DESTROYED !!!]
fs finish] recycle fs
end
```

```
to compshell :map                          ;decides enemy's shots,
(local "x "y)                              ;  erases your ships if hit.
pu seth 270 make "shot first :map
make "x item 1 :shot make "y item 2 :shot
setpos (se :x :y)
if or memberp se :x :y :T memberp (se :x :y) :TT [go "E]
if or memberp se :x :y :TTT memberp (se :x :y) :TTTT [go "E]
setpos se :x :y st
fd 2 bk 2 ts type char 7 fs ht shell
label "E setpos se :x :y st
ts type char 7 fs fd 2 bk 2 ht ts type char 7
   fs ht bk 24 rt 90 fd 36 lt 90 pe
repeat 9 [fd 48 lt 90 fd 2 lt 90 fd 48 rt 90 fd 2 rt 90]
pu kill compshell bf :map
end

to position                                ;draws random 'map' for enemy
make "map shuffle (list [-272 213] [-272 162] [-272 111] [-272 60]
[-272 9] [-272 -42] [-224 213] [-224 162] [-224 111] [-224 60]
[-224 9] [-224 -42] [-176 213] [-176 162] [-176 111] [-176 60]
[-176 9] [-176 -42] [-128 213] [-128 162] [-128 111] [-128 60]
[-128 9] [-128 -42] [-80 213] [-80 162] [-80 111] [-80 60] [-80 9]
[-80 -42] [-32 213] [-32 162] [-32 111] [-32 60] [-32 9] [-32 -42])
recycle ts setcursor [31 20] repeat 3 [type char 7]
repeat 28 [type []] setcursor [41 22] type [FIRE: f] fs compshell :map
end
```

NOTE: TYPE THE MAP-LIST IN AS ONE CONTINUOUS LINE, LOGO WILL WRAP IT FOR YOU. CHECK THE NUMBERS CAREFULLY.

```
to kill                                    ;keeps enemy's score.
fs ts make "k :k + 1 setcursor [76 25] type :k
if :k = 10 [setcursor [15 25] pr [YOUR FLEET DESTROYED !!!]
   repeat 500 [] fs finish]
recycle fs
end

to locsub                                  ;locates enemy submarine,
(local "e "f)                              ;  and starts game.
fs make "e first cursorx make "f first cursory
if :e > 78 [make "e 78]
make "L (se :e :f)
if or memberp :L :LL memberp :L :LLL [locsub]
if memberp :L :LLLL [locsub]
fs ts setcursor [15 25] type [WAR !!!]
repeat 5 [type char 32] type [YOUR HITS:]
setcursor [53 25] type [ENEMY FLEET]
repeat 6 [type char 32] type [HITS:]
fs aimguns
end

to cursorx                                 ;random X co-ords.
local "xaxis
make "xaxis shuffle [66 78 54 72 60 48]
op :xaxis
end
```

```
to cursory                                   ;random Y co-ords.
local "yaxis
fs make "yaxis shuffle [7 4 1 16 13 10] op :yaxis
end

to locdes                                    ;locates enemy's destroyer.
(local "e "f)
fs make "e first cursorx make "f first cursory
if :e > 72 [make "e 72]
make "locdes1 se :e :f make "locdes2 se (:e + 6) :f
if or memberp :locdes1 :LLL memberp :locdes2 :LLL [locdes]
if or memberp :locdes1 :LLLL memberp :locdes2 :LLLL [locdes]
make "LL (list :locdes1 :locdes2)
locsub
end

to locrus                                    ;locates enemy's cruiser.
(local "e "f)
fs make "e first cursorx make "f first cursory
if :e > 66 [make "e 66]
make "locrus1 (se :e :f) make "locrus2 (se :e + 6 :f)
make "locrus3 (se :e + 12 :f)
if or memberp :locrus1 :LLLL memberp :locrus2 :LLLL [locrus]
if memberp :locrus3 :LLLL [locrus]
make "LLL (list :locrus1 :locrus2 :locrus3)
locdes
end

to locbat                                    ;locates enemy's battleship.
(local "e "f)
fs ts setcursor [53 25] type [ENEMY FLEET DEPLOYING]
fs make "e first cursorx make "f first cursory
if :e > 60 [make "e 60]
make "locbat1 se :e :f make "locbat2 se (:e + 6) :f
make "locbat3 se (:e + 12) :f make "locbat4 se (:e + 18) :f
make "LLLL (list :locbat1 :locbat2 :locbat3 :locbat4)
locrus
end

to aimguns                                   ;erases used procs.
ts setcursor [31 20] type [SEARCHING FOR ENEMY FLEET...]
er [locbat locrus locdes locsub cursorx cursory]
fs make "c 48 make "d 1 position
end

to finish                                    ;winds up game.
recycle cs fs erall load "w
setcursor [19 27] type [Type 'w' to play again]
recycle throw "TOPLEVEL
end
```

"WARSHIP"

This is a very long listing, but well worth the effort. Type in a chunk and then have a rest, then check what you've typed in. By now you should be able to spot typing errors easily enough when you run the program. Nine times out of ten it's a missing colon before a variable, or a colon instead of a quote-mark. Check that you have the ship-drawing procedures correct before adding the 'fill' commands, or one little mistake and you will flood the screen.

It is important to load and run program 'RANSEED' (LIBRARY PROGRAMS, PART TWO) before playing 'WARSHIP', so that **shuffle** has a fresh seed to work from; otherwise you will get the same deployment of the enemy's ships for every first time you play the game in a session. Then erase 'RANSEED' – you don't need to run it more than once per session. You could easily make 'RANSEED' self-erasing: just put in 'er "ranseed' as the last instruction before 'end'.

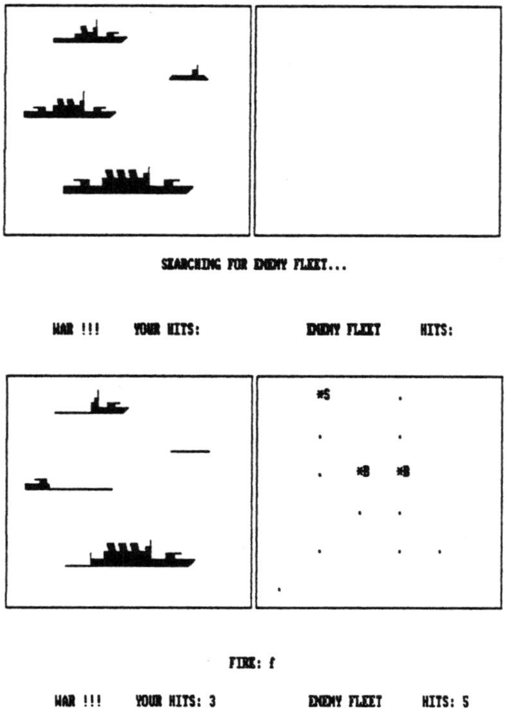

Figure III.8 (Top) WARSHIP begins: the home fleet is deployed, but the enemy is invisible, shrouded in fog. (Below) The heat of battle: the home fleet is in trouble

To play, all you need to do is type 'load "w w' and the game will run. When the 'sea' is drawn, you will see the legend DEPLOY YOUR FLEET (B,C,D,S). Place the turtle by using the cursor keys and enter B for Battleship (uses 4 spaces), C for Cruiser (3), D for Destroyer (2) and S for Submarine (1). Use SHIFT plus the letter to enter in upper case. Each ship will be drawn to the left-hand screen. The 'sea' is fenced in, so you will not be able to deploy outside the area, nor will you be able to cheat and enter more than one of each type of ship.

When you have deployed your fleet, press RETURN and the enemy fleet will be deployed (secretly) in the right-hand 'sea'. You will hear a fusilade of shots and the enemy will open fire on your fleet.

You may sight your guns by positioning the cursor with the cursor keys: fire by pressing 'f'. The enemy fleet will show up when you score a hit like this: *B

Your shots will be marked by dots. If the enemy scores a hit, your ships will disintegrate. It takes four shots to completely sink a battleship, three for a cruiser, and so on. When the enemy scores a hit, they get another go, since inevitably there is more randomness to their shooting than yours. You will find this makes it a tough game, but reasonably even.

At the end, when one or the other fleets has been destroyed, you may play another game by typing 'w' – the initial procedure 'w' will already have been loaded for you.

The enemy's shots are mapped using LOGO's list capabilities, so no two shots will fall in the same place. This makes for an exciting finish, since the enemy's accuracy increases alarmingly.

Happy shooting!

PART FOUR

REFERENCE

This section lists all the LOGO primitives and system properties available in Dr LOGO v 2.0 for the Amstrad PCW series, together with their meanings, syntax, and examples of their use. Primitives which are present in Dr LOGO, but which are not implemented for the PCW are noted, as are the few primitives which, though implemented, are of no practical use. The 'dot' commands are listed according to their alphabetical precedence, ignoring the leading dot. The arithmetic and Boolean signs, which cannot be indexed alphabetically, are listed at the end of the section. The same conventions apply as in the previous parts. The abbreviation 'REL PRIMS' stands for 'Related Primitives'.

and

Boolean logic operator. Outputs the value TRUE if all the input expressions are true. May only be used in prefix form. If there are more than two inputs, the operator and its inputs must be enclosed in round brackets.

SYNTAX: and *expression1 expression2*
(and and {and*N*} *expression1 expression2...expressionN*)

EXAMPLES:
```
?and 4 = 2 * 2 8 = 16 / 2
TRUE
?and 3 = 1 + 2 6 = 2 * 4
FALSE
?(and and 4 = 2 * 2 8 = 16 / 2 3 = 1 + 2)
TRUE
?
```

REL PRIMS: not, or, TRUE, FALSE

.APV (Associated Property Value)

System property. The value-property held in a global variable, or the value-properties of a list of the global variables present in the workspace.

SYNTAX: gprop "*variable* ".APV
glist ".APV

NOTE: The first returns the property value held in :*variable*, the second a list of all the global variables in the workspace.

EXAMPLES:
```
?make "a 10
?gprop "a ".APV
10
?to test
>local "b
>make "b 5
>end
test defined
?test
?gprop "b ".APV
b has no value
?glist ."APV
[a]
?
```
NOTE: .APV cannot return the value of a local variable.
REL PRIMS: pons

arctan (arctangent)

Arithmetic operator. Outputs an angle in degrees of the input number.

SYNTAX: arctan *number*

EXAMPLES:
```
?arctan 1
45
?arctan 6
80.5376777919742
?
```
REL PRIMS: cos, sin

ascii (American Standard Code For Information Interchange)

Character operator. Outputs the ASCII code of the first input character.

SYNTAX: ascii *character*

EXAMPLES:
```
?ascii "a
97
?ascii "alphabet
97                          ;ASCII value of first letter
?ascii bf "alphabet
108                         ;ASCII value of second letter
?
```
REL PRIMS: char

bf (but first)

List processing operator. Outputs all but the first element of an input word or a list.

SYNTAX: bf *input*

EXAMPLES:
```
?bf [1 2 3 4]
[2 3 4]
?bf "xyz
yz
?bf [[12] [3] [4 5 6]]
[[3] [4 5 6]]
?
```
REL PRIMS: bl, fput, lput, first, last

bk (back)

Turtle graphics operator. Takes one input, a number of units, and moves the turtle back that nummber of units, irrespective of the pen and turtle states. If the input is negative, it moves the turtle forward.

SYNTAX: bk *number*

EXAMPLES:

```
?bk 50
?bk -200                              ;equivalent to fd 200
?
```

REL PRIMS: fd, lt, rt

bl (but last)

List processing operator. Outputs all but the last element of an input word or a list.

SYNTAX: bl input

EXAMPLES:

```
?bl [1 2 3 4]
[1 2 3]
?bl "slope
slop
?bl "xyz
xy
?bl [[12] [3] [4 5 6]]
[[1 2] [3]]
?
```

REL PRIMS: bf, fput, lput, first, last

buttonp (buttonpress)

Primitive not implemented.

bye

System command. Takes no inputs. Returns control to CP/M.

SYNTAX: bye

EXAMPLES:

```
?bye
A>
```

NOTE: Everything in the LOGO workspace will be lost. The key-board will still be set to KEYS.DRL. To re-set the keyboard, run the file KEYS.CPM (see APPENDIX IV).

REL PRIMS:

catch

Flow-control command. Takes two inputs. The first is the catch label, the second is a list of instructions to be carried out following the catch declaration. Almost always used with the flow-control command throw. When a throw command with the same label is encountered, control passes to the instr-uction on the line after the catch.

SYNTAX: catch "*label* [*instructionlist*]

EXAMPLES:

```
?to test
>catch "here [check]
>type [A key has been pressed]
>end
?test defined
```

```
?to check
>if keyp [throw "here]
>check
>end
check defined
?test
...
A key has been pressed
?j                                  ;key 'j' was pressed
```

NOTE: When the label "error is used with catch, 'catch "error' intercepts any action the system might take to deal with the error, and throws control to TOPLEVEL. When the label '"TRUE' is used with catch, 'catch "TRUE' intercepts any throw, no matter what the throw label is. See CHAPTER 13 for details. See also ERRACT.

REL PRIMS: throw

changef (change filename)

File-handling operator. Changes the filename of a file on the default drive. Takes two inputs, the first is the new filename, the second is the old filename.

SYNTAX: changef "newfilename "oldfilename

EXAMPLES:

```
?changef "addsum "total
?dir "addsum
[ADDSUM]
?dir "total
[]
?
```

NOTE: May suffer from a system bug preventing the operator from working.

REL PRIMS: save, erasefile, load, edf

char (character)

ASCII-number operator. Takes one input, and ASCII number, and outputs the character or action corresponding to that input.

SYNTAX: char ascii number

EXAMPLES:

```
?type char 71
G
?pr char 10                         ;linefeed code

?(type char 119 char 111 char 114 char 100)
word
?
```

REL PRIMS:: ascii

clean

Screen-handling operator. Takes no inputs. Clears the screen and leaves the turtle where it is. Sets a split-screen.

SYNTAX: clean

EXAMPLES:

```
?tf
[0 0 0 PD 1 TRUE]
?fd 50 rt 90 clean
```

```
?tf
[0 50 90 PD 1 TRUE]
?
```

REL PRIMS: cs, ct, home

co (continue)

Flow-control operator. Takes no inputs. Continues program execution after a pause.

SYNTAX: co

EXAMPLES:

```
?to break
>pr [Take a break]
use
>pr [On with the work]
>end
break defined
?break
Take a break
pausing... in break: [pause]
break ?co
On with the work
?
```

REL PRIMS: pause

.contents

System operator. Takes no inputs. Outputs the contents of the workspace, including a list of all the primitives and system properties.

SYNTAX: .contents

EXAMPLES:

```
?.contents
[.DEF dirpic numberp arctan.....random fence label]
?
```

REL PRIMS: .PRM

copyoff

Printer control command. Takes no inputs. Stops output to printer initiated by a **copyon** command.

SYNTAX: copyoff

REL PRIMS: copyon

copyon

Printer control command. Takes no inputs. Copies all screen output to printer until a **copyoff** command is executed.

SYNTAX: copyon

REL PRIMS: copyoff

cos (cosine)

Arithmetic operator. Takes one input, an angle expressed in degrees, and outputs the cosine of that angle.

SYNTAX: cos angle

EXAMPLES:
```
?cos 60
0.5
?cos 44.5
0.713223278522491                    ;15 decimal places
?
```
REL PRIMS: sin, arctan

count

Enumerator. Takes one input, a word, number, or list, and outputs the total number of characters or elements.

SYNTAX:
```
count "word
count [list]
count number
```
EXAMPLES:
```
?count [A B C D E F]
6
?count [[2] [3] [4 5] 6]
4                         ;4 lists
?count "abc
3
?count 45678
5
```
REL PRIMS:

cs (clear screen)

Graphics screen operator. Takes no inputs. Clears the screen and homes the turtle to [0 0], seth 0. Sets a split-screen.

SYNTAX: cs

REL PRIMS: clean, ct, home

ct (clear text)

Text screen operator. Takes no inputs. Clears the text screen and homes the cursor to [0 0] in a full text-screen, or to the top left of the text portion of a split-screen.

SYNTAX: ct

REL PRIMS: cs, clean

cursor

Text screen operator. Takes no inputs. Returns the current cursor co-ordinates as a list in the form [*X co-ord* *Y co-ord*].

SYNTAX: cursor

EXAMPLES:
```
?to cursorpos
>setcursor [14 10]
>show cursor
>end
cursorpos defined
?cursorpos
[14 10]
?
```
REL PRIMS: setcursor

.DEF (defined)

System property. The definition-property of a procedure (*ie* the text), or a list of all the procedures in the workspace.

SYNTAX: gprop "procedurename ".DEF
glist ".DEF

EXAMPLES:
```
?gprop "cursorpos ".DEF
[[] [setcursor [14 10]] [show cursor]]
?gprop "tan
[[:ang] [op (sin :ang) / (cos :ang)]]
?glist ".DEF
[break cursorpos tan]
?
```

NOTE: The list at the beginning of the procedure list is a list of the parameters to the procedure (an empty list if there are no parameters).

REL PRIMS: po, poall, pots, text

define

Procedure-defining operator. Takes two inputs, a name and a list of instructions, and outputs a procedure of that name, having as its contents that list of instructions.

SYNTAX: define "name [instructionlist]

EXAMPLES:
```
?to make.proc
>make "name "new.proc
>make "deflist (list [] [local "a] [make "a rc] [pr ascii
:a])
>define :name :deflist
>end
make.proc defined
?make.proc
?pots
to make.proc
to new.proc
?new.proc
115                          ;user input is 's'
?
```

REL PRIMS:

defaultd (default drive)

Drive operator. Takes no inputs. Returns the name of the default drive.

SYNTAX: defaultd

EXAMPLES:
```
?defaultd
A:
?setd "m: defaultd
M:
?
```

REL PRIMS: setd

.deposit

System operator. Takes two decimal inputs, a memory location, and a byte value in the range 0..255. Puts the value given by the second input into the location given by the first input.

SYNTAX: .deposit *memory-location byte-value*

EXAMPLES:

```
?.deposit 64503 19
?.deposit 64500 305
.deposit doesn't like 305 as input
?
```

NOTE: To change the file extension, use locations 7542, 7543, 7544. The file extension '.LOG' is currently:

```
7542 76        ;L
7543 79        ;O
7544 71        ;G
```

If this file extension is changed, the file will not be recognised by the LOGO interpreter. See APPENDIX IX.

REL PRIMS: .examine

dir (directory)

Drive operator. Takes no inputs, or optionally a drive-letter, and/or optionally a filename, and outputs a list of all the LOGO *text* files on the default drive, or on the nominated drive, or a named file or an empty list if the named file is not present on the drive. The ? wildcard is recognised.

SYNTAX: dir {"*driveletter*} {"*filename*} {"????????}

EXAMPLES:

```
?dir
[ADLET HEX LOOP ASC ADDITION]
?dir "m:
[TEST]
?dir "a????                    ;ADDITION not shown, only
[ADLET ASC]                    ;  files of up to 5 letters.
?dir "????????                 ;entirely equivalent to dir.
[ADLET HEX LOOP ASC ADDITION]
?dir "hex
[HEX]
dir "dec
[]
?
```

NOTE: Only LOGO text files with the .LOG extension will be shown. Other files will not be shown, even though they may be present on the disk.

REL PRIMS: dirpic

dirpic (directory of picture files)

Drive operator. Takes no inputs, or optionally a drive-letter, and/or optionally a picfilename, and outputs a list of all the LOGO *picfiles* on the default drive, or on the nominated drive, or a named picfile or an empty list if the named picfile is not present on the drive. The ? wildcard is recognised.

SYNTAX: dirpic {*driveletter*} {*picfilename*} {????????}

EXAMPLES: (See **dir**)

NOTE: Only LOGO picfiles with the .PIC extension will be shown. Other files will not be shown, even though they may be present on the disc.

REL PRIMS: dirpic

dot

Graphics operator. Takes one input, a list of an X turtle co-ordinate and a Y turtle co-ordinate, and prints a one pixel dot at that position.

SYNTAX: dot [*X co-ordinate Y co-ordinate*]

EXAMPLES:

```
?dot [-100 50]
?
```

NOTE: The above example plots a dot 100 pixels to the left of, and 50 pixels above, the centre of the screen, provided the screen is in graphics mode. If the screen is in text mode, no dot is plotted.

REL PRIMS: dotc

dotc (dot current)

Graphics operator. Takes one input, a list of an X turtle co-ordinate and a Y turtle co-ordinate, and returns 1 if a dot has been plotted at that position, 0 if it has not.

SYNTAX: dotc [*X co-ordinate Y co-ordinate*]

EXAMPLES:

```
?dotc [-100 50]
1
?dotc [75 -30]
0
?
```

REL PRIMS: dot

ed (edit)

Editing command. Takes a single input, a procedure name, or a list of procedure names, puts the input into the edit buffer and displays the contents in the editing screen.

SYNTAX:
ed
ed "*procedurename*
ed [*list of procedures*]

EXAMPLES:

```
?ed "test
...
?ed [test action print]
...
```

NOTE: If there is insufficient space in the edit buffer to accept all the procedures listed, an error-message to that effect will be generated and control thrown back to TOPLEVEL. If 'ed' is entered without any inputs, a blank editing screen is put up. One or more procedures may then be written in the normal way. Variables cannot be edited.

REL PRIMS:: edall, edf

edall (edit all)

Editing command. Takes no inputs. Loads all the procedures and global variables in the workspace into the edit buffer and displays the contents in the editing screen. Variables cannot be edited.

SYNTAX: edall

EXAMPLES:

```
?edall
...
```

NOTE: If there is insufficient space in the edit buffer to accept all the procedures in the workspace, an error-message to that effect will be generated and control thrown back to TOPLEVEL. Use **recycle** before **edall** to prevent crashing.

REL PRIMS: ed, edf

edf (edit file)

Editing command. Takes one input, the name of a LOGO text file on the default drive, or optionally on a nominated drive, and puts the contents of that file into the edit buffer and displays the contents in the editing screen. When <EXIT> is pressed, the new version of the file, with the original filename, is saved to disc, over-writing the original version.

SYNTAX: edf "*filename*

EXAMPLES:

```
?edf "test
...
?edf "m:designer
...
```

NOTE: If there is insufficient space in the edit buffer to accept the file, an error-message to that effect will be generated and control thrown back to TOPLEVEL. It is possible to swap disks whilst the file is in the editor: the correct filename will still be written to disk.

REL PRIMS: ed, edall

emptyp (empty property)

Property evaluator. Takes one input and returns TRUE if the input is an empty word or list.

SYNTAX: emptyp *input*

EXAMPLES:

```
?emptyp "something
FALSE
?emptyp []
TRUE
?emptyp 7
FALSE
?emptyp "
TRUE
?emptyp [nothing]
FALSE
?
```

REL PRIMS: equalp, listp, namep, numberp, wordp

end

Definition marker. Delineates the end of a procedure. No other commands may be entered on the same line or after it.

REL PRIMS: to

.ENL (extension to line)

System property. The position-property of line extensions (remarks following a semi-colon) and the content-property of those extensions. .ENL cannot be used as an operator, but is included in returns from .FMT (qv).

EXAMPLES:
```
?gprop "revon ".FMT
[.FMT [[0 .ENL ;reverses palette] [12 .ENL ;escape code]]]
?
```
NOTE: '0' indicates that there are no words before the first remark line (the definition line is not included in the word-count). **.ENL** indicates the following text is the line extension. '12' is the word count from the start of the first line of the procedure to the beginning of the next line that has an extension. Round and square brackets are counted as words.

REL PRIMS: .FMT, noformat, .REM, .SPC

equalp (equal property)

Property evaluator. Takes two inputs, tests them for equality, and returns TRUE if they are exactly equal.

SYNTAX: equalp *input1 input2*

EXAMPLES:
```
?equalp 6 6
TRUE
?equalp "six 6
FALSE
?equalp [1 3 4 7] [1 3  5 7]
FALSE
?equalp count [1 3 4 7] count [1 3 5 7]
TRUE
?
```
NOTE: May be used with variables where the values may not be known to test for equality. Entirely equivalent to **=**.

REL PRIMS: emptyp, listp, namep, numberp, wordp

er (erase)

Procedure operator. Takes one input, the name of a procedure, or a list of procedure names, and erases the input procedure or procedures.

SYNTAX: er "*procedurename*
er [*list of procedures*]

EXAMPLES:
```
?er "test
?er [proc2 allvalue action]
?
```
REL PRIMS: erall, ern, erasefile, erasepic

erall (erase all)

Workspace operator. Takes no inputs. Erases all procedures and variables in the workspace, but not properties.

SYNTAX: erall

EXAMPLES:
```
?erall
?pots
?pons
?pps
buttercup's flower is yellow
daisy's flower is white
?
```
NOTE: Properties can only be erased with **remprop** (qv), or by leaving LOGO with **bye** and re-booting.

REL PRIMS: er, ern, erasefile, erasepic

erasefile

File-handling operator. Takes one input, the name of a file on the default drive, or optionally on a named drive, and erases the file. The ? wild-card is recognised.

SYNTAX: erasefile {"*drive*} "*filename*

EXAMPLES:

```
?erasefile "test
?erasefile "m:test
?erasefile "r????          ;erases all 5-letter files
                           ; beginning 'r'.
?erasefile "????????       ;erases all .LOG files
?
```

NOTE: Use with care: no confirmation is requested.

REL PRIMS: er, erall, erasepic, ern

erasepic (erase picfile)

Picfile-handling operator. Takes one input, the name of a picfile on the default drive, or optionally on a named drive, and erases the picfile. The ? wild-card is recognised.

SYNTAX: erasepic {"*drive*} "*filename*

EXAMPLES:

```
?erasepic "drawing
?erasepic "b:graphic
?erasepic "d???????        ;erases all 8-letter picfiles
                           ; beginning 'd'
?
```

NOTE: Use with care: no confirmation is requested.

REL PRIMS: er, erall, erasefile, ern

ERRACT (error action)

Error operator. Takes no inputs. Normally has the value FALSE. When **ERRACT** is made TRUE, run-time error messages are suppressed and pauses inserted.

SYNTAX:

```
make "ERRACT "TRUE
make "ERRACT "FALSE        ;returns to default value.
er "ERRACT                 ;returns to default value.
```

EXAMPLES:

```
?to debug
>catch "error [action]
>end
debug defined
?to action
>make :a ascii rc
>pr :a
>end
action defined
?make "ERRACT "TRUE
?debug
pausing... in action: :a
action
?
```

NOTE: No further execution of the program will take place until **co** entered. The program may be edited or continued.

REL PRIMS: co, error, pause

error

Error operator and label. Takes no inputs. (1) Used as a label to catch and throw, intercepts any action the system might take in dealing with errors. (2) Used as an operator after a 'catch "error throw "error' action, outputs a list whose elements describe the error number and the error.

SYNTAX: (1): catch "error [*next action*]
(2): op error

EXAMPLES:

```
?to mistake
>pr A
>end
?mistake defined
?to "trap
>catch "error [mistake]
>end
trap defined
?trap                              ;no error message, program
?to print.error                    ;  stops.
>catch "error [mistake]
>op error
>end
print.error defined
?print.error
pausing... in mistake: pr A
mistake?co
[35 [I don't know how to A] mistake [pr A] pr A]0
?
```

NOTE: The procedure may be edited, or any other action taken from within the pause.

REL PRIMS: co, ERRACT, pause

ern (erase named variable)

Variable operator. Takes a single input, a variable name, or a list of variable names, and erases the named variable or variables from the workspace.

SYNTAX: ern "*variablename*
ern [*list of variablenames*]

EXAMPLES:

```
?ern "a
?make "b 6
?:b
6
?ern "b
?:b
b has no value
?pons
input is y
var is 18
file is action
?ern [input file var]
?pons
?
```

REL PRIMS: er, erall, erasefile, erasepic

.examine

Memory operator. Takes one input, the number of a memory location, and returns the value of the byte stored at that address. Both the operator and the byte value are in decimal.

SYNTAX: .examine *location*

EXAMPLES:
```
?.examine 64504
9
?.examine 64503
49
?
```

NOTE: The byte value at the examined address may be changed with the command **.deposit** (qv). See APPENDIX IX.

REL PRIMS: .deposit

FALSE

Boolean logic value. Returned by a comparison test when the result of that test is not true. May be assigned to certain primitives.

SYNTAX: make "*primitive* "FALSE

EXAMPLES:
```
?6 > 7
FALSE
?equalp 2 4
FALSE
?[8] = [8]
TRUE
?make "REDEFP "FALSE
?
```

REL PRIMS: TRUE

fd (forward)

Turtle graphics command. Takes one input, a number of units, and moves the turtle forward that number of units in the direction of the current turtle heading, irrespective of the pen state. If the input is negative the turtle moves back.

SYNTAX: fd units

EXAMPLES:
```
?tf
[0 0 0 PD TRUE]
?fd 50
?make "num 100
?fd :num
?tf
[0 150 0 PD TRUE]
?
```

REL PRIMS: bk, rt, lt

fence

Turtle graphics command. Takes no inputs. Restricts the turtle, whether visible or not, to the visible screen. If the turtle tries to leave the visible screen, an error maessage is generated.

SYNTAX: fence

EXAMPLES:
```
?sf
[0 FS 10 WINDOW .46875]
?fence sf
[0 FS 10 FENCE .46875]
?fd 1000
turtle out of bounds
?
```
REL PRIMS: window. wrap

fill

Graphics command. Takes no inputs. Fills the area containing the turtle if the penstate is pd and if the area is bounded by continuous lines, or the full screen if the area is not so bounded.

SYNTAX: fill

EXAMPLES:
```
?pd fill                   ;switches pixels on
?pu fill                   ;no action
?pe fill                   ;switches pixels off
?
```
NOTE: If the area is already filled, 'pe fill' will erase the area fill. If used with **px**, **fill** will unfill a filled area and fill an unfilled area. In other words, fill in this case works in exactly the same way as line-drawing with **px**. The slightest 'hole' in the boundary of the area being filled will allow the 'fill' to escape and flood the entire screen.

REL PRIMS: pd, pe, pu, px

first

List and word processing operator. Takes one input, a list or a word, and outputs the first element of that input.

SYNTAX: first [*list*]
first "*word*

EXAMPLES:
```
?first [a b c d]
a
?first 4321
4
?first "APPLE
A
?first [[1] [2] [3]]
[1]
?first first [name address]
n
?
```
REL PRIMS: bf, bl, fput, last, lput

.FMT (format)

System property. The formatting-property of a procedure, or a list of formatted procedures. Indentations are returned as .SPC statements and remarks as .ENL statements, and removed lines as **.REM** statements.

SYNTAX: glist ".FMT
gprop "*procedurename* ".FMT
plist "*procedurename*

EXAMPLES:

```
?to revon                              ;reverses palette
>(type (word char 27 "b0 char 27 "c6))  ;escape codes
>end
?revon defined
?glist ".FMT
[revon dec high]
?gprop "revon ".FMT
[[.ENL . ;reverses palette][0 .SPC . 3][12 .ENL ;escape
codes]]
?plist "revon
[.DEF [[] [(type (word char 27 "b0 char 27 "c6))]] .FMT [[0
. ENL . ;reverses palette][0 .SPC . 3][12 . ENL . ;escape
codes]]
?
```

NOTE: 'glist "revon' outputs a list of all procedures with formatting (indentations, line extensions, or removed lines). For an explanation of '[0 .SPC . 3]', see **.SPC**. For an explanation of the return from 'plist "revon', see **.ENL**. For an explanation of the .DEF statement, see **.DEF**. See also **.REM**.

REL PRIMS: .DEF, .ENL, noformat, .REM, .SPC

fput (first put)

List and word processing operator. Takes two inputs and outputs a list or a word in which the first input is added to the front of the second input.

SYNTAX: fput *input1 input2*

EXAMPLES:

```
?fput "rain "bow
rainbow
?fput "foot [ball]
[foot ball]
?fput [x] [yz]
[[x] yz]
?make "a "subject
?fput :a [verb object]
[subject verb object]
?
```

NOTE: When used in procedures **fput** must be assigned, thus: 'make "temp fput first :alist :temp'.

REL PRIMS: first, last, lput

fs (full screen)

Screen command. Takes no inputs. Makes the entire screen over to graphical input. Text input will not be printed.

SYNTAX: fs

EXAMPLES:

```
?fs
?sf
[0 FS 10 WINDOW .46875]
?
```

NOTE: Certain text commands will still be accepted, although not printed to the screen. The rule is that text commands will be obeyed unless their execution requires text to be printed, in which case no action will be taken.

REL PRIMS: ss, ts

glist (get list)

List and property processing operator. Takes one input and outputs a list of all the properties associated with that input.

SYNTAX: glist "*input*

EXAMPLES:

```
?glist ".PRM
[dirpic numberp arctan.....random fence label]
?glist ".APV                    ;a list of all variables in
[a try file]                    ;  the workspace.
?pots
to proc1
to test
to action
?glist ".DEF                    ;a list of all the procedures
[proc1 test action]             ;  in the workspace.
?
```

NOTE: 'glist ".DEF' is useful in programs, where the command **pots** would not work. Similarly 'glist ".APV' should be used in programs instead of **pons.**

REL PRIMS: gprop, plist

go

Flow-control operator. Takes one input, the name of a label in the same procedure. Passes control forwards or backwards to the instruction folowing the label name.

SYNTAX: go "*labelname*

EXAMPLES:

```
?make "a 0
?to jump
>if :a = 5 [go "here]
>make "a :a + 1 type :a
>jump
>label "here
>pr [jump made]
>throw "TOPLEVEL                ;if this throw is not made,
>end                            ;  the program will loop back
jump defined                    ;  5 times and print the
?jump                           ;  message each time.
12345jump made
?
```

REL PRIMS: label

gprop (get property)

Property processing operator. Takes two inputs, the first being the name of an object, the second being the name of a property of that object. Outputs the value contained in the named property.

SYNTAX: gprop "*object* "*property*

EXAMPLES:

```
?make "a 5
?gprop "a ".APV
5
?gprop "jump ".DEF
[[] [make "a 0] [if :a = 5 [go "here]] [make "a :a + 1 type!
:a] [label "here] [jump] [pr [jump back made]]]
?
```

NOTE:	In the definition list, the line has wrapped since it is too long, indicated by the exclamation mark (!).
REL PRIMS:	glist, plist

home

Turtle graphics command. Takes no inputs. Puts the turtle in the centre of the sceen, with X and Y co-ordinates of 0 and an absolute heading of 0. The command 'setpos [0 0] seth 0' is entirely equivalent to **home**.

SYNTAX: home

EXAMPLES:

```
?pd st seth 90 setpos [100 -30]
?tf
[100 -30 90 PD 1 TRUE]
?home tf
[0 0 0 PD 1 TRUE]
?
```

REL PRIMS: setpos, seth, setx, sety

ht (hide turtle)

Turtle graphics command. Takes no input. Hides the turtle. Speeds up drawing operations considerably, but does not otherwise affect them.

SYNTAX: ht

EXAMPLES:

```
?st tf
[0 0 0 PD 1 TRUE]              ;turtle shown, ie TRUE.
?ht tf
[0 0 0 PD 1 FALSE]
?
```

REL PRIMS: st

if

Conditional logic operator. Takes one input, or optionally more, and outputs a truth value, or values of the conditional test. It requires a list, or optionally lists, of instructions to be carried out if the result of the conditional test is TRUE, and optionally if it is FALSE. If there is no second list, and the output is FALSE, control is passed to the next line of the program.

SYNTAX: if *condition* [*instructionlist1*] {[*instructionlist2*]}

EXAMPLES:

```
?make "a 6 make "b 10
?if :a > :b [pr :a] [pr :b]        ;test returns FALSE
10
?if (:a * 10) = (:b * 6) [pr (:a * 10)]   ;test returns TRUE
?60
?
```

REL PRIMS: and, FALSE, not, or, TRUE

.in

System operator. Takes one input, the number of a CP/M port, and outputs the decimal byte value held at that port.

SYNTAX: .in *port*

EXAMPLES:

```
?.in 248
7
?
```

NOTE: A difficult primitive to use, since it may interfere with CP/M operations and cause the system to crash. It is necessary to know what ports to address to use the command safely.

REL PRIMS: .out

int (integer)

Arithmetic operator. Takes one input, a real number, and rounds it down to the nearest whole number.

SYNTAX: int *realnumber*

EXAMPLES:

```
?int 2.5
2
?int (2.4 * 3.1)                  ;real result is 7.44
7
?make "a 6.75 make "b 2.7
?int (:a / :b)                    ;real result is 2.5
2
?
```

REL PRIMS: quotient, remainder, round

item

List and word processing operator. Takes two inputs, the first an integer indicating the position of the enumerated element in the second input, which may be a word,list or number.

SYNTAX: item *number* [*list*]
item *number* "*word*
item *number number*

EXAMPLES:

```
?item 3 "number
m
?item 4 3241
1
?item 2 [name address1 address2 address3]
address1
?item 4 [a [bc] d [e [f g]] h]
[e [fg]]
?item 1 item 2 item 4 [a [bc] d [e [f g]] h]
fg
?
```

NOTE: To make the list of lists clearer, here it is broken down:

```
item        1  2   3      4    5
level 1    [a [bc] d [e [f g]] h]
item           1      2   3    4
level 2       [bc]   [e [...]] h]
item                  1   2    3
level 3               e [f g]  h
item                      1
level 4                  f g
```

REL PRIMS: piece

keyp (key press)

Keyboard input operator. Takes a keypress from the keyboard as input and returns TRUE when a key is pressed Contains the value FALSE at TOPLEVEL. Once a key has been pressed, keyp retains the value TRUE until contro passes back to TOPLEVEL, when its value is reset to FALSE.

SYNTAX: keyp

EXAMPLES:

```
?keyp
FALSE
?to test.key :num
>pr [Press a key to stop counting]
>if keyp [stop]
>(type "loop :num [])
>test.key :num + 1
>end
test.key defined
?test.key
loop 1 Press a key to stop counting
loop 2 Press a key to stop counting
loop 3 Press a key to stop counting
?b                              ;key b has been pressed
```

NOTE: Introducing a pause in the program resets keyp. The command **co** will allow program execution to continue. In the above example, instead of the line 'if keyp [stop]', insert 'i. keyp [cont]', and add this procedure:

```
?to cont
>pr [Type 'co' to continue] pause
>next-action
>end
?
```

REL PRIMS: rc, rl, rq

label

Flow control operator. Takes one input, a name. When a 'go "labelname' command is encountered, control is passec forwards or backwards to the label of the same name, provided it is in the same procedure.

SYNTAX: label "name

EXAMPLES:

```
?to jump
>if :a = 5 [go "here]
>make "a :a + 1 type :a
>jump
>label "here
>pr [jump made]
>throw "TOPLEVEL
>end
jump defined
?make "a 0
jump
12345jump made
?
```

REL PRIMS: go

last

List and word processing operator. Takes one input, a list or a word, and outputs the last element of that input.

SYNTAX:
last "*word*
last [*list*]

EXAMPLES:
```
?last [a b c d]
d
?last 4321
1
?last "APPLE
E
?last [[1] [2] [3]]
[3]
?last last [name address]
s
?
```

REL PRIMS: bf, bl, first, fput, lput

lc (lower case)

Word processing operator. Takes one input, a character or a word or a list of words in the range A..Z, and outputs the equivalent character in the range a..z.

SYNTAX: lc "*word*

EXAMPLES:
```
?lc "UPPER
upper
?lc "lower
lower
?make "a "Q
?lc :a
q
?lc 32FILE7
lc doesn't like 32 as input
?lc "32FILE7                      ;a case where a number must be
32fil7                            ;  declared as a word.
?
```

REL PRIMS: uc

list

List processing operator. Takes one or more inputs and outputs those inputs as a list. If the number of inputs is more or less than two, the operator and its inputs must be enclosed in round brackets.

SYNTAX:
list "*input1* "*input2*
(list "*input1* "*input2* ..."*inputN*)

EXAMPLES:
```
?(list "single)
[single]
?list "one "two
[one two]
?(list [a] [b] [c])
[[a] [b] [c]]
?(list "list1 [list2] [list2])
[list1 [list2] [list3]]
?
```

REL PRIMS: se, word

listp (list property)

List processing evaluator. Takes one input and outputs TRUE if that input is a list.

SYNTAX: listp "*input*

EXAMPLES:
```
?listp [x y z]
TRUE
?listp "alist
FALSE
?listp [1]
TRUE
?listp []
TRUE
?
```

REL PRIMS: equalp, list, namep, numberp, wordp

load

File handling command. Takes one input, the name of a file on the default drive, or optionally on a named drive, and loads the contents of that file into the workspace.

SYNTAX: load {"*drive*} "*filename*

EXAMPLES:
```
?load "proc1
proc1 defined
proc2 defined
proc3 defined
?load "UPD
file not found
?load "upd
upd defined
?load "m:test
test defined
?
```

NOTE: The command 'load "filename' loads everything that was in the workspace when the file was saved, including global variables and properties.

REL PRIMS: changef, edf, erasefile, erasepic, loadpic, save, savepic

loadpic (load picfile)

Picfile handling command. Takes one input, the name of a picfile on the default drive, or optionally on a named drive, and loads that picfile to the screen.

SYNTAX: loadpic {*drive*} "*picfilename*

EXAMPLES:
```
?loadpic "graph
?loadpic "b:plan
?
```

NOTE: **loadpic** loads and displays a picfile to that part of the screen given over to graphics.

REL PRIMS: changef, edf, erasepic, erasefile, load, save, savepic

local

Variable operator. Takes one or more inputs, the names of variables local to the procedure in which they are declared and to procedures called by that procedure. Local variables may be passed to the called procedures as parameters to those procedures. If more than one local variable is declared, then both the operator and its inputs must be enclosed in round brackets.

SYNTAX: local "*variablename*
(local "*variablename1* "*variablename2...*" *variablenameN*)

EXAMPLES:

```
?to procedure1
>local "a
>make "a 8 pr :a
>end
?procedure1 defined
?procedure1
8
?:a
a has no value
?make "a 6
?to procedure2
>(local "a "b)
>make "a 2 make "b 10
>(pr :a :b)
>end
procedure2 defined
?procedure2
2 10
?:a
6
?:b
b has no value
?to procedure3
>local "num
>make "num 12
>procedure4 :num
>end
procedure3 defined
?to procedure4 :num
>pr :num
>end
procedure4 defined
?procedure3
12
?:num
num has no value
?
```

NOTE: In the second example, the value of :a as a global variable is not affected by the creation of a local variable :a, which takes precedence over the global during the execution of the procedure. However, once 'procedure2' is over, global :a re-appears with its own value intact. In the third example, 'procedure3' creates a local variable :num and assigns to it the value 12. This is passed to 'procedure4' as a parameter. The parameter names in the two procedures need not be the same. Local variables can be created as parameters and need not in that case be expressly declared as local. In the program TAN, the declaration line 'tan :ang' creates a local variable :ang which has not been previouly declared. When the program finishes, the variable :ang will disappear.

REL PRIMS: make

lput (last put)

List and word processing operator. Takes two inputs and outputs a list or a word in which the first input is added to the end of the second input.

SYNTAX: lput *input1 input2*

EXAMPLES:
```
?lput "hog "hedge
hedgehog
?lput "club [golf]
[golf club]
?lput [x] [yz]
[yz [x]]
?make "a "object
?lput :a [subject verb]
[subject verb object]
?
```

NOTE: When used in procedures **lput** must be assigned, thus: 'make "temp lput first :alist :temp'.

REL PRIMS: first, fput, last

lt (left)

Turtle graphics operator. Takes one input, an angle in degrees, and turns the relative turtle heading that number of degrees to the left.

SYNTAX: lt *angle*

EXAMPLES:
```
?tf
[0 0 0 PD 1 TRUE]
?lt 75 tf
[0 0 285 PD 1 TRUE]
?
```

REL PRIMS: rt, seth

make

Variable operator. Takes two inputs, a variable name and a value, and assigns the value to the variable-name. The variable will be global unless previously declared as local.

SYNTAX: make "*variablename value*

EXAMPLES:
```
?make "num 6
?:num
6
?make "num :num + 9
?:num
15
?make "colour "YELLOW
?:colour
YELLOW
?make "alist (list "table "chair "desk)
?:alist
[table chair desk]
?
```

REL PRIMS: local

memberp (member property)

Word and list processing evaluator. Takes two inputs and returns TRUE if they are both exactly the same.

SYNTAX:
memberp "*element* [*list*]
memberp "*item* "*list*
memberp *figure number*

EXAMPLES:
```
?memberp "A "ABC
TRUE
?memberp "a "ABC
FALSE
?memberp "duct "introduction
TRUE
?memberp [2] [[1] [2] [3]]
TRUE
?memberp [2] [1 2 3]
FALSE
?memberp 10 471086
TRUE
?memberp 10 [4 7 1 0 8 6]
FALSE
?
```

REL PRIMS: equalp, listp, namep, numberp, wordp

namep (name property)

Variable evaluator. Takes one input, a name, and outputs TRUE if a variable of that name exists in the workspace.SYNTAX: namep "*variable-name*

EXAMPLES:
```
?make "a "var
?namep :a
TRUE
?namep "var
TRUE
?namep :var
FALSE
?
```

NOTE: :var is not a name, it is a variable. The name of that variable is "a.

REL PRIMS: emptyp, equalp, listp, numberp, wordp

nodes

Workspace evaluator. Takes no input. Returns the number of nodes (useable workspace memory) remaining.

SYNTAX: nodes

EXAMPLES:
```
?nodes
3634
?nodes
3632
?recycle nodes
3634
?
```

NOTE: **nodes** does not necessarily return the true space remaining. Use recycle to do a garbage collection before using nodes.

REL PRIMS: recycle

noformat

System operator. Removes all formatting (line extensions , 'removed-lines', and all indentations throughout all procedures in the workspace.

SYNTAX: noformat

EXAMPLES:

```
?plist "revon
[.FMT [[0 . ENL . ;reverses palette] [0 .SPC . 3] [12 . ENL . ;escape codes]] .DEF [[] [(type (word char 27 "b0 char 27 "c6))]]]
?noformat
?plist "revon
[]
?
```

NOTE: This operator needs to be used with great caution, since removing indents may alter the operation of some programs. 'Removed lines' will disappear completely, which may not be intended. Checking with **.FMT** is advisable before using noformat.

REL PRIMS: .ENL, .FMT, .REM, .SPC

not

Boolean logic operator. Takes one input and inverts the truth value of that input. The operator may be used in prefix form only.

SYNTAX: not *expression*

EXAMPLES:

```
?3 = 2 + 1
TRUE
?not 3 = 2 + 1
FALSE
?not (4 = 2 + 1)
TRUEO
?not equalp "house "flat
TRUE
?not "TRUE = "FALSE
TRUE
?
```

REL PRIMS: and, if, or, TRUE, FALSE

notrace

Tracing command. Takes no inputs. Turns off program evaluation initiated by trace. Should always be entered on a line by itself.

SYNTAX: notrace

EXAMPLES:

```
?trace
?procedure2
[1] Evaluating procedure2
[1] making a 2
[1] making b 10
2 10
?notrace
?procedure2
2 10
?
```

REL PRIMS: nowatch, trace, watch

nowatch

Tracing command. Takes no inputs. Turns off program evaluation initiated by watch. Should always be entered on a line by itself.

SYNTAX: nowatch

EXAMPLES:

```
?watch "procedure2
?procedure2
[1] In procedure2, ( local "a "b )
[1] In procedure2, make "a 2
[1] In procedure2, make "b 10
[1] In procedure2, ( pr :a :b )
2 10
?nowatch
?procedure2
2 10
?
```

REL PRIMS: notrace, trace, watch

numberp (number property)

Number evaluator. Takes one input and outputs TRUE if that input is a number.

SYNTAX: numberp *input*

EXAMPLES:

```
?numberp 12
TRUE
?numberp "a
FALSE
?make "a 8
?numberp :a
TRUE
?numberp 12x436
FALSE
?
```

REL PRIMS: equalp, listp, memberp, namep, wordp

op (output)

Procedure output operator. Takes one input and outputs the value of that input to the calling procedure. Stops execution of the procedure in which it operates.

SYNTAX: op *value*

EXAMPLES:

```
?to test
>make "a output              ;answer assigned before the
>(pr [Answer is] :a)         ;  call is made
>end
test defined
?to output
>make "b cos 30
>op :b
>(pr [cos 30 is] :b)
>end
output defined
?test
Answer is 0.866025388240814
?
```

NOTE: Line 2 of 'test' assigns the result of the execution of procedure 'output' to the variable named "a. The program jumps to 'output', runs it and take the output from 'op :b' back to 'test' in line 3, where the instruction 'pr [answer is] :a' is executed. The line '(pr [cos 30 is] :b)' is never reached. All calls involving **op** must have the value output by **op** assigned in some way. This would not work:

```
?to test
>output
...
to output
make "b cos 30
>op :b
...
```

An error message 'I don't know what to do with 0.866025388240814 in test: output' would be generated. It is possible to assign more than one value to **op** by assigning to it a list of values.

REL PRIMS:

or

Boolean logic operator. Takes two, or optionally more, inputs and outputs TRUE if any of the input expressions is true. If there are more than two inputs, the operator and all its inputs must be enclosed in round brackets. Can only be used in prefix form.

SYNTAX: or *expression1 expression2*
(or {or} {or*N*} *expression1 expression2...expressionN*)

EXAMPLES:

```
?or 3 = 10 * 0.3 8 = 16 / 4
TRUE
?(or or 16 > (2 * 9) 3.5 = 24 / 6 4 * 8 / 10 = 3.2)
TRUE
?
```

NOTE: The values in the examples are:

```
1) 3=10*.3
   3=3            TRUE      )
   8=16/4                   ) or returns TRUE
   8=4            FALSE     )
2) 16>(2*9)
   16>18          FALSE     )
   3.5=24/6                 )
   3.5=4          FALSE     ) or returns TRUE
   4*8/10=3.2               )
   10=10          TRUE      )
```

REL PRIMS: and, FALSE, not, TRUE

.out

System operator. Takes two inputs, the location of a CP/M port and a byte value, both in decimal. Inputs the byte value into the CP/M port.

SYNTAX: .out *port value*

EXAMPLES:

```
?.out 248 8          ;screen blanked out.
.out 248 7           ;screen display restored.
?
```

NOTE: A very tricky operator to handle. Knowledge of the CP/M ports and their functions is essential. See TUTORIAL 14.

REL PRIMS: .in

paddle

Primitive not implemented.

pal

Primitive not implemented.

pause

Run-time operator. Takes no inputs. Enforces a pause in run-time execution of a program.

SYNTAX: pause

EXAMPLES:

```
?to break
>pr [take a break]
>pause
>pr [on with the work]
>end
break defined
?break
take a break
pausing... in break: [pause]
break ?co
on with the work
?
```

NOTE: From a pause state, editing may be carried out, variables tested, etc, and the program resumed afterwards. If you wish to abandon the program, the only way out of the pause is to cause an error message by, for example, mistyping **co** ('c' + <RETURN> is sufficient). Pressing <STOP> will not overcome a pause. Normally if **co** is entered the program will leave the pause state and run on until it is completed.

REL PRIMS: co

pd (pen down)

Turtle graphics command. Takes no inputs. Puts the pen down, enabling lines to be drawn when the turtle is moved. The pen colour is always 1.

SYNTAX: pd

EXAMPLES:

```
?pe tf
[0 0 0 PE 1 TRUE]
?pd tf
[0 0 0 PD 1 TRUE]
?
```

REL PRIMS: pe, pu, px

pe (pen erase)

Turtle graphics command. Takes no inputs. Makes the pencolour the same as the background colour, turning off any pixels it passes over, effectively erasing previously-drawn lines.

SYNTAX: pe

EXAMPLES:
```
?pd tf
[0 0 0 PD 1 TRUE]
?pe tf
[0 0 0 PE 1 TRUE]
?
```

REL PRIMS: pd, pu, px

piece

Word and list processing operator. Takes three inputs, the first two a range and the third a word or list. Outputs those elements of the word or list within the range described by the first two inputs.

SYNTAX: piece *number number word*
piece *number number list*

EXAMPLES:
```
?piece 4 6 "element
men
?piece 2 5 283579
8357
?piece 2 3 [one two three four five]
two three
?
```

REL PRIMS: item

plist (property list)

Property processing operator. Takes one input, the name of an object or a procedure, and outputs a list of properties associated with the object, together with the values.

SYNTAX: plist "*object*
plist "*procedure*

EXAMPLES:
```
?pprop "terrier "colour "brown
?plist "terrier
[colour brown]
?plist "procedure1
[.DEF [[] [local "a] [make "a 8 pr :a]]]
?
```

REL PRIMS: glist, gprop, pprop, remprop

po (print out)

Print command. Takes one input, a procedure name, or a list of procedure names, and prints out the definitions of those procedures.

SYNTAX: po "*procedurename*
po [*procedurename1 procedurename2...procedurenameN*]

EXAMPLES:
```
?po "jump
to jump
make "a 0
if :a = 5 [go "here]
```

```
make "a :a + 1 type :a
jump
label "here
pr [jump made]
end
?
```

REL PRIMS: poall, pons, pops, pots

poall (print out all)

Print comand. Takes no inputs. Prints out the text of all procedures and the values of all global variables in the workspace.

SYNTAX: poall

EXAMPLES:

```
?poall
to jump
make "a 0
....etc.
```

REL PRIMS: po, pons, pops, pots

pons (print out names)

Print command. Takes no inputs. Prints out all the global variables present in the workspace and their values.

SYNTAX: pons

EXAMPLES:

```
?make "x 32 make "y 10
?pons
x is 32
y is 10
?
```

REL PRIMS: pops, pots, pps

pops (print out procedures)

Print command. Takes no inputs. Prints out the definitions of all the procedures in the workspace.

SYNTAX: pops

EXAMPLES:

```
?pops
to jump
if :a = 5 [go "here]
make "a :a + 1 type :a
...etc.
```

REL PRIMS: po, poall, pons, pots, pps

pots (print out titles)

Print command. Takes no inputs. Prints out the titles (names) of all the procedures in the workspace.

SYNTAX: pots

EXAMPLES:

```
?pots
to jump
to example
to loop :st :en :step
to abs :n
```

REL PRIMS: po, poall, pons, pops, pps

pprop (put property)

Property processing operator. Takes three inputs, the first the name of an object, the second a property of that object, and the third the value of that property.

SYNTAX: pprop "*object* "*property* "*value*

EXAMPLES:
```
?pprop "labrador "colour "black
?pprop "terrier "colour "brown
?pprop "labrador "coat "short
?plist "labrador
[coat short colour black]
?gprop "terrier "colour
brown
?
```

REL PRIMS: glist, gprop, plist, remprop

pps (print properties)

Print command. Takes no inputs. Prints out all the objects properties and values in the workspace, and adds some grammar.

SYNTAX: pps

EXAMPLES:
```
?pps
labrador's colour is black
terrier's colour is brown
labrador's coat is short
?
```

REL PRIMS: pons, pops, pots

pr (print)

Print command. Takes one or more inputs, which may be words or lists, prints them to the screen and then executes a line-feed and carriage-return. If there is more than one input, the command and all its inputs must be enclosed in round brackets.

SYNTAX:
pr "*word*
pr [*list*]
(pr "*input1* "*input2*..."*inputN*)

EXAMPLES:
```
?pr "anything
anything
?pr [A complete sentence]
A complete sentence
?(pr "wine "glass)
wine glass
?pr "number pr "one
number
one
?make "a 12 make "b 13 make "c 14
?(pr :a :b :c)
12 13 14
?
```

REL PRIMS: show, type

.PRM (primitive)

System property. The memory-location-property of a primitive. Enables alterations to machine code to be made in order to modify the action of primitives. May also be used to return a list of primitives in the system, but not system properties. See the program STARTUP in PART THREE for examples.

SYNTAX: gprop "*primitive* ".PRM
glist ".PRM

EXAMPLES:
```
?gprop "keyp ".PRM
7710
?glist ".PRM
[dirpic numberp arctan...random fence label]
?
```

REL PRIMS:

pu (pen up)

Turtle graphics command. Takes no inputs. Puts the pen up, enabling the turtle to move without drawing lines.

SYNTAX: pu

EXAMPLES:
```
?pd tf
[0 0 0 PD 1 TRUE]
?pu tf
[0 0 0 PU 1 TRUE]
?
```

REL PRIMS: pd, pe, px

px (pen XOR)

Turtle graphics command. Takes no inputs. Puts the pen in Exclusive Or mode and reverses the state of any pixel the pen passes over.

SYNTAX: px

EXAMPLES:
```
?pd tf
[0 0 0 PD 1 TRUE]
?px tf
[0 0 0 PX 1 TRUE]
?
```

REL PRIMS: pd, pe, pu

quotient

Arithmetic operator. Takes two inputs, two numbers, and outputs the result of integer division of the first number by the second. Any remainder is discarded.

SYNTAX: quotient *dividend divisor*

EXAMPLES:
```
?quotient 12 4
3
?quotient 20 8
2
?20 / 8
2.5
?quotient 13.38 4
3
?
```

NOTE: In the last example quotient first reduces the real to an integer, performs integer division and discards the remainder. Maximum input 32767. For greater numbers use 'int (*dividend/divisor*)'.

REL PRIMS: int, remainder, /

random

Arithmetic operator. Takes one input, an integer, and outputs a pseudo-random number between zero and one less than the input number.

SYNTAX: random integer

EXAMPLES:
```
?random 100
52
?random 100
14
?
```

NOTE: The numbers output by **random** will always be exactly the same and in the same sequence if **random** is run immediately after LOGO is booted, since the system 'seed' is always the same on booting. The solution is to use program RANSEED (in PART TWO). To eliminate the possibility of an output of zero from **random**, use the line '(random integer) + 1' which ensures that zero cannot be returned. It is equally well possible, using this method, to obtain random numbers between any two numbers. Thus to get randon numbers between and including, say, 50 and 60, enter the line '(random 11) + 50'. The operator **rerandom** resets the random seed, so that a sequence of random numbers may be repeated exactly to check the operation of a program.

REL PRIMS: rerandom

rc (read character)

Input operator. Takes one input, any character capable of being typed in at the keyboard, and outputs TRUE if a key is pressed. If used in a procedure, it must be assigned to a variable or compared. **rc** does not require <RETURN> to be pressed and does not output the input character.

SYNTAX: make "*variable* rc

EXAMPLES:
```
?"make "inp rc
...                              ;the letter 'D' is pressed
?:inp
D
?
...
pr [Press S to save, any other key to continue]
if rc = "S [save "program]
...
```

NOTE: In the second example the input is not assigned to a variable. This is quite in order.

REL PRIMS: rl, rq

recycle

Workspace operator. Takes no inputs. Enforces garbage collection, *ie* clears the memory of 'dead' data.

SYNTAX: recycle

EXAMPLES:

```
?nodes
1214
?er [proc1 proc2 action loop]
?nodes
1214
?recycle
?nodes
1823
?
```

NOTE: Garbage collection is also carried out automatically, but this can slow up program execution. **recycle** should be inserted from time to time in programs which use a lot of temporary memory. A good place to do this is when there is a need for a pause - perhaps to read user instructions. Recycling takes between 1 and 3 seconds to complete.

REL PRIMS: nodes

REDEFP (redefine primitive)

System operator. Has the value FALSE when the system is booted and remains inactive in that state. When made TRUE, enables primitive names to be redefined, and primitives themselves to be eliminated.

SYNTAX: make "REDEFP "TRUE

EXAMPLES:

```
?to dir
dir is a primitive
?make "REDEFP "TRUE
?to dir
>end
dir defined
?dir "a:
I don't know how to dir
?
```

NOTE: The primitive 'dir' now has no meaning. The only way to reverse this is to reset the computer and re-boot LOGO. Using REDEFP with primitives that are not implemented or unwanted enables extra workspace to be created. See program SPACER in PART TWO. After using REDEFP it should be returned to its inactive state with 'make "REDEFP "FALSE or erase it from the workspace with 'ern "REDEFP'.

REL PRIMS:

.REM (removed line)

System property. The 'removed-line' property of a procedure. **.REM** cannot be used as an operator, but is included in returns from **.FMT** (qv).

EXAMPLES:

```
?to test :ang
>pr sin :ang
>;pr cos :ang
>end
?gprop "test ".FMT
```

```
[.FMT [[0 .REM . ;pr cos :ang]]]
?
```

NOTE: The figure '0' indicates the word-count (not including the definition line) to the removed line, which has been prevented from operating by the semi-colon at its head. *cf* .ENL. **noformat** erases all 'removed lines'.

REL PRIMS: .ENL, .FMT, .SPC

remainder

Arithmetic operator. Takes two inputs, both integers, and outputs the remainder, if any, left after integer division of the first input by the second.

SYNTAX: remainder *dividend divisor*

EXAMPLES:

```
?remainder 12 5
2
?remainder 12 6
0
?remainder 12 2.5
0
?
```

NOTE: In the last example, remainder reduces the divisor to an integer before performing the division. Maximum input 32767 . For greater numbers use '*dividend* – (int (*dividend* / *divisor*)) * *divisor*.

REL PRIMS: quotient, /

remprop (remove property)

Property processing operator. Takes two inputs, an object and a property of that object, and removes the property named in the second input from the property-list of the first input.

SYNTAX: remprop "*object* "*property*

EXAMPLES:

```
?pprop "USA "capital "Washington
?pprop "USSR "capital "Moscow
?pps
USA's capital is Washington
USSR's capital is Moscow
?remprop "USSR "capital
?pps
USA's capital is Washington
?
```

REL PRIMS: glist, gprop, plist, pprop

repeat

Repetition operator. Takes two inputs, a number and an instruction list, and repeats the insructions contained in the list the number of times required by the input number.

SYNTAX: repeat *number* [*instructionlist*]

EXAMPLES:

```
?              ?make "alist (list "a "b "c "d "e)
?repeat 3 [make "alist bf :alist] pr :alist
[d e]
?
```

REL PRIMS:

rerandom (reset random)

Random number operator. Resets the seed for random operations to its boot-up value, allowing repeat testing based on a pre-defined number sequence.

SYNTAX: rerandom

REL PRIMS: random, shuffle

rl (read list)

Input operator. Takes any input from the keyboard and outputs it as a list. If used in a procedure, it must be assigned to a variable or compared. No action is taken until <RETURN> has been pressed.

SYNTAX: make "*variablename* rl
if rl = *list* [*instruction list*]

EXAMPLES:

```
?make "inlist rl
...                          ;input is 'tea coffee cocoa
?:inlist
[tea coffee cocoa]
?if rl = [yes] [pr "YES]
...                          ;input is [yes]
YES
?show rl
rl has no value
?
```

NOTE: Inputs to **rl** must not be entered as lists, unless lists of lists are required. **rl** itself turns the input into a list.

REL PRIMS: rc, rq

round

Arithmetic operator. Takes one input, a real number, and outputs the nearest whole number.

SYNTAX: round *real-number*

EXAMPLES:

```
?round 2.4
2
?round 16.8
17
?round 8.5
9
?round 20.49
20
?
```

NOTE: LOGO only takes into account the first decimal place when rounding. In arithmetic 20.49 would round up to 20.5, thence to 21. Decimals in the range (0.0)..(0.4) are rounded down, those in the range (0.5)..(0.9) are rounded up.

REL PRIMS: int

rq (read quote)

Input operator. Takes an input string from the keyboard and outputs it in the same form in which it was entered. It must be assigned to a variable or compared. No action is taken until <RETURN> has been pressed.

SYNTAX: make "*variablename* rq
if rq = "*quote* [*instruction list*]

EXAMPLES:
```
?make "inp rq
....                        ;input is 'number=1429'
?:inp
number=1429
?if rq = "quite "right [pr "YES]
...                         ;input is 'quite right'
YES
?:rq
rq has no value
?
```
REL PRIMS: rc, rl

rt (right)

Turtle graphics operator. Takes one input, an angle in degrees, and turns the relative turtle heading that number of degrees to the right.

SYNTAX: rt *angle*

EXAMPLES:
```
?tf
[0 0 0 PD 1 TRUE]
?rt 75 tf
[0 0 75 PD 1 TRUE]
?
```
REL PRIMS: lt, seth

run

Program command. Takes one input, an instruction list, and executes those instructions.

SYNTAX: run *instruction-list*

EXAMPLES:
```
?test.key                   ;see entry on keyp
Press a key to stop printing
Press a key to stop printing
Press a key to stop printing
?d                          ;key 'd' pressed
```
REL PRIMS:

save

File-handling command. Takes one input, the name of a file, and saves everything in the workspace to the default drive, or optionally to a named drive, as a file of the input name.

SYNTAX: save "{*drive*} *filename*

EXAMPLES:
```
?save "sample
?dir
[SAMPLE]
?save "m:test
?save "m:test
file already exists
?dir "m:
[TEST]
?
```
REL PRIMS: changef, edf, erasefile, erasepic, load, loadpic, savepic

savepic (save picfile)

Picfile-handling command. Takes one input, the name of a picture file, and saves the screen to the default drive, or optionally to a named drive, as a picfile of the input name.

SYNTAX: savepic "{drive} picfilename

EXAMPLES:

```
?savepic "graph
?savepic "b:picture
?savepic "graph
file already exists
?dirpic
[GRAPH]
?
```

REL PRIMS: changef, edf, erasefile, erasepic, load, loadpic, save

se (sentence)

Word and list processing operator. Takes one or more inputs and outputs them as a list. If any of the inputs is a list, **se** first strips away the first-level brackets. If the number of inputs is more or less than two, the operator and all its inputs must be enclosed in round brackets.

SYNTAX: se *input1 input2*
(se *input1 input2...inputN*)

EXAMPLES:

```
?se "one "two
[one two]
?make "x 34 make "y 18
?se :x :y
[34 18]
?(se [total] "is 412)
[total is 412]
?(se "one)
[one]
?se [level one list] [[level two list]]
[level one list [level two list]]
?
```

NOTE: In the last example, only the outer brackets are removed from '[[level two list]]'. **se** then wraps the entire input in brackets.

REL PRIMS: list, word

setbg (set background)

Graphics command. Takes one input, a number, and sets the background colour of the screen to the input number.

SYNTAX: setbg *number*

NOTE: The background colour of the PCW monochrome screens must always be 0. **setbg** will not accept any other input. The primitive is of no practical use and should be ignored.

setcursor

Text screen command. Takes one input, a list of X Y cursor coordinates, and sets the cursor to that position.

SYNTAX: setcursor [*X co-ordinate Y co-ordinate*]

EXAMPLES:

```
?setcursor [45 15]
?cursor
```

```
[45 15]
?make "x 30 make "y 10
?setcursor se :x :y
?cursor
[30 10]
?
```

NOTE: **setcursor** will only work properly within a program. In command mode the X co-ordinate will always revert to 1.

REL PRIMS: cursor

setd (set default)

File-handling command. Takes one input, a drive name, and sets that drive as the default drive.

SYNTAX: setd "*drive*

EXAMPLES:

```
?defaultd
A:
?setd "m:
?defaultd
M:
?
```

REL PRIMS: defaultd

setpal (set palette)

Primitive not implemented.

setpc (set pencolour)

Graphics command. Takes one input, a number, and sets the pen to the colour corresponding to that number.

SYNTAX: setpc *number*

NOTE: With PCW monochrome screens, **setpc** will only accept two pencolours, 0 and 1. 0 is equivalent to the background colour, 1 is the normal pencolour. The primitive is of no practical use whatsoever and should be ignored.

setpen

Graphics operator. Will not accept inputs for monochrome screens. The primitive is of no practical use whatsoever and should be ignored.

setpos (set position)

Turtle graphics command. Takes one input, a list of two real numbers, the X and Y turtle co-ordinates, and moves the turtle to that position.

SYNTAX: setpos [*X co-ordinate Y co-ordinate*]

EXAMPLES:

```
?tf
[0 0 0 PD 1 TRUE]
?setpos [100 -30] tf
[100 -30 0 PD TRUE]
?make "x -250 make "y 17
?setpos se :x :y
?tf
```

```
[-250 17 0 PD 1 TRUE]
?
```

REL PRIMS: setx, sety

setscrunch

Screen command. Takes one input, a number, and sets the vertical and horizontal aspects of the screen to that aspect ratio.

SYNTAX: setscrunch *number*

EXAMPLES:

```
?sf
[0 SS 10 WINDOW .46875]
?setscrunch 1 sf
[0 SS 10 WINDOW 1]
?
```

NOTE: The default setting of .46875 draws a round circle to screen and the dedicated PCW dot matrix printer. Some very odd effects can be achieved by setting a different aspect ratio. Some printers may work better with a setting of 0.5. Various adjustments may need to be made to suit the particular machine.

REL PRIMS:

seth (set heading)

Turtle graphics command. Takes one input, an angle in degrees, and sets the absolute heading of the turtle to that angle. The absolute heading of 0° (or 360°) is pointing vertically up towards the top of the screen.

SYNTAX: seth *angle*

EXAMPLES:

```
?seth 90 tf
[0 0 90 PD 1 TRUE]
?seth 280 tf
[0 0 280 PD 1 TRUE]
?
```

REL PRIMS: lt, rt

setsplit

Screen command. Takes one input, an integer, and sets the text part of a split screen to that number of rows.

SYNTAX: setsplit *integer*

EXAMPLES:

```
?sf
[0 SS 10 WRAP .46875]
?setsplit 3 sf
[0 FS 3 WRAP .46875]
?
```

REL PRIMS: fs, ss, ts

setx (set X co-ordinate)

Turtle graphics command. Takes one input, a number, and moves the turtle to a position corresponding to the input X co-ordinate and the existing Y co-ordinate.

SYNTAX: setx *number*

EXAMPLES:
```
?tf
[0 0 0 PD 1 TRUE]
?setx 100 tf
[100 0 0 PD 1 TRUE]
?
```
REL PRIMS: setpos, sety

sety (set Y co-ordinate)

Turtle graphics command. Takes one input, a number and moves the turtle to a position corresponding to the input Y co-ordinate and the existing X co-ordinate.

SYNTAX: sety *number*

EXAMPLES:
```
?tf
[0 0 0 PD 1 TRUE]
?sety -70 tf
[0 -70 0 PD 1 TRUE]
?
```
REL PRIMS: setpos, setx

sf (screen facts)

Screen command. Takes no inputs. Outputs the screen state as a list. Item 1 is the background colour (always 0), item 2 is the screen mode (**ss fs ts**), item 3 is the number of text lines in a split screen, item 4 is the screen state (**window wrap fence**), and item 5 is the aspect ratio of the screen.

SYNTAX: sf

EXAMPLES:
```
?sf
[0 SS 5 FENCE .46875]
?
```
REL PRIMS: fence, fs, setscrunch, ss, tf, ts, window, wrap

show

Print command. Takes one input, a word or a list, prints it to the screen and then executes a line-feed and carriage-return. Does not strip the outer brackets from a list.

SYNTAX: show "*word*
show [*list*]

EXAMPLES:
```
?show "output
output
?show [This is a list]
[This is a list]
?make "a (list 6) show :a
[6]
?(show :a :b)
[6]
I don't know what to do with :b
?
```
REL PRIMS: pr, type

shuffle

List operator. Takes one input, a list, and outputs that list in random order.

SYNTAX: shuffle [*list*]

EXAMPLES:
```
?make "alist [1 2 3 4 5 6]
?shuffle :alist
[3 1 6 5 2 4]
?
```

NOTE: **rerandom** resets the seed for **shuffle** to its start-up value.

REL PRIMS: random, rerandom

sin (sine)

Arithmetic operator. Takes one input, an angle in degrees, and outputs the sine of that angle.

SYNTAX: sin *angle*

EXAMPLES:
```
?sin 45
.707
?sin 60
.866
?
```

REL PRIMS: arctan, cos

.SPC (spaces)

System property. The space-indent property of a procedure and a word-count up to that point, excluding the definition line. Round and square brackets are counted as words. .SPC cannot be used as an operator, but is returned in an **.FMT** statement.

EXAMPLES:
```
?gprop "revon ".FMT
[[0 .ENL . ;reverses palette] [0 .SPC . 3] [13 .ENL .
;escape code]]
?
```

NOTE: For an explanation of '[0 .ENL . ;reverses palette]' see **.ENL.** '0' is the word-count up to the first indentation (not including the definition line). '3' is the number of spaces in the indent.

REL PRIMS: .ENL, .FMT, noformat, .REM

ss (split screen)

Screen command. Takes no inputs. Sets the screen to a mixed text and graphics mode, in the proportion set by setsplit (qv). The upper part of the screen is given over to graphics, the lower to text. Commands entered at the ? command prompt are printed to the text (lower) part of the screen. All graphics commands are printed to the graphics (upper) part of the screen.

SYNTAX: ss

EXAMPLES:
```
?ts sf
[0 TS 10 WINDOW .46875]
?ss sf
[0 SS 10 WINDOW .46875]
?
```

REL PRIMS: fs, ts

st (show turtle)

Turtle graphics command. Takes no input. Shows the turtle. Slows down drawing operations considerably, but does not otherwise affect them.

SYNTAX: st

EXAMPLES:
```
?ht tf
[0 0 0 PD 1 FALSE]          ;turtle hidden, ie FALSE.
?st tf
[0 0 0 PD 1 TRUE]
?
```

REL PRIMS: ht

stop

Flow-control command. Takes no inputs. Stops execution of the procedure in which it is executed and throws control back to the calling procedure, or to **TOPLEVEL** if none.

SYNTAX: stop

EXAMPLES:
```
?to test1
>make check 1
>work :check
>pr [Program completed]
>end
test1 defined
?to work :check
>pr :check
>if :check = 5 [stop]
>work :check + 1
>end
work defined
?test1
1
2
3
4
5
Program completed
?
```

NOTE: When :check reaches 5, the procedure is stopped and control is thrown back to the instruction following the call. When 'test' ends, as it was called from **TOPLEVEL**, control is thrown back there.

text

Definition print command. Takes one input, a procedure name, and outputs the definition of that procedure as a list.

SYNTAX: text "*procedurename*

EXAMPLES:
```
?text "work
[[:check] [pr :check] [if :check = 5 [stop]] [work :check +
1]]
?
```

REL PRIMS: .DEF, po, poall

tf (turtle facts)

Turtle graphics command. Takes no inputs. Outputs a list of facts relating to the turtle, of which items 1 and 2 are the X and Y co-ordinates of the turtle, item 3 is the absolute turtle heading, item 4 is the pen-state (**pu pd px pe**), item 5 is the ink colour (always 1 with monochrome screens), and item 6 is the turtle visibility: TRUE=visible, FALSE=hidden.

SYNTAX: tf

EXAMPLES:

```
?tf
[0 0 0 PD 1 TRUE]
?setpos [120 -40] seth 270 pu ht tf
[120 -40 270 PU 1 FALSE]
?
```

REL PRIMS: sf

thing

Variable operator. Takes one input, the name of a variable, and outputs the value contained in that variable. Nested values may be examined.

SYNTAX: thing "*variable*

EXAMPLES:

```
?make "a 10
?thing :a
10
?make "a "b
?make "b "c
?make "c "d
?thing :a
:b
?thing thing :a
:c
?thing thing thing :a
:d
?
```

REL PRIMS: .APV

throw

Flow-control command. Takes one input, a catch-label, and passes control to the instruction following the catch.

SYNTAX: throw "*label*

EXAMPLES:

```
?to test2
>catch "here [check]
>type [A key has been pressed]
>end
?test2 defined
?to check
>if keyp [throw "here]
>check
>end
check defined
?test2
...
A key has been pressed
?
```

REL PRIMS: catch, label

to

Definition marker. Takes one input, a procedure name, and optionally parameters to the procedure. The declaration must be completed by the 'end' marker.

SYNTAX: to *procedure-name*

EXAMPLES:

```
?to example :x
>pr :x
>end
example defined
?
```

REL PRIMS: end

TOPLEVEL

System label. Takes no inputs. Used as a throw-label, passes control back to the highest level of the system, ie: the command prompt, bypassing all other instructions. Pressing the <STOP> key will always return control back to **TOPLEVEL.**

SYNTAX: throw "TOPLEVEL

EXAMPLES:

```
?to halt.prog
>pr [Enter a number 1..5}
>if rc = 5 [throw "TOPLEVEL]
>halt.prog
>end
halt.prog defined
?halt.prog
...                                ;...when 5 is typed
?
```

REL PRIMS: stop, throw

tones

Primitive not implemented.

towards

Turtle graphics command. Takes one input, a list of the X and Y co-ordinates of a point in the graphics screen, and outputs the absolute turtle heading of that point from the present turtle position. Does not affect the turtle heading or position.

SYNTAX: towards [*X co-ordinate Y co-ordinate*]

EXAMPLES:

```
?tf
[0 0 0 PD 1 TRUE]
?towards [100 -100]
135
?seth towards [50 50] tf
[0 0 45 PD 1 TRUE]
?
```

REL PRIMS: seth

trace

Program analyser. Takes no inputs. Outputs to screen a run-time analysis of the execution of a program and depths of calls. Enables the values of local variables to be examined. Cancelled by **notrace**.

SYNTAX: trace

EXAMPLES:

```
?trace
?test1
[1] Evaluating test1
[1] Making "check 1
[2] Evaluating work
[2] check is 1
1
[3] Evaluating work
[3] check is 2
2
[4] Evaluating work
[4] check is 3
3
[5] Evaluating work
[5] check is 4
4
[6] Evaluating work
[6] check is 5
5
Program completed
?
```

NOTE: **trace** may be used in conjunction with **watch** (qv).

REL PRIMS: notrace, watch, nowatch

TRUE

Boolean value. Takes no inputs. Returned by a comparison test when the result of that test is true. May be assigned to certain primitives, and may be used as a catch-label in error tracing.

SYNTAX: make "primitive "TRUE

EXAMPLES:

```
?6 > 4
TRUE
?equalp (2 * 16) 32
TRUE
?[11] = 11
FALSE
?make "REDEFP "TRUE
?:REDEFP
TRUE
?
```

NOTE: In a conditional test, either TRUE or FALSE is output, though not seen within a program. If the condition is met, the output of the conditional test is TRUE.

REL PRIMS: FALSE

ts (text screen)

Screen command. Takes no inputs. Makes the full screen over to text input. Graphical input will not be printed. The turtle may be moved but will not show.

SYNTAX: ts

EXAMPLES:

```
?fs sf
[0 FS 10 WINDOW .46875]
?ts sf
[0 TS 10 WINDOW .46875]
?
```

NOTE: Certain graphics commands will still be accepted, *eg* **cs** will still clear the entire screen, including text display. In this case the text screen will be lost.

REL PRIMS: fs, ss

type

Print command. Takes one or more inputs, which may be words or lists, and prints the contents of the input to the screen. If there is more than one input, the command and all its inputs must be enclosed in round brackets.

SYNTAX: type "*word*
type [*list*]
(type "*word1* "*word2...*"*wordN*)

EXAMPLES:

```
?type "Example
Example
?type [A list of words]
A list of words
?type [a [bc] d [[ef] g] h]
a [bc] d [[ef] g] h
?type "wine type "glass
wineglass
?type "cow "hide
cow
I don't know what to do with hide
?(type word "cow "hide)
cowhide
?make "a 3 make "b 11
?(type :a [] :b)
3 11
?
```

REL PRIMS: pr, show

uc (upper case)

Word processing operator. Takes one input, a character or a word or a list of words, in the range a..z, and outputs the equivalent character or characters in the range A..Z. Entirely equivalent to subtracting 32 dec (20 hex) from the ASCII value of the input character, if the input is within the given range. Characters outside the range are unaffected.

SYNTAX: uc *input*

EXAMPLES:

```
?uc "lower
LOWER
```

```
?uc "uPpEr
UPPER
?make "a "q
?uc :a
Q
?uc "32file7
32FILE7
?
```

REL PRIMS: lc

wait

Primitive not implemented.

watch

Program analyser. Takes no inputs, or optionally one input, a procedure name, or a list of procedure names, and outputs each instruction of the procedure in turn, waiting for a <RETURN> to be entered before the next instruction is executed. Cancelled by **nowatch**.

SYNTAX: watch {"*procedurename*}
watch {[*list of procedurenames*]}

EXAMPLES:

```
?watch "halt.prog
?halt.prog
[1] In halt.prog, pr [Enter a number 1..5]         ;<RETURN>
[1] In halt.prog, pr Enter a number 1..5
1                                                  ;1 entered
[1] In halt.prog, if rc = 5 [throw "TOPLEVEL]      ;<RETURN>
[1] In halt.prog, halt.prog                        ;<RETURN>
[1] In halt.prog, pr [Enter a number 1..5]         ;<RETURN>
[1] In halt.prog, pr Enter a number 1..5
5                                                  ;5 entered
[1] In halt.prog, if rc = 5 [throw "TOPLEVEL]      ;<RETURN>
[1] In halt.prog, throw "TOPLEVEL
?
```

REL PRIMS: notrace, nowatch, trace

where

Word and list processing operator. Takes no inputs. Outputs the position of the item which was the subject of the last **memberp** test, but only if that test was successful.

SYNTAX: where

EXAMPLES:

```
?memberp "w "flower
TRUE
?where
4
?memberp "petal "flower
FALSE
?where
?memberp 12 6912478
TRUE
?where
3
?
```

NOTE: **where** will only be updated if the result of the **memberp** test is TRUE, otherwise it will return a null value.

REL PRIMS:

window

Graphics command. Takes no inputs. Permits the turtle to move off the visible screen, which is regarded as a window onto a theoretically infinite turtle world.

SYNTAX: window

EXAMPLES:

```
?sf
[0 FS 10 FENCE .46875]
?window sf
[0 FS 10 WINDOW .46875]
?
```

NOTE: The viewport co-ordinates are:
X axis, left..right −350..349
Y axis, bottom..top 250..−249
The turtle moves more slowly when not within the visible screen.

REL PRIMS: fence, wrap

word

Word-processing operator. Takes one or more inputs, a word or words, and concatenates the given inputs: that is they are linked together without spaces. If there are more or less than two inputs, the operator and all its inputs must be enclosed in round brackets.

SYNTAX: word "*input1* {"*input2*}
(word "*word1* "*word2...*" *wordN*)

EXAMPLES:

```
?word "d "o
do
?word 6 8
68
?(word "A)
A
?(word "sum char 32 68 "+ 27 "= 68 + 27)
sum 68+27=95
?word [5] [7]
word doesn't like [5] as input
?word first [5] first [7]
57
?
```

REL PRIMS: list, se, wordp

wordp (word property)

Word-processing operator. Takes one input and outputs TRUE if that input is a word. Numbers are regarded as words in a **numberp** test.

SYNTAX: wordp *input*

EXAMPLES:

```
?wordp "name
TRUE
?wordp 239
TRUE
```

```
?wordp [239]
FALSE
?wordp [words]
FALSE
?
```

NOTE: *To distinguish between words and numbers, the primitive* **numberp** should be used.

REL PRIMS: listp, namep, numberp

wrap

Graphics command. Takes no inputs. Confines the turtle to the physical (visible) screen. If the turtle attempts to move off the physical screen, it will immediately reappear at the diametrically opposed position on the other side of the screen.

SYNTAX: wrap

EXAMPLES:

```
?sf
[0 FS 10 WINDOW .46875]
?wrap sf
[0 FS 10 WRAP .46875]
?
```

REL PRIMS: fence, window

+ (plus)

Arithmetic operator. Takes two inputs, numerical values, and outputs the sum of those inputs. May be used in infix or prefix form. May be used with variables.

SYNTAX: *input1 + input2*
+ input1 input2

EXAMPLES:

```
?34 + 73
107
?+ + 27 15 30
72
?make "p 35 make "q 78
?op :p + :q
113
?
```

NOTE: Whilst + may be used as a prefix to positive numbers, its inclusion is unnecessary. In the absence of a sign, positive is assumed.

REL PRIMS: quotient, remainder, * , / , -

- (minus)

Arithmetic operator. Takes two inputs, numerical values, and outputs the result of subtracting the second input from the first. May be used in infix or prefix form. When used as a negative quantity sign, there must be no space between the operator and the number. May be used with variables.

SYNTAX: *input1 - input2*
- input1 input2

EXAMPLES:

```
?14 - 8
6
```

```
?- 55 9
46
?18 - -9
27
?
```

NOTE: The minus quantity of 9 is expressed as '-9', whereas subtracting 9 from *number* is expressed as '*number* - 9'. The two are not synonymous in LOGO.

REL PRIMS: quotient, remainder, *, /, +

*** (asterisk)**

Arithmetic operator. Takes two inputs, numerical values, and outputs the product of multiplying the first input by the second. May be used in infix or prefix form. May be used with variables.

SYNTAX: *multiplicand * multiplier*
** multiplicand multiplier*

EXAMPLES:

```
?14 * 21
294
?* 5 19
95
?
```

REL PRIMS: quotient, remainder, / , + , -

/ (slash)

Arithmetic operator. Takes two inputs, real numbers or integers, and outputs the real number result of dividing the first input by the second. May be used in infix or prefix form. May be used with variables.

SYNTAX: *input1 / input2*
/ input1 input2

EXAMPLES:

```
?25 / 4                   ;real division
6.25
?quotient 25 4                 ;integer division
6
?/ 82 9
9.11111111111111               ;real numbers to 15 dec places
?
```

REL PRIMS: quotient, remainder, * , + , -

NOTE: With the above four operators, normal arithmetical precedence is observed, but brackets are recognised. * and / take precedence over + and -, but expressions inside round brackets take precedence over expressions outside the brackets. Brackets may be nested.

EXAMPLES:

```
?3 * 6 + 2
20
?3 * (6 + 2)
24
?(23 * ((4 - 9) + (8 * 5))) / 16
50.3125
?
```

. (full stop)

Decimal point. Indicates where the decimal point is in real numbers. May also be used as a full-stop in text without a backslash prefix.

SYNTAX: *number.fraction*

NOTE: There must be no space separator between the decimal point and either the number or it's decimal fraction. Fractions entered without a leading zero will be given one by the interpreter. Thus .54 will be represented as 0.54. However whole numbers will be stripped of any leading zeroes. Thus 008 will be represented as 8. Prefixing with a backslash will preserve the input zero if required, thus: \08 will be printed with the leading zero in place.

> (greater than)

Boolean comparator. Takes two inputs and outputs TRUE if the first input is greater than the second. May be used in infix or prefix form. May be used with variables, or characters. In words only the first character is compared.

SYNTAX:
input1 > input2
> input1 input2

EXAMPLES:

```
?104 > 97
TRUE
?> 12 11
TRUE
?6 > 8
FALSE
?make "a 15 make "b 7
?> :a :b
TRUE
?"a > "A                        ;ASCII a=97, A=65 (decimal)
TRUE
?"BIG > "small                  ;ASCII B=66, s=115 (decimal)
FALSE
?
```

REL PRIMS: < , =

< (less than)

Boolean comparator. Takes two inputs and outputs TRUE if the first input is less than the second. May be used in infix or prefix form. May be used with variables, or characters. In words only the first character is compared.

SYNTAX:
input1 < input2
< input1 input2

EXAMPLES:

```
?67 < 73
TRUE
?< 1001 1002
TRUE
?7 < 6
FALSE
?make "x 78 make y 94.6
?< :x :y
TRUE
?2545 < "A                      ;ASCII 2=50, A=65 (decimal)
TRUE
```

```
?45 < 45
FALSE
?
```

REL PRIMS: >, =

= (equals)

Boolean comparator. Takes two inputs and outputs TRUE if the first input is precisely equal to the second. May be used in prefix or infix form.

SYNTAX: *input1 = input2*
= input1 input2

EXAMPLES:

```
?33 + 7 = 40
TRUE
?12 - 5 = 7
TRUE
?= 91 92
FALSE
?
```

REL PRIMS: >, <, equalp

: (colon)

Syntax indicator. Used in two forms: (1) as a prefix to a variable name, delineates the name as a variable holding a value, and (2) as a suffix to a letter, delineates a drive.

SYNTAX: :*variablename*
driveletter:

EXAMPLES:

```
?make "a 10
?:a
10
?setd "b:
?defaultd
B:
?dir "m:
[RON ROF HEX]
?
```

REL PRIMS:

" (double-quote mark)

Syntax indicator. When used immediately preceding a word, it delineates a name, an object, a property, a value, or a system property. Figures need not have a quote-mark preceding them, but optionally may.

SYNTAX: "*name*

EXAMPLES:

```
?make "var 13
?gprop "var ".APV
13
?pprop "house "semi_detached "three_bedrooms
?glist "house
[semi_detached three_bedrooms]
?pr (word 4 ". 0 5 2)
4.052
?(type "" "wild " "horses "")
" wild  horses "
```

```
?type "" type "wild type " type "horses type ""
"wildhorses"
?
```

REL PRIMS:

NOTE: May be used to indicate a null value, *eg* 'pr "' executes a line-feed and carriage-return without printing anything.

[] (square brackets)

Syntax indicator. Delineates a list. Lists may be nested. An empty list still exists as a list and is represented as '[]'.

SYNTAX: [*item1 item2...itemN*]

EXAMPLES:

```
?pr [chicken cow duck horse]
chicken cow duck horse
?pr [1 4 9 [3 [6]] 5]
1 4 9 [3 [6]] 5
?(list "a "b "c "d)
[a b c d]
?
```

REL PRIMS: ()

() (parentheses)

Arithmetic and system delimiter. May be used with numbers to alter precedence, or as a word and list processing delimiter.

SYNTAX: (*input1* + *input2*) * *input3*

(list *input1 input2...inputN*)

EXAMPLES:

```
?4 + 11 * 3
37
?(4 + 11) * 3
45
?pr (word "not "with "standing)
notwithstanding
?(type "The "Way "Of "The "World)
The Way Of The World
?
```

REL PRIMS: []

(space)

Syntax delimiter. One space must be used to separate every instruction, word, list, variable, etc. Arithmetical expressions need not have separators between them.

EXAMPLES:

```
?make "a 20
?make "a20
Not enough inputs to make
?4*12=96/2
TRUE
?repeat 5 [(type "A [])]
A A A A A
?fd100
I don't know how to fd100
?(type "B char 32 "B)
B   B                           ;3 spaces
?
```

\ (backslash)

Operator canceller. Used before any arithmetical operator or system delimiter (other than space) it cancels the meaning of the operator or delimiter and allows it to be used as a text character.

SYNTAX: *operator*

EXAMPLES:

```
?type "*
type doesn't like * as input
?type "\*
*
?
```

NOTE: The backslash can be printed using f3, or <ALT><Q>.

; (semi-colon)

Operation separator. The interpreter will ignore any text which follows, and is on the same line as, the semi-colon, enabling remarks to be entered in the text. <RETURN> delimits the remark. A semi-colon inserted at the beginning of a program line will prevent execution of that line.

EXAMPLES:

```
...
make "inp rc  ;single character assigned
if :inp = "X [stop]  ;  to variable :inp.
...
```

NOTE: In the above example, there needs to be a minimum of one space and a maximum of two spaces between the end of the instruction line and the semi-colon. If more spaces are entered, the interpreter will still close them up to one or two spaces. Remarks take up memory space, and are best used for print-outs and then erased before the program is run if space is at a premium.

REL PRIMS: .ENL, .FMT, .REM

! (exclamation mark)

System indicator. When a line is too long a '!' will be entered automatically in column 90 to indicate that the line is continued on the next row down.

NOTE: Wrapping lines should be avoided if possible for clarity's sake, and is almost always unnecessary.

APPENDIX I

PRIMITIVES AND SYSTEM PROPERTIES

---

and
.APV
arctan
ascii

bf
bk
bl
*buttonp
bye

catch
changef
char
clean
co
.contents
copyoff
copyon
cos
count
cs
ct
cursor

.DEF
define
defaultd
.deposit
dir
dirpic
dot
dotc

ed
edall
edf

emptyp
end
.ENL
equalp
er
erall
erasefile
erasepic
ERRACT
error
ern
.examine

FALSE
fd
fence
fill
first
.FMT
fput
fs

glist
go
gprop

home
ht

if
.in
int
item

keyp

label

last
lc
list
listp
load
loadpic
local
lput
lt

make
memberp

namep
nodes
noformat
not
notrace
nowatch
numberp

op
or
.out

*paddle
*pal
pause
pd
pe
piece
plist
po
poall
pons
pops
pots

pprop
pps
pr
.PRM
pu
px

quotient

random
rc
recycle
REDEFP
.REM
remainder
remprop
repeat
rerandom
rl
round
rq
rt
run

save
savepic
se
setbg
setcursor
setd
*setpal
setpc
setpen
setpos
setscrunch
seth
setsplit

setx
sety
sf
show
shuffle
sin
.SPC
ss
st
stop

text
tf
thing
throw
to
TOPLEVEL
*tones
towards
trace
TRUE
ts
type

uc

*wait
watch
where
window
word
wordp
wrap

* Primitives marked thus are not implemented.

APPENDIX II

THE EDITING COMMANDS

COMMAND	EFFECT
CURSORS:	move up a line.
	move down a line.
	move right one character.
	move left one character.
LINE	move to beginning of line.
EOL	move to end of line.
DOC	move to end of edit buffer.
ALT + DOC	move to top of edit buffer.
RELAY	move to top of edit buffer.
PAGE	move to end of page.
ALT + PAGE	move to top of page.
[+] (set key)	move to top of page.
DEL-)	delete character under cursor.
(-DEL	delete previous character.
ALT + DEL-)	erase to EOL.
COPY or PASTE	recall the last line deleted.
EXIT	finish editing and define all procedures in the edit buffer.
STOP	abandon edit without defining procedures.

The editor will accept approximately 700-800 nodes of program material, which amounts on average to about 2 pages of 29 lines per page, or just over 1150 characters and space separators in all. When the edit buffer is full, the system will beep and will refuse to acept more entries. The solution is to reduce the edit buffer content, <EXIT>, re-enter the editor with less content, and continue editing.

edf "*filename*

entered in command mode will load the file *filename* from the default or named drive straight into the editor. If no file of that name exists, an empty file *filename* will be created on the default or named drive and control will be passed to the editor. On pressing <EXIT> the file will be saved to disk automatically. The contents of the workspace will not be affected. Disks may be swapped between loading and saving.

edall will occasionally lock up the computer on exit. Always use **recycle** before entering **edall** to prevent this. As an alternative select procedures to edit and enter them as a list, eg:

?ed [*procdure1 procedure2...procedureN*]

ed entered without inputs will take you into an empty edit screen.

When an error is encountered during run-time execution, type 'ed' and you will be taken into the editor with the appropriate procedure loaded. Occasionally LOGO will get it wrong, in which case press <STOP> and load the correct procedure into the editor with 'ed "*procedure-name*'.

Pressing <STOP> in the editor causes an exit to the command prompt without defining any of the procedures currently in the editor and thus abandoning any changes which may have been made.

APPENDIX III

ERROR MESSAGES

NO.	MESSAGE	POSSIBLE CAUSE / ACTION
2	Number too big	Split the sum into smaller parts.
7	Can't find label...	Line missing, or catch and throw not in same program path.
11	I'm having trouble with the disk	Disk wrong type for drive, maybe a B: disk in the A: drive, or the disk may be full.
12	Disk full	Use a fresh disk and repeat save.
13	Can't divide by zero	Check your arithmetic.
14	I can't find that drive	Wrong drive letter entered.
15	File *file* already exists	Erase the file on disk, or choose a new name.
17	File *file* not found	Try another disk.
23	I'm out of space	Erase something to make more space. Try **recycle**.
28	Out of LOGO stack during garbage collection	Probably the program is too big for the available space: try breaking it up into smaller bits.
29	Not enough inputs to list	Check the syntax: possibly brackets are missing, or **piece** or **item** with a higher number than the number of elements in the list.
34	Turtle out of bounds	Turtle moving off-screen in 'fence' or moving a long way off-screen in 'window'.
35	I don't know how to...	Undefined procedure; wrong syntax, quite possibly a missing colon before a variable name.
36	...has no value	Unassigned variable: check with **pons**.
37	) without (	Check round brackets: go into edit mode, the cursor will show the error.
38	I don't know what to do with...	Unassigned variable, probably a value from an **op** command.
39	Primitive not implemented	Don't use it!

41 ...doesn't like...as input	Check syntax: the input is wrong in some way, possibly out of range, or the wrong type.
42 ...didn't output to...	Wrong input: similar to 41.
45 The word is too long	Be less loquacious!
46 My edit buffer is full	Edit smaller program chunks: probably trying to use **edall** when the program is too big to fit into the editor.
47 If wants []'s around instructions	Check syntax: go into edit mode, the cursor will show where the error is.
74 Out of LOGO stack space	Find another algorithm that uses less stack: usually caused by multi-recursive procedures, or complicated and repetitious arithmetic.
Can't find catch for...	Usually because the **catch** and **throw** are not in the same program path. The throw must be in the path initiated by the catch action.
...is a primitive	Primitive names must not be used as procedure names.
...is not true or false	Check the conditional test and re-write it so that the answer must be either TRUE or FALSE.
...isn't a name or procedure	Check the entry and amend it.
I can't...while loading a file	Remember, you can't type ahead.
...doesn't like an empty word as input	A variable isn't functioning as it should: it has somehow got a null value.
I need more memory to run LOGO	Unlikely to occur on the PCW, unless you have re-written the memory addresses of the operating system.
I don't have any LOGO nodes left	Recycle, or reduce workspace content.
Can't...from the editor	Leave the editor and execute the command in command mode.
Please turn on the printer	Printer not connected.
Can not run in this environment	Boot up CP/M: Dr LOGO will not run under any other operating system. Possibly trying to access a memory address outside LOGO's boundaries.
LOGO system bug	That's honesty for you! Nothing you can do about it - except try another way round the problem. Possibly caused by the user hacking the system.

APPENDIX IV

CP/M COMMANDS

The following commands are the LOGO versions of the CP/M Escape Commands. They should be entered exactly as set out here, whether used from within programs or from the command line. Names in brackets following the functions, thus: (RON), are LIBRARY PROGRAMS from PART TWO.

COMMAND	EFFECT
(type word char 27 0)	Disables the status line. (STOF)
(type word char 27 1)	Enables the status line. (STON)
(type word char 27 "A)	Moves the cursor up one line.
(type word char 27 "B)	Moves the cursor down one line.
(type word char 27 "C)	Moves the cursor right one column.
(type word char 27 "D)	Moves the cursor left one column.
(type word char 27 "E)	Clears the screen. Equivalent to cs.
(type word char 27 "H)	Moves the cursor to [0 0].
(type word char 27 "I)	Moves the cursor up one row, scrolling the text down if necessary.
(type word char 27 "J)	Erases to the end of the page.
(type word char 27 "K)	Erases to the end of the line.
(type word char 27 "L)	Inserts a line, scrolling text down a line.
(type word char 27 "M)	Deletes the line with the cursor on it. Lines below are scrolled up to fill the gap.
(type word char 27 "N)	Deletes the character under the cursor.
(type word char 27 "d)	Clears the screen up to the cursor position.
(type word char 27 "e)	Enables the cursor blob. (CUROF)
(type word char 27 "f)	Disables the cursor blob. (CURON)
(type word char 27 "j)	Saves the cursor position. (SAVEC)
(type word char 27 "k)	Restores the cursor position saved by the previous command. (RESTC)
(type word char 27 "l)	Erases all the characters on the line.
(type word char 27 "o)	Erases the line up to and including the cursor.
(type word char 27 "p)	Turns on reverse video. (RON)
(type word char 27 "q)	Turns off reverse video. (ROF)
(type word char 27 "r)	Turns on underline. (ULON)
(type word char 27 "u)	Turns off underline. (ULOF)
(type word char 27 "v)	Selects word-wrap.
(type word char 27 "w)	Cancels word-wrap.
(type word char 27 "x)	Sets screen to 24X80 mode.
(type word char 27 "y)	Leaves 24X80 mode.

In addition the following characters may be used:

type char 7	BEL (bleep).
type char 8	Backspace.
type char 10	Line-feed.
type char 12	Form-feed
type char 13	Carriage-return.

PRINTER CONTROL

There are some CP/M printer commands which can be used directly from LOGO, but some of the most important do not work, and the ones that do are at best a fragile way of controlling the printer. This is best done by writing a printer file and using SETLST.COM to set the file before LOGO is loaded. Alternatively, leave LOGO with 'bye', set up the printer file and re-enter LOGO, thus:

A>setlst *printerfile*
A>logo

The CP/M program SETLST.COM and the required printer file must both be on the default drive. Better still, put the 'setlst' line into your PROFILE.SUB. The following files are suggested printer files for program print-out and label-printing.

SETPRINT.FIL (Suitable for program listings)

```
^'ESC'l^'8'          ;left margin at 8
^'ESC'c              ;continuous printing
^'ESC'C^'66'         ;page length 66
^'ESC'N^'5'          ;bottom margin 5
^'ESC'M'             ;Elite typestyle
^'ESC'm^'1'          ;High Quality print
{^'ESC'd'            ;make current settings the default}
```

Type the listing in using a word-processor (any program that can output an ASCII file), or use RPED which automatically outputs ASCII files. With LocoScript use the Save ASCII option (page-image). With Protext enter in Program mode. The up-arrow ^ is obtained by pressing <EXTRA><u>. The printer status bar may be used to execute form- and line- feeds, and to toggle between Draft and High Quality.

Save the file as SETPRINT.FIL and, unless you have already done so, copy SETLST.COM from your system disks to M: using:

A>pip
*m:=a:setlst.com

Put your LOGO start of day disk in A: and enter:

*a:=m:setlst.com

Insert this line in your PROFILE.SUB file:

setlst setprint.fil

and it will be loaded up every time you boot LOGO. Use the LOGO program PQ to print listings. This will be found in PART TWO.

SETLABEL.FIL

This file is suitable for printing labels using the DATABASE program from PART THREE. Save as an ASCII file.

```
^'ESC'l^'7'              ;left margin 7 (adjust the figure to suit)
^'ESC'c                  ;continuous printing
^'ESC'C^'9'              ;page length 9 (top of label to top of next)
^'ESC'm^'1'              ;High Quality print
```

Save the file as an ASCII file called SETLABEL.FIL. Call it up by leaving LOGO with 'bye', at the A> prompt enter:

setlst setlabel.fil

Re-enter LOGO by typing 'logo'. 'Re-set' on the printer status bar will re-set the printer to the default, ie SETPRINT.FIL. The up-arrow (^) is <EXTRA><u>.

KEYS.CPM

When leaving LOGO with 'bye' and working on a CP/M program, the keys are still set up for LOGO (keys.drl). The following file will re-set the keys to the normal CP/M settings.

```
66 N     "^C"
02 N S   "^Z"
00 N S   "^Q"
73 N S   "^S"
77 N S   "^P"
16 N     "^G"
75 N     "^H"
10 N     "^U"
03 N     "^W"
20 N     "^]"                          ;close square bracket
14 N     "^_"                          ;underline character
23 N     "^V"
15 N     "^A"
06 N     "^F"
05 N     "^F"
01 N     "^R"
79 N     "^'30'"
16     A "^K"
76 N     "^\"                          ;backslash is <EXTRA><1/2>
79     A "^E"
72     A "^X"
72 N     "^'#8A'"
13 N     "^'#8F'"
13   S   "^'#90'"
E  #8A   "^'8'^G
E  #8F   "^F^B^B"
E  #90   "^F^B"
08 N     "^'27'"
16 N     "^G"
11 N     "^Y"
```

This file should be entered in the same way as the others, and saved as an ASCII file called KEYS.CPM. The up-arrow (^) is <EXTRA><u>. You must have SETKEYS.COM on your start of day disk (see above and INTRODUCION for details).

To re-set the keys to CP/M settings on leaving LOGO, enter at the prompt:

```
A>setkeys keys.cpm
```

and the keys will be back to normal. Alternatively put the line in your PROFILE.SUB file as the last line. Then every time you exit from LOGO the keys will be re-set automatically.

LOGO.SUB

In case you can't find the file LOGO.SUB, or have lost it, it is an ASCII file and consists of only two lines:

```
setkeys keys.drl

logo
```

APPENDIX V

PICFILE PRINTING AND CONVERSION

LOGOPRNT.BAS

This file should be entered using BASIC, RPED, or a word-processor which can save as ASCII. Save as LOGOPRNT.BAS. When run in BASIC it will print out an A4 size bit-image picture of your LOGO picfile on a dot-matrix, ink-jet, or laser printer.

```
10 REM To print A4 size LOGO pictures.
20 PRINT CHR$(27)+"E"+CHR$(27)+"H"
30 PRINT TAB(28)"*****  LOGO PICTURE PRINTER  *****":PRINT
40 PRINT:PRINT TAB(20)"PUT DISK IN DEFAULT DRIVE":PRINT
50 PRINT TAB(20)"LOAD A4 PAPER IN PRINTER":PRINT
60 PRINT TAB(20);:LINE INPUT "ENTER FILENAME (without .PIC ext): ";pf$
70 pf$=pf$+".pic"
80 PRINT:PRINT:PRINT"Printing..."
90 OPTION NOT TAB
100 j=126:k=3
110 LPRINT CHR$(27);"A";CHR$(8);CHR$(27);"c";CHR$(27);"C"
120 OPEN "R",1,pf$,1
130 FIELD 1,1 AS b$
140 FOR x=1 TO 90
150 a=1
160 LPRINT CHR$(27);"L";CHR$(j);CHR$(k)
170 WIDTH LPRINT 255
180 FOR y=22358+x TO 128+x STEP -90
190 GET 1,y
200 FOR z=1 TO 2
210 IF a=10 THEN a=1:GOTO 240
220 LPRINT b$;b$;
230 a=a+1
240 NEXT z
250 NEXT y
260 FOR i=1 TO 78:LPRINT CHR$(8);:NEXT i
270 LPRINT SPACE$(78);:LPRINT
280 NEXT x
290 PRINT:PRINT"Printing completed."
300 END
```

LOGOSCRN.BAS

This program converts a LOGO picfile to a format suitable for direct loading into MICRODESIGN2/3 and STOP PRESS DTP programs. Save as LOGOSCRN.BAS. In MICRODESIGN the file is a "screen" type with a .SCR extension. In STOP PRESS it is an .SPC file (change the file extension in line 90 from .SCR to .SPC). It takes some time to convert the 32 lines, but a running count is printed to screen. Make sure that there is enough room on the disk containing the LOGO picfile, as the converted file will be saved to it. The converted file will occupy the same space as the LOGO original, *ie* 173k drives: 23k, 706k drives: 24k.

```
10 REM To convert LOGO picfiles for DTP programs
20 PRINT CHR$(27)+"E"+CHR$(27)+"H"
30 PRINT TAB(27) "*****  LOGO PICFILE CONVERSION  *****":PRINT
40 PRINT TAB(14)"LOGO picfile conversion to MD and STOP PRESS format":PRINT
50 PRINT:PRINT "Enter a filename without .PIC extension:  ";
60 ON ERROR GOTO 0
70 LINE INPUT picf$:picf$=UPPER$(picf$)
80 IF picf$="" THEN GOTO 120
90 scr$=picf$+".SCR":picf$=picf$+".PIC"
95 REM substitute ".SPC" for STOP PRESS in line 90
100 IF FIND$(picf$)<>"" THEN GOTO 120
110 PRINT "Input file '";picf$;"' not found":GOTO 50
120 OPEN "R",1,picf$:OPEN "O",2,scr$
130 DIM a$(8):PRINT "Please wait... "
140 GET #1,2:c%=128
150 FOR line%=1 TO 32
160 FOR row%=1 TO 8:a$(row%)=""
170 b%=90-LEN(a$(row%))
180 IF c%>=b% THEN GOTO 210
190 IF c%>0 THEN a$(row%)=a$(row%)+INPUT$(c%,1)
200 GET £1:c%=128:GOTO 170
210 a$(row%)=a$(row%)+INPUT$(b%,1):c%=c%-b%
220 NEXT row%
230 FOR col%=1 TO 90
240 FOR row%=1 TO 8:PRINT #2,MID$(a$(row%),col%,1);:NEXT row%
250 NEXT col%
260 PRINT CHR$((line% MOD 10)+48);:NEXT line%
270 PRINT:CLOSE:PRINT:PRINT "Conversion completed. File is saved as ";scr$
280 END
```

APPENDIX VI

KEYBOARD CODES

The following are the codes returned by the non-alphanumeric keys. If a keypress is required by a program, it may be useful to use one of these instead of one of the alphanumeric keys. It is important to note that these are different codes from the keyboard codes used by SETKEYS.COM: they are the ASCII codes which the keys return in LOGO.

[+]	234	LINE	255	<-DEL	248	f7	240
[-]	28	EXCH	29	DEL->	252	f8	249
EXIT	253	FIND	29	TAB	247	UNIT	NULL
RELAY	238	DOC	232	f1	241	PARA	NULL
ENTER	243	PAGE	234	f2	242	CURSORS:	
RETURN	243	COPY	231	f3	239	up	240
WORD	250	PASTE	231	f4	244	down	242
CHAR	250	CUT	235	f5	245	right	250
EOL	251	CAN	248	f6	246	left	254

The following Control Commands may be used in command mode:

Press <ALT> with:

G	STOP	Q	backslash
I	TAB	S	split screen
L	full screen	T	text screen
M	carriage return	Z	pause

The following keypresses may be used in command mode:

f1, f2	pause
f3, f4	backslash
TAB	cursor jumps right four columns (not a true tab, but useful for indenting)

APPENDIX VII

LOGO VERSION EQUIVALENTS

LOGO is a highly portable language: programs which run on one implementation can usually be run on another with very little adaptation. However there are some differences in primitive names; the following are the main alternatives. Most other implementations require upper case input.

Dr LOGO	OTHER	Dr LOGO	OTHER
and	ALLOF	listp	LIST?
	BOTH	load	READ
arctan	ATAN	loadpic	LOADPICT
bk	BACK	numberp	NUMBER?
	BD	namep	THING?
bf	BUTFIRST	or	ANYOF
bl	BUTLAST		EITHER
cs	CLEARSCREEN	op	OUTPUT
ct	CLEARTEXT	px	PENREVERSE
dir	CATALOG	pr	PRINT
emptyp	EMPTY?	pu, pd	PENUP, PENDOWN
equalp	EQUAL?	rt	RIGHT
erall	ERPS	savepic	SAVEPICT
ern	ERNAME	se	SENTENCE
fd	FORWARD	seth	HEADING
fence	EDGES	setcursor	CURSOR
fs	DRAW	setpos	SETXY
	FULLSCREEN	ss	SPLITSCREEN
home	CENTRE	tf	TURTLESTATE
if... [...]	IF...THEN...	ts	NODRAW
if... [...][...]	IF...THEN...ELSE	type	PRINT1
item 1 tf	XCOR	window	NOEDGES
item 2 tf	YCOR	wordp	WORD?
keyp	RC?	>	GREATER
lt	LEFT	<	LESS

In addition, the following commands may be found:

COMMAND	MEANING
background, bg	show background colour.
bury	protects the named package from erall, pops, save, etc.
buttonp	TRUE if joystick button is pressed.
clearinput	clears the memory of characters input but not yet read.
definedp	TRUE if input is a procedure.
ent	sets the tone envelope.
env	sets the volume envelope.
iftrue, ift	action which follows is executed if result of 'test' is true.
iffalse, iff	action which follows is executed if result of 'test' is false.
package	sets a name and contents of a package of procedures, etc.
paddle	outputs the orientation of the joystick.
pal	outputs the palette colours set by setpal.
pen	show the pen–state, visibilty, colour, nib and type.
pencolor, pc	show the pen colour.
primitivep	TRUE if input is a primitive.
product	outputs the product of the input numbers.
randomize	sets a random number seed.
release	releases sound channels previously set to 'hold'.
setpal	sets the palette colours.
setpc	sets the pen colour.
setpen	sets the pen number.
shownp	TRUE if turtle is shown.
sum	outputs the sum of the input numbers.
sqrt	square root
test	runs a conditional argument.
tt	prints text at turtle position.
unbury	removes protection given by bury.
wait	pauses the program for the input number of cycles.

APPENDIX VIII

PRIMITIVE MEMORY LOCATIONS

(	440	item	2831	remprop	5712
pause	486	last	2913	glist	5734
repeat	567	list	2965	noformat	5861
op	608	listp	3022	define	5884
stop	614	lput	3039	text	6034
run	623	memberp	3153	edall	6054
not	629	numberp	3390	ed	6101
and	656	se	3427	po	6248
or	665	wordp	3573	poall	6302
co	775	word	3586	pots	6323
if	792	piece	3706	pons	6351
arctan	897	where	3949	pops	6383
cos	929	uc	3958	erall	6415
sin	952	lc	3969	er	6436
int	975	rq	4444	ern	6445
*	1057	rc	4488	bk	6950
random	1187	rl	4522	clean	6972
quotient	1291	show	4555	cs	6978
remainder	1340	catch	4575	dot	6990
rerandom	1413	error	4674	fd	7020
round	1420	throw	4687	tf	7039
+	1507	label	4766	sf	7122
−	1516	go	4772	ht	7229
/	1785	nodes	5043	home	7235
<	1794	.contents	5054	lt	7241
>	1800	trace	5087	rt	7258
shuffle	1997	notrace	5096	setbg	7272
ascii	2140	watch	5239	seth	7290
bf	2157	nowatch	5179	setpc	7304
char	2186	local	5273	setpen	7318
count	2207	make	5251	setpos	7454
equalp	2375	namep	5334	setx	7484
emptyp	2655	thing	5379	sety	7511
=	2735	gprop	5517	st	7538
first	2744	plist	5540	towards	7544
bl	2668	pprop	5555	keyp	7710
fput	2774	pps	5592	.in	7719

.out	7732
.examine	7753
.deposit	7765
setsplit	7783
ss	7906
ts	7937
fs	7953
wrap	8027
ct	8033
cursor	8039
setcursor	8065
setscrunch	8132
edf	9505
load	9717
save	9786
erasefile	9889
changef	9947
dir	10014
defaultd	10108
setd	10136
pr	10203
type	10209
recycle	15829
)	21660
pd	28058
pu	28073
pe	28081
px	28096
window	28743
fence	28772
pal	30649
setpal	30652
copyon	30655
copyoff	30718
tones	30813
wait	30816
buttonp	30819
paddle	30822
fill	31041
dotc	31078
erasepic	31366
dirpic	31375
loadpic	31384
savepic	31474

APPENDIX IX

LOGO AND MACHINE CODE

Although it is difficult to incorporate machine code in LOGO, it is not impossible. This is by no means an exhaustive examination of the subject, but it may be useful as the basis for further experimentation. First of all, by machine code in this context we mean data bytes produced by assembly-language programs. It is no easy thing to know where one can safely load the data without crashing the system. The area 0008..0099 hex (8..153 decimal) is reasonably safe. But miss out bytes 0030..0032 and bytes 0038..003A. Storage space for 140 bytes of data is not exactly massive, but it's a start. On no account use the first 7 bytes (0000h–0007h) as they are essential to both CP/M and LOGO. For example all BDOS calls are made to, and redirected from, 0005h.

Having stored the data in the given area, the next problem is retrieving it and using it within a program. What is needed is some sort of 'call' function. The answer is to invent a new primitive which has as its data the machine code data you wish to use. First a useful memory-scanner:

```
to memscan
(local "addr1 "addr2 "peek "range)
make "peek [] ct
pr [Enter START ADDRESS, END ADDRESS:]
make "range rl
make "addr1 first :range make "addr2 last :range
scanner :addr1 :addr2
end

to scanner :addr1 :addr2
local "inp
repeat (:addr2 - :addr1) + 1 [make "inp .examine :addr1
   (type :addr1 char 32) pr :inp
   make "peek lput :inp :peek make "addr1 :addr1 + 1]
memscan
end
```

This program will print out a given range of memory locations, together with the byte value stored at each location. It loops back so that you can enter fresh locations. Addresses must be in decimal. Leave it with <STOP>.Now to the meat. The following program asks for a list of machine code data to be input, together with a 'call' name (a new primitive in effect) and a start address to store the data.

```
to data
(local "poke "addr)
ct pr [Enter MACHINE CODE DATA:]
make "poke rl
pr [Enter START ADDRESS:]
make "addr rq
hack :addr :poke
end
```

```
to hack :address :poke
if emptyp :poke [stop]
.deposit :address first :poke
hack :address + 1 bf :poke
end
```

This program will poke the data into memory and create a new primitive. It is now necessary to put the name of the new primitive into the appropriate memory location. This cannot be done from within the program:

?pprop "*name* ".PRM *start-address*

The following two data lists may be used to test the program. The first list will set the numeric keypad to output the numbers instead of the cursor keys. It is entirely equal to pressing <ALT><RELAY>:

Data: 1 32 16 205 90 252 221 0 205 90 252 218 0 201
Name: numlok

Now enter:

?pprop "numlok ".PRM *start-address*

Get out of it with <ALT><RELAY>, which is a toggle, or by entering:

?.deposit start-address 0

If you now enter 'numlok' nothing will happen.

This data was chosen, not because it is of much use, but because it's very easy to test various areas of memory with the function. Try '8' as the start address to kick off with.

The second data list will execute a screen-dump (on the PCW dot-matrix printer only) from within a program when the new primitive **dump** is run, which can be very useful.

Data: 205 90 252 114 20 201
Name: dump

Enter:

?pprop "dump ".PRM "start-address

and enter 'dump' any time you want a screen-dump. It also works from within a program: just put in the line 'type dump' wherever you want the screen-dump to happen. If you've already deposited the 'numlok' data, use 22 as the start address, or try 30649, the location occupied by **pal**.

It is perfectly possible to use memory space occupied by primitives that you don't need, or which are of no use, such as **setpen** and **setbg**. It's matter of trial and error.

Get the start address from the look-up table above, and get the values of, say, 15 bytes from there using 'memscan'. Now try entering '.deposit 0' at 'address + 15'. Keep doing this, decreasing the address by 1 and testing the primitive each time until it no longer works or the program crashes. Put back the original value into the byte at which the primitive failed, and there you have it. Keep a note of anything you discover, because all these changes only last until you leave LOGO - unless of course you want to get to work with SID and write the data in directly.

Beware of **buttonp** and **paddle:** if you crash into **fill**, which lives right next door, you'll probably fill the screen. But don't worry, crashing soon becomes a way of life when you start playing around in memory!

The old primitive can be given a new name in the usual way with **.PRM**. Using these methods it is possible to store quite a considerable amount of machine code; you can custom-make it for yourself if you're into assembler. If you're not, look through the computer mags and adapt BASIC listings with DATA statements in them.

APPENDIX X

BIBLIOGRAPHY

"Apple Logo"
Harold Abelson
Byte/McGraw-Hill 1982

"Artificial Intelligence"
Patrick Henry Winston
Addison-Wesley 1977

"Artificial Intelligence, An Introductory Course"
ed. A. Bundy
Edinburgh University Press 1980

"Getting Started With Basic And Logo"
F.A.Wilson
Bernard Babani 1988

"Guide To Logo"
Boris Allan
Amsoft 1985

"Lisp"
Patrick Henry Winston and Berthold Klaus Paul Horn
Addison-Wesley 1981

"Logo - A Language For Learning"
Anne Sparrowhawk
Pan Books Ltd 1984

"Logo For Beginners"
W.S.Penfold
Bernard Babani 1988

"Logo Programming"
Peter Ross
Addison-Wesley Publishing Co. 1983

"Mindstorms, Children, Computers and Powerful Ideas"
Seymour Papert
Harvester Press

"The Logo Pocketbook"
Martin Sims
Glentop Publishers Ltd 1989

"Turtle Geometry, The Computer As A Medium For Exploring Mathematics"
Harold Abelson and Andrea diSessa
MIT Press 1981

"Using Logo On The Atari ST"
Martin Sims
Glentop Publishers Ltd 1986

INDEX

Words for the wise - from
Sigma Press

Sigma publish what is probably the widest range of computer books from any independent UK publisher. And that's not just for the PC, but for many other popular micros – Atari, Amiga and Archimedes – and for software packages that are widely-used in the UK and Europe, including Timeworks, Deskpress, Sage, Money Manager and many more. We also publish a whole range of professional-level books for topics as far apart as IBM mainframes, UNIX, computer translation, manufacturing technology and networking.

A complete catalogue is available, but here are some of the highlights:

Amstrad PCW

The Complete Guide to LocoScript and Amstrad PCW Computers – Hughes – £12.95
LocoScripting People – Clayton and Clayton – £12.95
The PCW LOGO Manual – Robert Grant – £12.95
Picture Processing on the Amstrad PCW – Gilmore – £12.95
See also Programming section for *Mini Office*

Archimedes

A Beginner's Guide to WIMP Programming – Fox – £12.95
See also: *Desktop Publishing on the Archimedes* and *Archimedes Game Maker's Manual*

Artificial Intelligence

Build Your Own Expert System – Naylor – £11.95
Computational Linguistics – McEnery – £14.95
Introducing Neural Networks – Carling – £14.95

Beginners' Guides

The New User's PC Book – Croucher – £12.95
Alone with a PC – Bradley – £12.95
The New User's Mac Book – Wilson – £12.95
PC Computing for Absolute Beginners – Edwards – £12.95

DTP and Graphics

Designworks Companion – Whale – £14.95
Ventura to Quark XPress for the PC – Wilmore – £19.95
Timeworks Publisher Companion – Morrissey – £12.95
Timeworks for Windows Companion – Sinclair – £14.95
PagePlus Publisher Companion – Sinclair – £12.95
Express Publisher DTP Companion – Sinclair – £14.95
Amiga Real-Time 3D Graphics – Tyler – £14.95
Atari Real-Time 3D Graphics – Tyler – £12.95

European and US Software Packages

Mastering Money Manager PC – Sinclair – £12.95
Using Sage Sterling in Business – Woodford – £12.95
Mastering Masterfile PC – Sinclair – £12.95
All-in-One Business Computing (Mini Office Professional) – Hughes – £12.95

Game Making and Playing

PC Games Bible – Matthews and Rigby – £12.95
Archimedes Game Maker's Manual – Blunt – £14.95
Atari Game Maker's Manual – Hill – £14.95
Amiga Game Maker's Manual – Hill – £16.95
Adventure Gamer's Manual – Redrup – £12.95

General

Music and New Technology – Georghiades and Jacobs – £12.95
Getting the Best from your Amstrad Notepad – Wilson – £12.95
Computers and Chaos (Atari and Amiga editions) – Bessant – £12.95
Computers in Genealogy – Isaac – £12.95
Multimedia, CD-ROM and Compact Disc – Botto – £14.95
Advanced Manufacturing Technology – Zairi – £14.95

Networks

$25 Network User Guide – Sinclair – £12.95
Integrated Digital Networks – Lawton – £24.95
Novell Netware Companion – Croucher – £16.95

PC Operating Systems and Architecture

Working with Windows 3.1 – Sinclair – £16.95
Servicing and Supporting IBM PCs and Compatibles – Moss – £16.95
The DR DOS Book – Croucher – £16.95
MS-DOS Revealed – Last – £12.95
PC Architecture and Assembly Language – Kauler – £16.95
Programmer's Technical Reference – Williams – £19.95
MS-DOS File and Program Control – Sinclair – £12.95
Mastering DesqView – Sinclair – £12.95

Programming

C Applications Library – Pugh – £16.95
Starting MS-DOS Assembler – Sinclair – £12.95
Understanding Occam and the transputer – Ellison – £12.95
Programming in ANSI Standard C – Horsington – £14.95
Programming in Microsoft Visual Basic – Penfold – £16.95
For **LOGO**, *see Amstrad PCW*

UNIX and mainframes

UNIX – The Book – Banahan and Rutter – £11.95
UNIX – The Complete Guide – Manger – £19.95
RPG on the IBM AS/400 – Tomlinson – £24.95

HOW TO ORDER

Order these books from your usual bookshop, or direct from:

SIGMA PRESS,
1 SOUTH OAK LANE, WILMSLOW, CHESHIRE, SK9 6AR

PHONE: 0625 – 531035
FAX: 0625 – 536800

PLEASE ADD £1 TOWARDS POST AND PACKING FOR ONE BOOK. POSTAGE IS FREE FOR TWO OR MORE BOOKS.

CHEQUES SHOULD BE MADE PAYABLE TO SIGMA PRESS.

ACCESS AND VISA WELCOME

24 HOUR ANSWERPHONE SERVICE.